A NEW MILLENNIUM AT SOUTHWARK CATHEDRAL

INVESTIGATIONS INTO THE FIRST TWO THOUSAND YEARS

Frontispiece   Millennium excavations at Southwark Cathedral, by Ptolemy Dean, architect to the project

For Archbishop Emeritus Desmond Tutu
and Dr Nelson Mandela

A New Millennium at Southwark Cathedral

Investigations into the first two thousand years

David Divers, Chris Mayo, Nathalie Cohen and Chris Jarrett

Pre-Construct Archaeology Limited, Monograph No. 8

PCA Monograph Series

1   Excavations at Hunt's House, Guy's Hospital, London Borough of Southwark
     By Robin Taylor-Wilson, 2002
     ISBN   0-9542938-0-0

2   Tatberht's Lundenwic: Archaeological Excavations in Middle Saxon London
     By Jim Leary with Gary Brown, James Rackham, Chris Pickard and Richard Hughes, 2004
     ISBN   0-9542938-1-9

3   Iwade: Occupation of a North Kent Village from the Mesolithic to the Medieval period
     By Barry Bishop and Mark Bagwell, 2005
     ISBN   0-9542938-2-7

4   Saxons, Knights & Lawyers in the Inner Temple: Archaeological Excavations in Church Court & Hare Court
     By Jonathan Butler, 2005
     ISBN   0-9542938-3-5

5   Unlocking the Landscape: Archaeological Excavations at Ashford Prison, Middlesex
     By Tim Carew, Barry Bishop, Frank Meddens and Victoria Ridgeway, 2006
     ISBN   0-9542938-4-3

6   Reclaiming the Marsh: Archaeological excavations at Moor House, City of London
     By Jonathan Butler, 2006
     ISBN   0-9542938-5-1

7   From Temples to Thames Street – 2000 Years of Riverside Development: Archaeological Excavations at the
     Salvation Army International Headquarters
     By Timothy Bradley and Jonathan Butler, 2008
     ISBN   978-0-9542938-6-4

Published by Pre-Construct Archaeology Limited
Copyright © Pre-Construct Archaeology Limited 2009

ISBN   978-0-9542938-7-1

Typesetting and layout by Trevor Ashwin at World Tree
Printed and bound by the Lavenham Press

Front cover: Millennium excavations at Southwark Cathedral, by Ptolemy Dean, detail from frontispiece
Back cover: Recording ledger slabs in the retro-choir; kiln remains to the north of the Cathedral; the Roman roadside ditch

Contents

Contributors

Principal authors (PCA)	David Divers, Chris Mayo and Chris Jarrett
Principal author (SCARP)	Nathalie Cohen
Additional authors (SCARP)	Gustav Milne, Simon Roffey
Volume manager and editor	Victoria Ridgeway
Academic adviser	Barney Sloane
Project manager	Peter Moore
Post-excavation managers	Frank Meddens and Victoria Ridgeway
Graphics (PCA)	Josephine Brown
Graphics (SCARP)	Sophie Lamb (MoLAS) and Chrissie Harrison
Finds illustrations	Cate Davies, Helen Davies and Michael Miles
Photography (PCA)	Cheryl Blundy, Strephon Duckering, Tudor Morgan-Owen and Richard Young
Photography (SCARP)	Ken Walton (Institute of Archaeology, UCL) and Mike Webber (Museum of London)
Roman pottery	Malcolm Lyne
Medieval and post-medieval pottery	Chris Jarrett
Clay tobacco pipe	Chris Jarrett
Building Material	Ken Sabel
Small finds	Märit Gaimster
Glass	John Shepherd and Sarah Carter
Human bone	Natasha Dodwell and Kathelen Sayer
Animal bone	Philip Armitage
Environmental analysis	Alys Vaughan-Williams
Coffin furniture	Duncan Sayer
French translation	Agnès Shepherd
German translation	Sylvia Butler
Index	Trevor Ashwin
Series editor	Victoria Ridgeway

Figures

Summary

The Millennium Project at Southwark Cathedral was one of many schemes conducted across the country to mark the beginning of the new millennium. The work involved cleaning and conserving the fabric of the Cathedral, landscaping and reorganisation of the churchyard, and the construction of new buildings on its northern side. This provided an opportunity to revisit the scene of earlier excavations, undertaken by Graham Dawson in the late 1960s and early 1970s, and to explore elements of the Cathedral fabric through excavation and standing building recording.

The archaeological story of Southwark Cathedral begins in the first years of Roman occupation, with the construction of a road heading southwest from a crossing point of the Thames, which provided access to the city of *Londinium,* close to modern London Bridge. The final intended destination of this road to the southwest remains unknown, though the excavations provided the potential to explore more fully its origins, construction and adjacent buildings. Artefacts and ecofacts provide insights into the lifestyle of the inhabitants, amphorae fragments may reflect the wine drunk by road builders whilst wild fruits and nuts may have supplemented a diet based on cattle, sheep and pig, as well as pulses and grains such as barley.

Although a Saxon origin for the Cathedral is suspected, no definite evidence for such was forthcoming. Pitting, of 10th- and 11th-century date may be associated with an early church, but could equally reflect a gradual expansion of occupation close to the crossing point of the Thames prior to the establishment of the Augustinian Priory of St Mary in 1106. Piecemeal excavations in small trenches around the perimeter of the Cathedral revealed elements of the foundations and fabric of the building, whilst a student training program set up by the Institute of Archaeology, University College London enabled the recording of various elements of the Cathedral's fabric.

The results of the different strands of evidence have been pulled together here into a narrative, which takes the form of a 'tour' around the Cathedral. This begins in the medieval nave and progresses through the building and out into the cloisters of the priory unusually situated to the north of the church, but here providing access to the Thames. Finds and historical data are woven into the description of the church and associated buildings. The re-examination of skeletal remains recovered by Dawson from the chapter house provides some insight into the wealthy lifestyle and rich diet of the priors.

The priory church survived the dissolution remarkably well. However, although the church escaped demolition, it did suffer a period of neglect. The cloisters and ancillary buildings north of the church fell into private ownership and were converted to domestic and industrial use, new buildings were constructed within the former precinct and ultimately even against the church fabric itself. The church, rededicated to St Saviour, deteriorated until the early 17th century when parishioners acquired the church and began a series of repairs. An examination of the post-medieval church fabric follows a similar structure to that of the priory church.

The archaeological investigations provided an opportunity to examine some of the secular buildings surrounding the post-Reformation church and also revealed elements of the burial grounds. Interpretation of the recorded upstanding and buried remains is augmented by a wealth of historical sources including numerous plans and copious illustrations of the area, many of which are reproduced here, giving an indication of the changing fortunes of Southwark Cathedral through time.

Evocative of the change in use of the former priory buildings is the conversion of the former chapter house to a pot house for the manufacture of Delftware; this, earliest kiln, was subsequently extended to the east, using the north transept wall in its construction. The publication includes a detailed report on the form of the kilns, the products of the pot house and methods of manufacture.

Following a consideration of the results of the fieldwork the volume concludes with a vision for the future of the Cathedral, provided by Richard Griffiths, with an illustration of the construction of the new buildings by Ptolemy Dean, both architects to the project. This also provides a guide to surviving archaeological remains preserved during the construction works, which are visible around the Cathedral.

No single publication could encompass every aspect of Southwark Cathedral's 2000 years of fascinating history, and this volume covers only a small portion of that story. However, it is hoped that this publication provides something of interest to the student of church architecture, archaeologist and visitor to Southwark Cathedral alike.

Acknowledgements

Pre-Construct Archaeology would like to thank The Chapter of the Cathedral Church and Collegiate Church of St Saviour and St Mary Overie, Southwark who kindly funded the archaeological fieldwork and the post-excavation analysis, which has resulted in this publication. Also CoLAT for providing funding to enable the integration of work carried out by SCARP into this volume. Special thanks go to the Dean, the Very Reverend Colin Slee, Anne Burgess, Roy Horsecroft, Sarah King, Matthew Knight, the vergers, especially Paul Timms, and the entire cathedral staff. Thanks also to the Millennium Commission who partly funded the Cathedral's Millennium Project.

Pre-Construct Archaeology would also like to thank the project team for their help and co-operation throughout the fieldwork, especially Graham Preston, Brian Lawrence, Ptolemy Dean. Richard Griffiths, Dominic Echlin and Guy Neville. Thanks also to the main contractors, Walter Lilly, especially Paul Andrews, Mike Dolling, Ian Edwards and Mike Parker; and to Foundation and Exploration Services Ltd for their hard work, especially Norman Kitchener, Bob Hide and Bob Skinner.

The authors would like to thank Dave Beard, Sarah Gibson, Harvey Sheldon and Dr. Richard Gem for their help and advice, and Peter Moore as the Project Manager. Thanks also to Frank Meddens and Victoria Ridgeway for managing the post-excavation program.

Big thanks to the site staff for their hard work; Mark Bagwell, Jon Balderson, Tony Baxter, Mark Beasley, Tim Bradley, John Brown, Jon Butler, Tim Carew, Nick Crank, Toby Cuthbertson, Lorraine Darton, Anna Deeks, Simon Deeves, Strephon Duckering, Ruth Duckworth, Gary Evans, Colin Forcey, Astrid Hatam, Sam Hatrick, Anne George, Gavin Glover, Jack Green, Ireneo Grosso, Sean Jackson, Chris Jarrett, Ben Lammas, Jim Leary, Adam Lord, Shane Maher, Chris Mayo, Natasha Mulder, Gef Parsons, Mick Parsons, Ashley Pooley, Alan Rae, Mark Randerson, Derrick Roberts, Victoria Ridgeway, Freya Sadarangani, Dan Slater, James Taylor, Jo Thomas, Steve Townsend, Will Valentine, Phil Wert, Justin Wiles, Hanne Wooldridge, Elliott Wragg and Ken Yandall.

Many of the above would also like to thank My Tea Shop, Luncheonette and the Wheatsheaf public house, for sustenance throughout the project and the many people who showed interest in the archaeology and history of the Cathedral and its environs.

The Southwark Cathedral Archaeological Research Project (SCARP) was initiated by Gustav Milne, who provided support and encouragement throughout the work. Mike Webber supervised the first season's recording with Nathalie Cohen, and Simon Roffey co-directed recording work from 1997–2000. Site survey was undertaken by Duncan Lees and Kate Pollard . Thanks are due to Sarah Gibson, and colleagues from MoLAS and UCL, who visited the site. From UCL, Dominique Quevillon recorded the moulded stone fragments, Karin Semmelman undertook on site stone typing and assessment and Rachel Foster examined the roof bosses. Nathalie Cohen would like to thank Dan Swift, for working at the site, transport, and extensive discussion of the results of the recording work over the last several years. Adrian Miles and Gustav Milne read and commented upon drafts of the text.

The site assistants, who produced the excellent drawn record presented in this report under difficult and dusty conditions were Alex Hall, Alex Langlands, Kathryn Thomas; Jon Binns, Clare Bridgewater, Jane Camps-Linney, Maria Cannata, Caroline Carter, Joanne Caulfield, Merry Collins, Neville Constantine, Simon Davis, Matt Easton, Henry Escudero, Julie Everett, William Fowler, Fiona Littlewood, Liz MacKillop, Sally McAleey, Rikki Osterlund, Katie Pack, Hannah Padley, Elissa Rauba, Matt Sears, Abigail Stokell, Joanna Taylor, Patrick Tomlins, Maria Vinnels, Tiziana Vitali and Sylvina Wood.

SCARP would also like to thank the parishioners and staff of Southwark Cathedral, in particular Paul Timms, Dean's Verger and Derek Turner, Canon's Verger. Graham Norwell, Aidan Platten and Marcus Smith (Choir and Chapter House Vergers) also helped the project providing access to the tower and triforium. Dr Peter Draper from the Fabric Advisory Committee provided help and advice during the project. The first two seasons work were funded by the F.A.C. while funding from the Royal Archaeological Institute and Medieval Archaeology Society supported the building recording work in the triforium. The London Archaeological Research Facility, and the Southwark and Lambeth Archaeological Excavation Committee provided funds for assessment and analysis work.

The editor and authors are greatly indebted to Barney Sloane for reading, commenting on and suggesting revisions to drafts of this text, particularly for his advice on the integration and presentation of excavated evidence and building recording. The editor would also like to thank Jonathan Butler for reading and commenting on a late version of this text, Josephine Brown for all her help with the graphics work for this project and Sally Mills for access to her MA dissertation (Mills 2004). Thanks also to Southwark Local Studies Library and the Guildhall Library, City of London for all their help with providing images for this publication and for allowing their reproduction.

Foreword

Archbishop Emeritus Desmond Tutu launched the appeal for Southwark Cathedral's Millennium Project in 1997. In April 2001 Dr Nelson Mandela opened the new buildings after attending a service in the cleaned and repaired Cathedral church. With their permission, this monograph is dedicated to those two electrifying men as our great friends. They represent all that has inspired people for centuries. Their lives are a reflection of the Gospel: Love, Forgiveness, Reconciliation, a profound understanding of Justice; they are men of integrity, truthfulness, resilience and fun. Christian faith, genuinely apprehended, is not for the faint hearted, neither is it dreary.

This monograph records the discoveries made as the Millennium Buildings were constructed, but also draws upon earlier work. It is an important publication, not because of its dedication (although no other Cathedral could lay claim to a project begun and ended by two such men); nor because of the archaeology here explored and discussed, hugely significant though that is. It is important because it links the ancient origins of this church with the present reality of its role and ministry. Cathedrals are dynamic buildings, they have organic life, they represent continuous change and development in fabric and in society, but they also revere tradition, depth, stability and permanence.

Archaeology is not an exact science. Everything in this publication is, in its own way, provisional. More discoveries, greater scholarship and new techniques will cast their illumination on this document and that is as it should be, the archaeology and the Cathedral Church have a great deal in common – far more than the fabric of which they are constituted. They relate a vibrant tale of community: the very stones are soaked in the character, prayer and unconventionality of Southwark. The constant growth of scholarship, critical study and new techniques in archaeology parallels the same growth in biblical study and the pilgrimage of faith.

I am indebted to this Cathedral's archaeologists because they have worked with enormous flexibility, showing an understanding of our present role whilst exposing successive layers of our origins. They have written this record of the past, they have enabled us to place past and present alongside each other. It is genuinely exciting. Anyone who thinks archaeology is dry as dust or irrelevant to our present is mistaken. It holds the secrets, it is the seedbed of our present experience.

I commend this publication to everyone: professional or amateur historian and lay person, in the skills and science of archaeological study. I believe the story that is told will inspire and encourage readers to a marvellous appreciation that we really do stand on holy ground in Southwark.

The Very Reverend Colin Slee
Dean of Southwark
March 2009

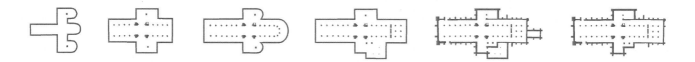

Chapter 1   Introduction

Southwark Cathedral, officially the Cathedral and Collegiate Church of St Saviour and St Mary Overie, in the London Borough of Southwark and county of Surrey, sits 300m south of the River Thames (TQ 3265 8040), just east of London Bridge and opposite the formerly walled City of London and Roman *Londinium*. The archaeological importance of this area has been known for many years and the obvious focus of the site is Southwark Cathedral itself, which evolved from 11th-century, possibly earlier, foundations into the important medieval priory of St Marie Overie, post-reformation parish church and most recently Cathedral. However the study area also lies within the historic heart of Southwark on the southern side of London Bridge, the crossing point of the Thames to the City of London, from Roman times onwards.

Today the Cathedral occupies a relatively low-lying position in the modern landscape; overlooked by buildings, roads and rail lines into London Bridge Station, a result of hundreds of years of occupation and development adjacent

to Borough High Street, the modern approach road to London Bridge (Fig. 1).

ARCHAEOLOGY, BUILDING RECORDING AND THE MILLENNIUM PROJECT

The Millennium Project at Southwark Cathedral was the impetus for the archaeological and architectural work described in this volume. As one of many schemes conducted across the country to mark the beginning of the new millennium, the project involved conservation and cleaning of the fabric of the Cathedral, landscaping and reorganisation of the surrounding churchyard, and the construction of new buildings on the church's northern side, linked by an underground passage into Montague Chambers, where the Cathedral's administrative offices are housed. The scheme was designed to embrace the regeneration of Southwark's riverside, which has seen the

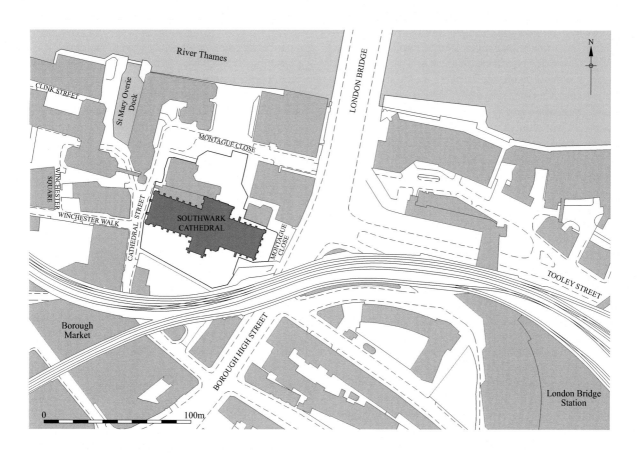

Fig. 1   The site location (scale 1:2,500)

semi-derelict landscape of late 19th- and 20th-century warehousing transformed to take on the challenges of the 21st century.

Due to the known archaeological potential of the site, the effect of any construction works on important archaeological remains had to be considered during the planning stage of the project. The new buildings were to be located on the northern side of the Cathedral where, between 1969 and 1973, Graham Dawson had previously undertaken archaeological excavations on behalf of the Southwark Archaeological Excavation Committee (SAEC) (Dawson 1971a; 1971b; 1976). A watching brief carried out on the excavation of three test-pits during November 1998, by Dave Beard, the archaeological consultant for the project, determined that elements of the significant remains identified during the previous excavations were still present. Three main phases of archaeological work were undertaken, determined by the redevelopment proposals. Phases 1 and 2 of the excavation work were undertaken to the north of the Cathedral building, in areas that were to be occupied by the new buildings, housing various facilities including an exhibition area, shop and refectory (see Fig. 5, Trenches 1 and 2). Although full excavation was carried out on these areas, various elements of the remains were preserved for display within the new building. Phase 3 involved a series of watching briefs and excavations on various service trenches around the Cathedral where the impact on buried deposits was generally much less and the depth of excavation was limited.

The archaeological work was carried out by Pre-Construct Archaeology Ltd (PCA) and monitored by Sarah Gibson of Southwark Borough Council. Phases 1 and 2 of the excavation were supervised by David Divers, while Phase 3 was largely supervised by Chris Mayo. The work was carried out alongside site work undertaken by the main contractors for the project, Walter Lilly, with Citex and Foundation and Exploration Services Ltd. The excavation and subsequent post-excavation program were generously funded by The Chapter of the Cathedral Church and Collegiate Church of St Saviour and St Mary Overie, Southwark with the financial assistance of the Millennium Commission who partly funded the Cathedral's Millennium Project.

Additionally, in June 1996, the London Archaeological Research Facility (LARF) accepted an invitation from the Fabric Advisory Committee of Southwark Cathedral to undertake the recording of the floor plan and ledger slabs at the east end of the Cathedral. Gustav Milne, of the Institute of Archaeology, University College London, set up a student training programme to record the floor and two seasons' work were carried out; in June 1996, the north and south transepts, the crossing and the retro-choir ledgers were recorded (supervised by Nathalie Cohen and Mike Webber, Museum of London) and in June 1997, the remaining slabs in the north and south aisles, the chancel and the high altar were the subject of investigation (supervised by Nathalie Cohen).

Due to the proficiency of the student teams there was also time during the first two seasons to examine some of the surviving medieval fabric within the building, and in late 1997, the Southwark Cathedral Archaeological Research Project (SCARP) was set up under the direction of Nathalie Cohen (Museum of London) and Simon Roffey (Institute of Archaeology) to record the medieval and post-medieval masonry of the east end of the Cathedral, and to interpret the early history and development of the priory buildings. The City of London Archaeological Trust (CoLAT) provided funding to enable the integration of this work into this publication.

Firstly, the internal and external fabric of the northeast transept chapel was recorded and became the subject of an undergraduate dissertation (Roffey 1998a; 1998b). During 1998 and 1999 the surviving medieval masonry in the triforium and tower was examined and three further dissertations on moulded stone fragments (Quevillon 1999), wooden roof bosses (Foster 2000) and a study of the development of the east end (Hall 2000) were undertaken. Elements and summaries of all of these documents are incorporated in this monograph. In 2000, during the final full season of student training, the wall monuments and chest tombs were recorded to complement the record made of the post-medieval ledger slabs and a study was undertaken of some of the doors of the Cathedral.

The first two seasons' work were funded by the Fabric Advisory Committee while funding from the Royal Archaeological Institute and Medieval Archaeology Society supported the building recording work in the triforium and the London Archaeological Research Facility, and the Southwark and Lambeth Archaeological Excavation Committee provided funds for assessment and analysis work.

Since the completion of the student training programme, SCARP has continued to undertake projects within the Cathedral, including further survey and a study of the early 15th-century tomb and chantry chapel of John Gower (Hines *et al* 2004). This volume aims to bring together the results of these archaeological and building recording projects.

BACKGROUND

Geology and topography

The landscape and natural environment of the area now occupied by Southwark Cathedral has witnessed significant and continual changes over the last few thousand years. The underlying geology of the site consists of London Clay, laid down some 50 million years ago when Southwark was part of a sub-tropical estuary. Above the London Clay are found the Shepperton Gravels, which were deposited by a fast-flowing river Thames during the latter stages of the last Ice Age (Gibbard 1994).

Following the end of the Ice Age, some 10,000 years ago, the north Southwark area consisted of a dynamic landscape with a series of shifting sand dunes forming within the Thames. These have been traced along the river from Westminster to Rotherhithe (Sidell *et al* 2000, 103–110), and, in the Southwark area, they had sufficiently stabilized to permit human activity upon them by the late Mesolithic period, some 5500–6500 years ago (Proctor and Bishop 2002). By this time the dunes would have formed into a series of islands, otherwise known as eyots, within the Thames, set within a landscape of river channels, marshes, mudflats and lakes, which would have provided a rich and varied habitat, ideally suited for a variety of activities throughout the prehistoric period. Since the last Ice Age there has been a persistent rise in sea levels, which has had the effect of slowing down the speed of flow of the river, raising its level and causing it to deposit a thick blanket of sediment. In north Southwark, this has resulted in the gradual submergence of the islands beneath a complex of sands, silts and peats.

Two main islands have been identified in Southwark and the site of Southwark Cathedral lies on the northernmost of these, which would have been a potential focus for early occupation (Fig. 2). Gravel deposits were recorded during the excavation at levels of approximately 1.2m OD immediately north of the Cathedral but dropped to 0.96m OD over a distance of c. 30m to the north, towards the Thames, and to 0.73m OD some 40m to the east, towards a natural inlet to the river. At the northern end of the site, the upper 0.2m of the gravel had been disturbed and reworked, possibly by floodwaters from the Thames.

The gravels were all overlain by 0.15–0.40m thick layer of very dark brown clay, described in previous excavations as 'chocolate clay' (Dawson 1976) which was recorded in Trenches 1 and 2 at levels between 1.33m and 1.23m OD and in Trench 3 at 1.21m OD. These clays, which are now attributed to a rise in river levels in the late pre-Roman period, are found elsewhere in north Southwark overlying the gravels at similar levels (Drummond-Murray et al 2002, 24; Cowan 2003). It is not clear if the Thames continued to rise gradually during the first millennium BC flooding the higher gravel islands later in the millennium as part of the same depositional process seen in lower-lying parts of Southwark where alluvial silts and clays are often over 1m thick, or alternatively if these clay deposits at Southwark Cathedral and elsewhere on the higher gravels are the result of separate events, perhaps resulting in the redeposition of estuarine sediments during the Iron Age (Watson et al 2001, 10). Although worked flint and prehistoric pottery were recovered from the clay there was no evidence for any occupation or activity on the site until the arrival of the Romans by which time the area appears to have been relatively habitable.

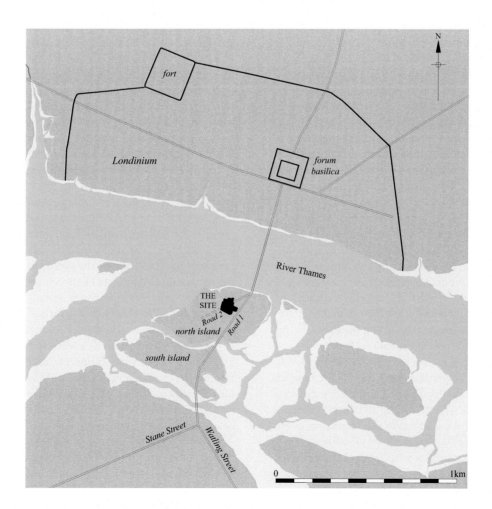

Fig. 2   The site in relation to the islands of north Southwark and *Londinium c.* AD 200 (scale 1:20,000)

Archaeological background

The diversity of environments found within north Southwark during the prehistoric periods has resulted in prolific evidence for occupation having been recorded here. The earliest evidence of human presence consists of various flint tools, including microliths that may have been used to form points and barbs on arrowheads, which appear to have been lost by transient Mesolithic hunter-gatherers some 5500–6500 years ago. These groups were no doubt making the most of the rich and abundant resources along the streams and islands that would have formed the landscape and environment of Southwark during that period.

During the latter parts of the Neolithic and throughout the Bronze Age, around 3000–5000 years ago, there is evidence that these mobile groups had started to engage in farming activities. As well as herding cattle and other livestock to and from the river, there are indications that the land was being ploughed; numerous examples of 'ard-marks', the scars cut into the sub-soil from primitive ploughs, have been recorded across the islands of north Southwark (Sidell *et al* 2002, 35–36). At Three Oak Lane, 1km to the east, the preserved wooden remains of a share from one of these primitive ploughs was recovered (Proctor and Bishop 2002). As well as witnessing farming, the north Southwark islands also became a focus for religious or ritual activities. This may best be demonstrated by the vast quantity of metalwork and other prestigious objects, including swords, spears and axes, which have been recovered from the Thames. These items may represent offerings made to the gods or to mark propitious events, and some evidence of these practices has been found in the vicinity of London Bridge (Sidell *et al* 2002, 62–63). Funerary activity is also represented; at Fenning's Wharf, located just the other side of London Bridge, a ring-ditch that may have been a ploughed-out roundbarrow was used as a focus of several cremation burials during the Bronze Age (Sidell *et al* 2002).

During the excavations at the Cathedral, 28 pieces of struck flint were recovered, including a pyramidal core characteristic of Mesolithic industries as well as a small quantity of prehistoric pottery of probable Bronze Age date. None of these came from contexts that were unequivocally prehistoric in date, the original prehistoric layers having been disturbed by later activity, but they do demonstrate that human groups were at least visiting the site from the Mesolithic period through to the Bronze Age.

Towards the end of the Bronze Age, rising river levels and the formation of extensive peat deposits progressively constrained activity on the islands, but there is increasing evidence that people were still living and farming along the higher points up until the advent of the Roman conquest.

The settlement of Southwark and the crossing point of the Thames have their origins in the early Roman period, the original bridge being located about 50m downstream of its modern counterpart. Roman settlement in Southwark initially developed during the AD 50s along the main road (generally known as Road 1), which more or less follows modern Borough High Street, a northern extension from Stane Street and Watling Street, which approached London from the south. Despite an early setback, when Roman Southwark appears to have been razed to the ground along with *Londinium* during the Boudiccan revolt of *c*. AD 60, the settlement continued to expand into the 2nd century, ultimately to occupy an area of *c*. 20–24ha (Perring and Brigham 2000, 147). Following the construction of the city wall around *Londinium* Southwark became the only substantial extra-mural area, although it appears to have contracted to an area around the bridgehead in the 4th century.

As settlement expanded other roads were constructed including one, (Road 2), which has no modern successor, leading southwest from the bridge and apparently continuing directly underneath the site of Southwark Cathedral. The destination of this road remains disputed; no archaeological evidence for it continuing to the southwest beyond the Cathedral has yet been found.

Roman settlement in Southwark is well studied in general and the frequency of archaeological interventions, particularly in recent years as a result of developer-funded excavations, has led to the production of numerous publications dealing with aspects of the settlement, complementing a wealth of shorter site-specific articles. It is not the intention of the authors to reproduce that work here, but to highlight the state of knowledge at the time of the excavations. The scene was set in the late 1970s with the publication of summaries of excavations in the 1970s and 1980s by the Southwark and Lambeth Archaeological Excavation Committee (SLAEC) and the Museum of London's Department of Greater London Archaeology (DoGLA) (Bird *et al* 1978; Hinton 1988) and has been supplemented in recent years by several monographs covering various aspects of the settlement (eg: Watson *et al* 2001; Drummond-Murray *et al* 2002; Cowan 2003, Hammer 2003; Yule 2005 as well as a wealth of shorter articles).

Although previous archaeological work has revealed much general evidence for the development of the area, not only for Roman Southwark, but also for the medieval priory and later post-medieval industries, supplementing a range of historical sources, the excavations most relevant to the site are those conducted between 1969 and 1973 along Montague Close, for many years a small lane sandwiched between large Victorian warehouses and the Cathedral itself (Dawson 1976). These excavations led to the discovery of the Roman road (Road 2) leading to the bridgehead. They also revealed features interpreted as elements of a Saxon Minster, medieval burials and structural elements of the priory, as well as 17th- and 18th-century tin-glaze pottery kilns. Details of Dawson's findings are discussed below in reference to the results of the recent excavations.

Despite its Cathedral status, and its long history, the Church of St Saviour in Southwark has received, until recently, comparatively little modern archaeological attention. Architectural elements of the Cathedral are described in detail in the RCHM volume of 1930, which identifies eight major building phases within the fabric of

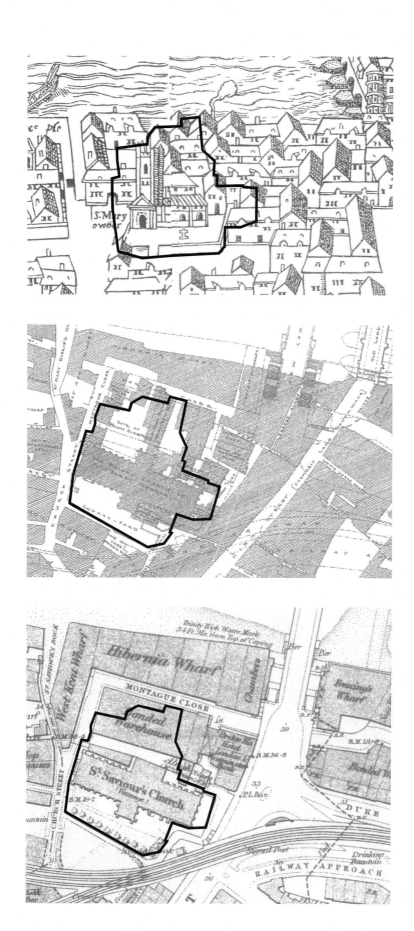

Fig. 3 The site in relation to Agas' map of c. 1562, Dollman's 1881 plan (showing early 19th-century buildings) and the 1st edition Ordnance Survey map of 1872 (Agas not accurately scaled, otherwise scale 1:2,000).

The Agas map is reproduced by kind permission of the publishers, Harry Margary at www.harrymargary.com, in association with the Guildhall Library, London. Dollman is reproduced by kind permission of Southwark Local Studies Library the church, and by Cherry and Pevsner (1983), while the history of the priory has been discussed by many different writers (see Taylor 1833; Thompson 1904; Stevens 1931; Higham 1955). A short introductory history is presented here and more detailed analyses are given in Chapters 3 and 4 below.

Given the location of the site near the Roman bridgehead it seems highly probable that, subsequent to Roman occupation and following a period of relative abandonment, settlement grew up around a ferry point prior to the construction of the bridge, and there may have been activity in the area of the site from at least the mid 9th century onwards (Carlin 1996, 9). However archaeological evidence for earlier Saxon activities in Southwark is elusive, amounting at best to a handful of pits excavated by Dawson, to the north of the Cathedral, interpreted by him as representing elements of a Saxon Minster. Although John Stow records legends of a 7th-century nunnery replaced by a 9th-century college of priests (Stow 1994, 52), the Cathedral's earliest surviving identified fabric dates from the early 12th century.

Whatever the earlier history of building here, the Domesday Book of 1086 records a *monasterium,* or Minster, on the site said to have been in existence during the reign of Edward the Confessor (1042–1066). The priory of St Mary was founded on this site in 1106, and is believed to be London's first Augustinian house (Luard 1866, 430), although the exact circumstances and nature of the foundation are obscure. Regularisation of the priory and the establishment of formal Augustine rule seems to have followed at a later date (possibly only a few decades later), and this accords well both with what is known about the lives of the founders of the priory and with the wider pattern of the foundation and development of early Augustinian houses.

Much of the 12th-century building was destroyed by fire in the early 13th century (Tyson 1925, 33), and rebuilding was still incomplete at the end of the 13th century. The surviving medieval fabric (see Chapter 3, below) reflects the extensive renovation necessitated by this damage and additionally that of the frequent episodes of flooding caused by the priory's proximity to the Thames; the structure as it survives today shows evidence of subsidence in several places. Further damage was caused by a fire in the south transept and parts of the choir in the 1390s and in 1469 the nave roof collapsed and was rebuilt in timber.

At the reformation the priory church was surrendered to King Henry VIII, to become the Parish Church of St Saviour and the parishes of St Margaret and St Mary Magdalene were amalgamated with it. As a result the priory buildings were put to new uses: the northeast transept chapel was used as a vestry and as a place where rates and taxes were assessed and paid (Stevens 1931, 50), while the retro-choir (which was also known as the Lady Chapel) was used in 1555 for the examination of some of the Marian martyrs (Stevens 1931, 61). During the later part of the 16th century, the retro-choir was leased out as a bakehouse, and ovens and kneading troughs were installed within

the building. Livestock was also housed in the retro-choir during this period (Concanen and Morgan 1795, 78) and the conventual buildings were granted to Sir Anthony Browne, who adapted the prior's house in the precinct as his residence. To the northeast of the chapter house a pot house was constructed, as identified by Dawson, for the manufacture of Delftware pottery, which is documented as being produced on the site from 1613 (initially within the chapter house itself). This is the earliest indication of what was to become one of Southwark's most important industries, and one that continued well into the 18th century. The schematic Agas map of *c.*1562 does not show an accurate representation of the form of the church; there is no nave and there appears to be a missing area between the tower crossing and the east end. However, it does show the former claustral buildings extending as far as the Thames to the north with the area to the northeast, between the church and London Bridge, densely occupied by buildings (Fig. 3a).

In the early 17th century, the church was repaired; the retro-choir was restored to the church in 1624 but a fire in 1676 damaged the eastern end of the church, and alterations and repairs continued to be made by the parishioners throughout the 18th century (Dollman 1881, 16).

It was not until the 19th century that the church was thoroughly restored by George Gwilt. Renovations were undertaken at the east end of the former priory church between 1818 and 1824 and both the chapel of St Mary Magdalene and the Bishop's Chapel were demolished at this time (RCHM 1930, 59). This was necessitated by the construction of the new London Bridge between 1823 and 1831. The routes of both old and new London Bridges are indicated on Dollman's survey of 1881, which illustrates the church and surrounding buildings as they were before demolition, in relation to the layout of the new bridge, buildings and infrastructure (Fig. 3b). In 1838 the now roofless nave was pulled down and rebuilt by Henry Rose (Cherry and Pevsner 1983, 564). This was subsequently replaced by a new nave in the Victorian Gothic style designed by Sir Arthur Blomfield and built by Thomas Rider (1890–7). The riverside location became increasingly valuable as wharfage during the later post-medieval period and by the end of the 19th century the whole area between the Cathedral and the river was dominated by large warehouses (Fig. 3c). In 1905, diocesan reorganization saw the parish church become a Cathedral and regain its earlier dedication as the Cathedral and Collegiate Church of St Saviour and St Mary Overie.

METHODOLOGY

The archaeological excavations

A watching brief undertaken on the excavation of three test-pits during November 1998, by Dave Beard, the archaeological consultant for the project, discovered that parts of the significant remains identified during Dawson's

Fig. 4   The evaluation in progress, looking west

The third phase of the project involved watching briefs and excavation undertaken during other works on the site including the construction of foundations, excavation of service trenches and general landscaping; a total of 21 interventions were investigated between February 2000 and April 2001.

The excavation areas were wholly determined by the proposed development and the mitigation strategy employed during these works ensured that, where possible, archaeological deposits remained *in situ;* the depths to which features were excavated being determined by the redevelopment proposals. Within Trench 1 isolated 'islands' of stratigraphy approximately 2m thick survived. Whilst these remains were mostly fully excavated, part of the Roman road, elements of medieval masonry and the pottery kiln were preserved *in situ* for permanent display in the new building, as were some brick warehouse walls. Trench 2 fell entirely within the footprint of the Victorian Bonded Warehouse (see Fig. 3c), the basements of which had truncated virtually all of the archaeology except cut features, or deposits slumped into them.

Interventions in Phase 3 were generally much more limited in scope and thus analysis of evidence from this phase of archaeological works involved a multi-faceted approach, combining the use of historical maps and sources with the archaeology, in order to present a coherent sequence. This approach has been necessitated not only by the complicated medieval and post-medieval history of the site, but also by the fact that much of this work involved small-scale investigations of key-hole trenches, rather than full-scale excavations as conducted in Phases 1 and 2. The main areas of excavation were the conjoining Trenches 3, 4 and 5 at the northwest corner of the Cathedral; Trench 3 being the only trench in the Phase 3 works to be excavated down to natural deposits. Trench 14 at the eastern end of the Cathedral revealed extensive medieval remains, which are now on display in the new herb garden. Medieval masonry was also recorded in many of the other trenches as were human burials although the extent to which these were excavated was determined by the nature of the works, most of the trenches being for the provision of drainage runs. A policy of leaving all skeletal remains as undisturbed as possible was also followed. In eight of the trenches (numbers 6, 7, 8, 9, 10, 11, 12 and 13) no archaeological finds were uncovered, due to the limited depth of excavation rather than the absence of archaeology in these locations (these trenches are therefore not numbered on Fig. 5).

The multi-faceted approach adopted in examining the archaeological evidence around the church provided a unique opportunity to test histories of the Cathedral, in particular the works of Francis Dollman, published in 1881 (see Fig. 3b). Dollman's work is amongst the most thorough architectural record and history of the Parish Church of St Saviour, and any reader cannot help but be impressed by its detail, not only regarding the church but also in placing the building in context with surrounding Southwark in the 19th century. The Millennium excavations have demonstrated that for the most part Dollman's record is

previous excavations were still present. Consequently Southwark Council's archaeological officer, Sarah Gibson, required an archaeological evaluation be undertaken to assess the extent of these remains. The evaluation involved the investigation of an area measuring a maximum of 10m north to south by 13m east to west immediately adjacent to the Cathedral's northeast transept chapel (Fig. 4), in part covering the area previously investigated by Dawson (1976). This established that most of the masonry features, the stone walls of the priory and the brick-built pottery kilns originally identified by Dawson remained *in situ* and, although much of the 'soft archaeology' had been removed, some areas between the old excavation trenches survived beneath cables and pipes.

Three main phases of excavation were undertaken. Phase 1 led on immediately from evaluation in what was to become Trench 1 and Trench 1a dug for the insertion of a lightwell for Montague Chambers, between May and September 1999. Trench 1 was essentially an extension of the evaluation trench and was contained within what had been Montague Close, between the Cathedral and the site of the Victorian warehouses (Fig. 5). Phase 2, the excavation of Trench 2, immediately to the north of Trench 1, was conducted during October and November 1999.

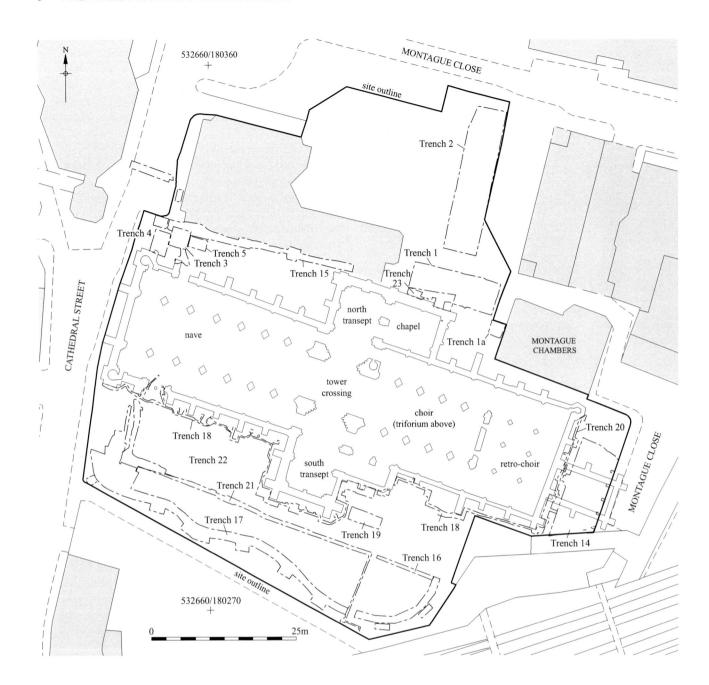

Fig. 5   Areas of archaeological investigation in relation to elements of the Cathedral church (scale 1:625)

Reproduced by permission of Ordnance Survey on behalf of HMSO. © Crown Copyright 2008. All rights reserved. Ordnance Survey Licence number 100020795

accurate; in the places where discrepancies do occur, it is possible to rationalize them with comparison to the archaeological sequence revealed at Southwark Cathedral.

Recovered artefacts and ecofacts including pottery, building materials, faunal remains, human remains and small finds from the site were examined, catalogued and assessed and where relevant the results of their analysis have been incorporated into this document. Detailed reports and catalogues have been produced and are held in the archive. Details of the methodologies used for analysing the pottery and human remains are presented below.

Roman pottery assemblages were quantified by numbers of sherds and their weights per fabric (Lyne 2003). These fabrics were identified using a x8 magnification lens

with inbuilt metric scale for determining the natures, sizes, forms and frequencies of added inclusions and classified using the system formulated by the Museum of London Archaeology Service (Davies *et al* 1994; Symonds and Tomber 1994). Two of the assemblages were large enough for quantification by Estimated Vessel Equivalents (EVEs) based on rim sherds (Orton 1975).

Saxon and medieval pottery was classified using the Museum of London Archaeology Specialist Services' pottery type codes. Pottery was quantified for each context by fabric, vessel shape and decoration using sherd counts (with fresh breaks discounted) and estimated vessel numbers and the information entered onto a database.

Selected articulated skeletal material was analysed to determine, where possible, the age and sex of the individual, his or her stature and any gross pathology. General methods used in the osteological evaluation of the material are those of Bass (1992), Buikstra and Ubelaker (1994) and Steele and Bramblett (1988). An assessment of age was based on the stages of dental eruption and epithyseal union, on the degree of dental attrition (Brothwell 1981) and where possible, on changes to the pubic symphysis (Brooks and Suchey 1990).

The sex of the individual was ascertained where possible from sexually dimorphic traits on the pelvis and the skull and from metrical data. No attempt was made to sex immature individuals. The living stature of the skeletons was, where possible calculated from the long bone lengths using the regression equation devised by Trotter and Gleser (1958).

The remains of sixteen individuals were recovered during excavations in 1969–1973. As there was no skeletal report available for these remains a brief analysis was undertaken to ascertain the age and sex of the individuals and any pathology present and is included below (Chapter 3). It should be noted that this was in no way intended to be a full osteological analysis of these remains.

A single-context recording system was used throughout the excavations and the building recording. During the post-excavation analysis the stratigraphic information was organised into chronological periods based on stratigraphic and dating evidence. In this text individual context numbers assigned during the excavation appear in square brackets (eg [100]), for clarity and to avoid confusion in the case of duplicate numbers from the two aspects of work those from the building recording project appear

without brackets, ledger slabs with the prefix 'L' (eg [L200]) moulded stone fragments are numbered thus: <M4>.

Various cartographic sources have been used to compile the figures used in this publication. In particular, two historical plans have been used: that of Dollman produced in 1881, which presents reconstructed plans of the church and adjacent buildings as they stood in the 1830s, prior to their partial demolition to make way for the approach to the new London Bridge; and the Royal Commission on Historical Monuments (RCHM) survey, published in 1930 (Dollman 1881; RCHM 1930). Additionally, recent Ordnance Survey maps, as well as engineers' survey plans produced for the Millennium Project have been used. PCA's archaeological trenches were related to the Ordnance Survey grid using a total station theodolite.

Generally in this publication both SCARP's building recording work and PCA's excavation trenches are shown in relation to the church as illustrated in the RCHM survey. However, in two areas of this publication the excavated remains have been related to Dollman's plan; both are associated with secular structures around the perimeter of the Cathedral, not elements of the fabric of the Cathedral itself. A delftware kiln was constructed against the northern wall of the chapel and, due to the RCHM plan recording later modifications to the north wall of the chapel (see below), the kiln evidence has been related to Dollman's plan (Fig. 109, Fig. 110, Fig. 112). Additionally remains of buildings recovered to the southeast of the Cathedral are shown as numbers 6 and 7 Chain Gate by Dollman (see Fig. 100) and thus the excavated remains have been related to his survey.

Because of the problems inherent in surveying a building the size of Southwark Cathedral, the many structural alterations which have been carried out to the

Fig. 6   Cleaning masonry on the north side of the triforium
©SCARP

fabric of the building, as well as the different levels of detail to which such a building may have been surveyed in the past, there were areas where historical plans of the Cathedral did not exactly match recent surveys. In particular the RCHM plan of the northeast corner of the Cathedral did not match any other plans, being slightly too far west, and thus the plan has been modified to match the Ordnance Survey and engineers' survey drawings. Additionally excavated evidence for the Lady Chapel (later the Bishop's Chapel) at the east end of the Cathedral matched Dollman's 1881 plan but not the RCHM survey, perhaps not surprisingly as it had been demolished by 1830 to make way for the construction of the new London Bridge. On the relevant figures (Fig. 56, Fig. 81, Fig. 122) the RCHM plan has been adjusted to match the excavated evidence of the Lady Chapel and Bishop's Chapel, and Dollman's plan.

The northeast corner of the northeast transept chapel also presented difficulties. It would appear that major work was carried out to the walls of the north aisle, north transept and north transept chapel which involved the construction of new buttresses and elements of wall facing. These were partly removed during the Millennium Project, and earlier elements of the Cathedral fabric were revealed resulting in differences in the thickness of the northern wall of the northeast transept chapel as shown on Dollman, RCHM and Ordnance Survey plans.

The building recording project

In order to accurately record the ledger stones a temporary grid was laid out using two 30m tapes set parallel. The inner edge of the walls and the outline of the ledger stones were then individually planned at a scale of 1:20 using off-sets from the grid (see Fig. 85). The locations of wall monuments and chest tombs were recorded in a series of measured sketch elevation drawings. Every memorial was individually numbered and described in a catalogue, which noted briefly the information contained upon it, and its condition (see Fig. 86).

Datum lines were emplaced on selected internal and external elevations of the northeast transept chapel and a plan of the outline of the floor was completed. In the triforium, the masonry was cleaned (Fig. 6) and datum lines were instated along the walls of the choir triforium, the retro-choir and the aisles and surveyed in by MoLAS Geomatics. Elevations and plans in both areas were hand drawn at scales of 1:10, 1:20 or 1:50 depending on the size of the masonry remains under investigation (see Fig. 38). A photographic corpus of black and white record shots, complemented with colour images, was also created.

THIS REPORT

This publication attempts to bring together the results of archaeological excavations and standing building recording into a coherent whole and additionally to integrate the results of analysis of recovered material. Chapter 2 deals with the evidence for exploitation of the area during the Roman period; the foundation and construction of Road 2 in the middle of the 1st century AD, its use, repair and modification and associated occupation evidence. This is followed by a study of the development of the church from a consideration of its documented Saxon origins, through the establishment of the priory in the 12th century to the Dissolution (Chapter 3). The study of the construction and development of the priory church, its associated buildings and their use takes the form of a 'tour' through the church and conventual buildings drawing on the evidence recovered both through archaeological excavation and the study of the buildings' fabric. Chapter 4 discusses the post-Reformation church using the same 'tour' approach, and also considers the increasing domestic and industrial use of the land around the church, again drawing on the evidence from standing buildings and archaeological investigation, in conjunction with contemporary illustrations and cartographic information. One aspect of this increasing encroachment of industry on the land between the church and the river is the establishment of a pot house in the early 17th century initially in the former chapter house, for the manufacture of Delftware. A small part of this early kiln and significant remains of later, 17th- and early 18th-century, kilns were uncovered during the excavations. The form of the kilns, technology used and products manufactured are discussed in Chapter 5. Chapter 6 draws conclusions about our current knowledge of the history and archaeology of the site based on the data presented in the preceding chapters and the volume concludes with a consideration of the new buildings in their modern setting by the architect, Richard Griffiths.

The archive

The site archives for both the work carried out by PCA and SCARP will be deposited in the London Archaeological Archive and Research Centre (LAARC), the archaeological element of the work under the site code MTA 99, and the historical building records under the site code SCA 96.

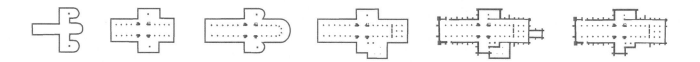

Chapter 2 The Roman Sequence

David Divers

with Philip Armitage, Sarah Carter, Märit Gaimster, Malcolm Lyne, John Shepherd and Alys Vaughan-Williams

It is generally accepted that Roman London developed from about AD 50, the location being selected as a crossing point of the Thames. The construction of the southern approach road to this crossing (Road 1) from Stane Street and Watling Street to the south would have been one of the first tasks for the Romans in what is now Southwark, probably during the early AD 50s (Drummond-Murray *et al* 2002, 14). It is not clear when the first bridge was built but excavations on the site of the Jubilee line extension suggest that it was in place by AD 50 and the northern bridgehead was certainly being developed by AD 52 (Brigham 2001, 23). South of the river, the actual bridgehead is more elusive as its remains are generally thought to have been destroyed by erosion in the medieval period, although there is some evidence for later 1st-century revetted embankments on Southwark's Thames frontage (Brigham 1998, 31). The actual location of the southern bridgehead has been

generally inferred by the alignments of Road 1 and Road 2, which joins it from the southwest (see Watson *et al* 2001, 33 and fig 15)

Excavations between 1969 and 1973 along Montague Close, carried out by SEAC under the direction of Graham Dawson, first discovered the subsidiary Roman Road 2 which crosses the site leading to the bridgehead, associated with gravel extraction pits and a roadside ditch, and later adjoined by clay and timber buildings (Dawson 1976) (Fig. 7.1). Also of significance are the excavations carried out in 1974 at the nearby Bonded Warehouse site by SLEAC where the same road, associated gravel extraction pits and a roadside ditch were recorded below what is currently the Mudlark pub (Fig. 7.2). These excavations also revealed evidence for clay and timber buildings having been built over the backfilled roadside ditch, and a stone wall on the same alignment as the road, probably of later Roman

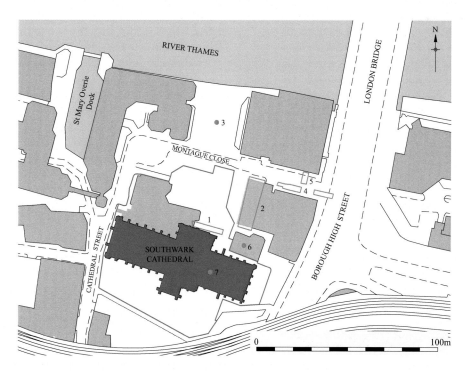

Fig. 7   Previous excavations along the line of Road 2 in the vicinity of the site 1) Montague Close, 2) Bonded Warehouse, 3) Hibernia Wharf, 4) District Heating Scheme, 5) Hibernia Chambers, 6) Montague Chambers, 7) The Cathedral crypt (scale 1:2,000)

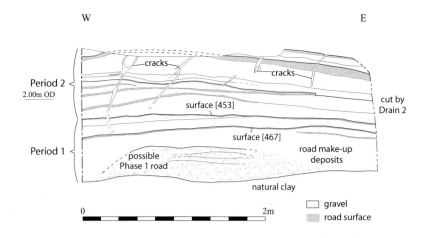

Fig. 8   South facing section through the road as seen in Trench 1; for location see Fig. 9 (scale 1:40)

date (Graham 1978). What appears to be the equivalent roadside ditch was also excavated at Hibernia Wharf (Fig. 7.3), along with more gravel pits and a clay and timber buildings constructed over the ditch (Richardson 1981, 49), though the results of this excavation remain as yet not fully published and the exact location of this observation is unknown. Further evidence of the road and associated buildings was found to the northeast on Tooley Street, during works for the District Heating Scheme (Graham 1978) (Fig. 7.4) and at Hibernia Chambers (Bird *et al* 1978, 23, fig. 5) (Fig. 7.5) and more evidence for buildings was found at Montague Chambers (Thompson *et al* 1998, 210) (Fig. 7.6). In addition a group of sculptures and inscriptions were found in the backfill of a well during excavations in the crypt of the Cathedral (Fig. 7.7). The excavation in the crypt revealed occupation layers dating to the 1st century and a 3rd-century Roman well, backfilled during the 4th century, with much dumped building debris as well as a group of sculptures. The statues are of Roman gods and deities; one inscription comes from a votive altar and a second from a tombstone (Hammerson 1978). It is likely that they are from a mausoleum rather than a temple, although the subsequent choice of location for the medieval priory may perhaps indicate an inherent religious significance to the site.

PERIOD 1: C. AD 50/55–70 ROAD CONSTRUCTION

In the Millennium excavations the road was the dominating Roman feature on the site. The excavations suggested that its initial construction involved dumping a layer of gravel up to 0.55m thick directly onto the natural clay (Fig. 8). The ground was probably relatively dry and firm at the time as there was no evidence of gravel sinking into the clay, and frequent root holes in the clay indicate that plants were colonising the area. The earliest, fragmented, evidence for a road surface indicated it was about 8m wide, with a cambered, metalled surface [467] at 1.75m OD. Pottery recovered from the make-up deposits

for the road would appear to suggest a date around AD 55–60 for its construction (see Fig. 14.1 – Fig. 14.4; Lyne 2003, Assemblage 3).

However, previous excavations at the adjacent Bonded Warehouse site revealed the earliest road (Phase 1) to be only 4.2m across at its maximum extent with cambered sides and a surface only 2.5m wide; this first phase of gravel construction being only 0.4m thick (Graham 1988, 239). At the Bonded Warehouse there was evidence that the road was subsequently widened, being extended slightly to the northwest (Phase 2). These original surfaces were not evident in plan during the Millennium excavations at the Cathedral, due to extensive truncation of the southwest side of the road. However, tip lines recorded in section within the early gravel dumps appear to reflect the original northwest edge of the road (Fig. 8) and may equate to the Phase 1 road identified at the Bonded Warehouse (although the road indicated in section during the Millennium excavations appears slightly narrower than that seen at the Bonded Warehouse).

The earliest road surface identified in plan [467] (see Fig. 10) appears to equate to the third phase of road construction at the Bonded Warehouse site. The pottery dating from the lowest road surface gravels suggests that these initial construction, resurfacing and widening events occurred over a short period of time, probably less than 10 years (Lyne 2003, Assemblage 3).

Gravel extraction pits

The gravel for the road was presumably derived from pits dug along its edge. On the north side of the road several pits were excavated. Three of these were dug into the surface of the natural clay underneath the northwestern side of the earliest identified road surface [467]. However if the road had initially been narrower and subsequently widened as indicated on the Bonded Warehouse site (Graham 1988), these would have actually been to the northwest of the original extent of the road (as indicated on Fig. 9), which strengthens the argument for an early

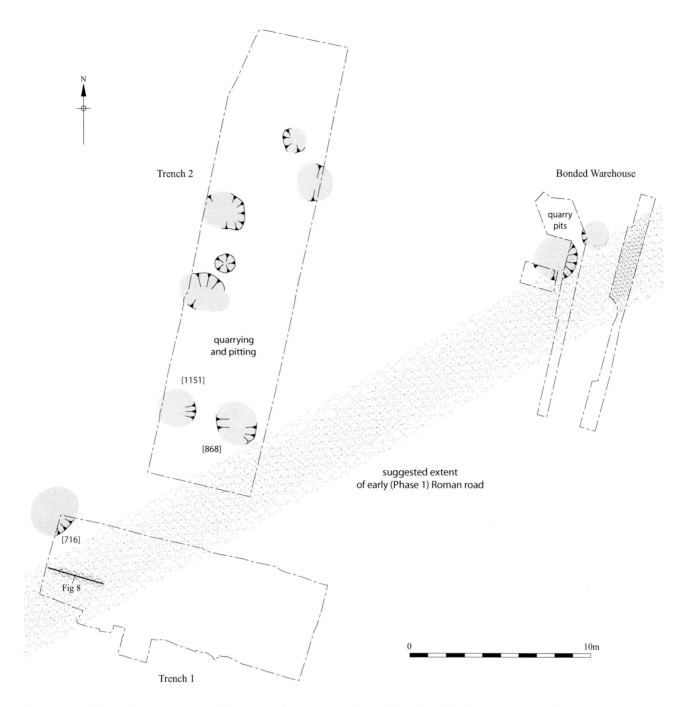

N

Trench 2

Bonded Warehouse

quarry
pits

quarrying
and pitting

[1151]

[868]

suggested extent
of early (Phase 1) Roman road

[716]

Fig 8

0   10m

Trench 1

Fig. 9   Early road construction and associated quarry pits; the width of road has been estimated from evidence seen
in section (Fig. 8) and observations of the Bonded Warehouse Phase 1 road (scale 1:200)

precursor, as indicated in section (Fig. 8), such as was
found at the Bonded Warehouse.

The largest of these extraction pits [868], which only
survived in a 0.7m wide strip between 19th-century
foundations, was 2.2m across east–west and about 0.9m
deep with steep, concave sides and a rounded base. It
contained large fragments of an imported, Gauloise
amphora, internally lined with resin, but also locally-
produced amphora in Sugar Loaf Court ware, indicating a
deposition date of AD 50/5–60 (Lyne 2003, Assemblage 1).
A second pit [1151] was circular, at least 1.7m in diameter
and contained a variety of imported and locally-produced

wares, dating to around AD 50–70 (Lyne 2003, Assemblage
2). A third quarry pit [716], recorded in the northwest
corner of Area 1, produced only one sherd of pottery dating
to AD 50–100. The presence of locally-produced wares
indicates that a Roman settlement in London was already
in existence by the time these pits were backfilled, probably
during the AD 50s.

Three more large pits excavated slightly further north
were probably also for gravel extraction. They were
typically over 2.0m in diameter and up to 0.8m deep with
concave sides and rounded bases. Their lower fills were
of gravel, while the upper fills were brown clay, making

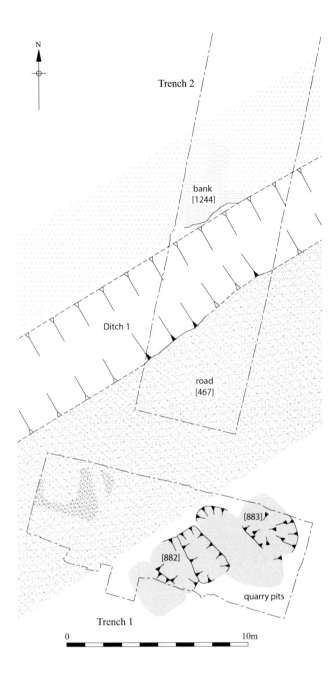

Fig. 10   Period 1 road with associated bank, ditch and pits (scale 1:200)

typically had a lower gravel fill, probably representing material fallen from the sides of the pits soon after they were dug with further brown silty clay fills suggesting the pits had been left open for some time, the colour deriving from the natural clay, which found its way back following the gravel extraction. These early deposits did not completely fill the pits, which would have remained visible for some time, being lower than the general ground level to the southeast. The pottery recovered from the quarry pits, which suggests a deposition date of AD 55–60, contained a high percentage of amphorae and flagons possibly used as containers for wine consumed by the road-builders.

It seems likely that the postulated original road, which was only 4.2m wide and 0.4m thick (Graham 1988) was probably constructed with gravel derived from the less systematic quarrying northwest of the road and that these southern pits were dug for a second or third phase of construction when the road was widened (as [467]); a suggestion strengthened by their close proximity to the southeastern edge of this road surface. Dating evidence from the pits again suggests that this occurred very soon after the road's initial construction, possibly some time in the late AD 50s or early AD 60s.

Ditch 1

A ditch 4.6m wide and 1.5m deep ran adjacent to the road's northwest edge. This was not a feature associated with the road in its earliest phase as it cut through some of the early gravel extraction pits while an associated bank covered others. The excavated gravel was presumably used for road construction, while the natural clay was used to create a bank [1244] on the northwest side of the ditch, which slumped slightly into the ditch in the west. The primary ditch fill was predominantly gravel, presumably derived from the natural gravels through which the ditch had been cut. Overlying this were several fills that were probably associated with the early silting of the ditch. The pottery, suggesting a c. AD 60–65 date for these primary fills, comprised a high proportion of storage vessels with resin sealant in their necks or on their shoulders, which indicates they would have contained both dry and liquid goods (eg Fig. 14.9, Fig. 14.11; Lyne 2003, Assemblage 5). A small wooden ball, c. 35mm in diameter and perhaps representing a toy, was recovered from the silty infilling of the ditch (Fig. 11).

Large stakeholes along both sides of the ditch were initially thought to represent several phases of revetment construction. On the northwest side of the ditch were four distinct rows of closely spaced stakeholes; the remnants of the upright timbers survived in some of the locations. The timbers were typically of unconverted oak roundwood (c. 100mm diameter) tapering to a point. The mineralised remains of horizontal on-edge planks, which appeared to have been nailed to the front (southeast) of the piles of the latest, most central, row of posts confirmed at least one phase of revetment construction. The revetment was built along the lower edge of the ditch to support its sides and

the edges difficult to see against the natural clay through which they had been dug. Two smaller pits in this area may have also been associated with this activity but would have produced very little gravel. These pits produced limited dating evidence; the absence of finds suggesting that they were relatively early. It is not clear whether they relate to the postulated initial phase of road construction or a later resurfacing or road-widening episode.

The most systematic gravel extraction was apparently slightly later and occurred to the southeast of the road where five adjacent sub-rectangular pits had been excavated, closely following the southeastern edge of the identified road surface [467] (Fig. 10). The pits ranged in size from 5.0m by 2.0m by 1.0m deep to 3.0m by 1.8m by 0.8m deep and had quite steep sides and flat bases. They

Fig. 11   Small wooden ball recovered from the primary infilling of Ditch 1 (1cm scale)

bank, indicating the ditch's importance for drainage, and reflecting an ongoing concern with keeping it clear and empty. An associated upcast bank was identified to the north of the ditch (Fig. 12).

Similar alignments of stakes excavated at Hibernia Wharf (SAEC 1973) were interpreted as piles for a building constructed on the backfilled ditch, which may also be the case on this site as they follow the same alignment as the wall of a later building (see below), and although some of the timbers and stakeholes appeared to be sealed below the associated bank, this appearance may be due to the bank slumping into the ditch. However, this cannot be the case with the latest line of stakes (illustrated in Fig. 12), which had planks nailed along its front, clearly forming a revetment and it is generally considered that here the stakes are more likely to represent revetting episodes. Several ditch fills were associated with the construction of these revetments produced pottery suggesting that the earliest revetments may have dated to AD 65–70 (see Fig. 14.14 – Fig. 14.15; Lyne 2003, Assemblage 6). None of the timbers produced a dendrochronological date. A dog skull recovered from one of these fills probably derives from a disturbed burial of a pet, although it could alternatively represent a votive offering associated with revetment construction.

On the southeast side, a similar line of stakes was found, close to the southern edge of the ditch, forming a revetment represented by the impressions of piles driven deep into the natural gravels. These also mirrored the projected wall alignment of a later building, although the requirement for such deep piles for a wall built over the upper edge of the ditch was probably unnecessary. The revetment probably functioned not to consolidate the sides of the ditch as with those built on the northwest side, but to hold back the road gravels that would have been up to 0.7m thick and prevent them slumping into the adjacent ditch. Deposits associated with the erection of the first of these revetments produced pottery suggesting a c. AD 65–70 construction date (Lyne 2003, Assemblage 6).

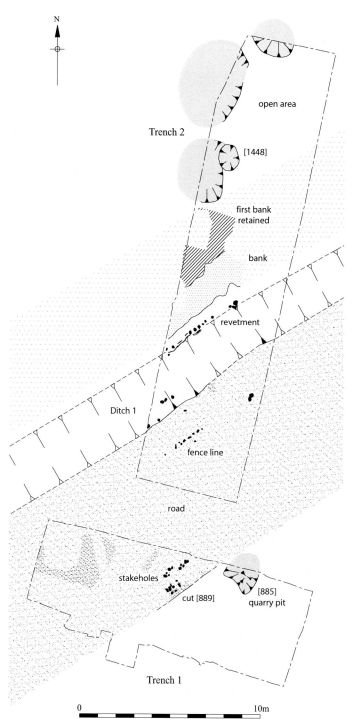

Fig. 12   Period 1 road in relation to Ditch 1 and modified bank (scale 1:200)

On the adjacent Bonded Warehouse excavations, a ditch to the north of the road was attributed to the 3rd phase of road construction, and was similarly dated. On that site a bank of sand dumped to widen the early road on its northwest had a near vertical edge, which, it was suggested, had originally been supported by a timber revetment (Graham 1988, 241).

Fig. 13   Ditch 1 during excavation, looking southwest

Fences

Several rows of stakeholes were found cutting through the lower layers of road gravel along both sides of the road, perhaps representing fences or posts protecting road users from a drop into the ditch or into the partially infilled pits or alternatively representing the location of stalls lining the road. They were mostly between 1.0m and 1.5m from the perceived edge of the road indicating the actual useable road surface was limited to the central 5.0m or 6.0m, and not the full 8.0m width. Many of the stakeholes were made with square or rectangular stakes, generally measuring about 60–100mm across.

Further resurfacing and gravel extraction

Several more refinements were made to the road during the pre-Flavian years although some of these produced little or no dating evidence. A fourth layer of gravel was added to the road with a new compacted surface 0.2m higher than its predecessor [453] (Fig. 8). A sixth pit [885] adjacent to the road on its southeast side, cut through the fill of one of the earlier gravel pits, which remained only partially filled at this time, may have provided some of the gravel for this, as may some of the pits to the northwest of the road. The new pit produced a relatively large pottery assemblage including olive-oil amphora sherds and a Verulamium Region Whiteware flagon (Fig. 14.16; Lyne 2003, Assemblage 7) suggesting a c. AD 60–70 date for its fill. It is possible that some of this pottery represents breakages from the putative roadside stalls suggested above.

The southeast edge of the road was defined by what appeared to be a straight vertical 'cut' [889] through the edge of the road gravels and the natural clay. The 'cut' was up to 0.5m deep with a flat base that extended c. 0.3m southeast to the edge of the partially filled gravel extraction pits. This presumably contained some sort of timber structure that would have supported the sides of the road gravel preventing collapse, possibly a road-side box drain.

Open area to the northwest of Ditch 1

The area to the northwest of the ditch appeared to remain little used; some pits continued to be dug here after the construction of the road and although a handful of postholes were recorded, no meaningful alignments could be identified. A layer of uncompacted gravel 0.1m thick in this area may have been dumped in an attempt to consolidate the underlying clay. Some of the larger pits in this area were probably dug for gravel needed during a later phase of road resurfacing, possibly in the decade AD 60–70 based on the few sherds of pottery recovered. A group of weathered cattle bones from one of these larger pits suggest that the pit had not been backfilled after excavation indicating the area was little used. A somewhat smaller pit [1448], which was too small for worthwhile gravel extraction, contained the skull of a horse. It is possible that the pit was deliberately dug for the deposition of the skull, possibly as a propitiatory offering.

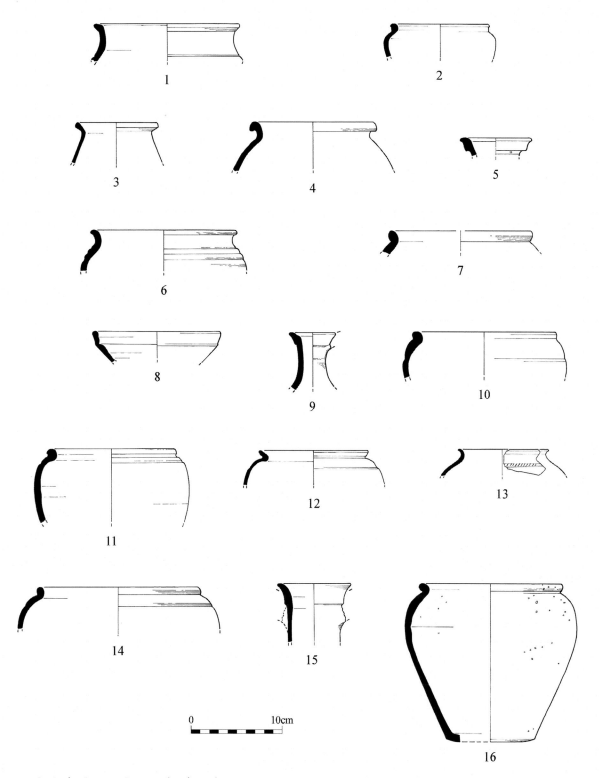

Fig. 14   Period 1 Roman Pottery (scale 1:4)

Period 1, catalogue of illustrated pottery

Assemblage 3. From the earliest road make-up deposits

Fig. 14.1   Rim from necked liquid storage-jar in grey AHSU fabric (Lyne and Jefferies 1979, Class 1A). *c.* AD 50–70.

Fig. 14.2   Small bead-rim jar in lumpy black Highgate Wood B fabric. The presence of resin on the shoulder of this vessel suggests use as packaging for some sort of local commodity. *c.* AD 43–70.

Fig. 14.3   Butt-beaker in very-fine cream-buff fabric with profuse silt-sized quartz and occasional silver mica and soft ferrous inclusions. *c.* AD 43–70.

Fig. 14.4   Hook-rimmed jar in hard sandfree blue-grey fabric fired brown with red margins. Three fresh sherds from this vessel are present. North Gaulish Greyware.

Assemblage 4. From gravel extraction pit [883] to the south of the road

Fig. 14.5   Collared flagon of Monaghan (1987) type 1E5.4 in white-slipped orange Hoo fabric. *c.* AD 43–70/80.

Fig. 14.6   Necked jar with double shoulder cordon in black ERSA fabric. *c.* AD 50–70.

Fig. 14.7   Bead-rim jar in Highgate Wood B fabric. *c.* AD 40–100.

Fig. 14.8   Gallo-Belgic platter copy in black Highgate Wood B fabric. *c.* AD 40–70.

Assemblage 5. From the primary fills of Ditch 1

Fig. 14.9   Complete top of collared flagon of Monaghan type 1E5.1 in white-slipped Hoo fabric with traces of resin sealant inside cupped rim. *c.* AD 43–70/80.

Fig. 14.10   Bead-rim jar in handmade black ERSI fabric with brown margins. *c.* AD 50–70.

Fig. 14.11   Another example in grey ERSB fabric fired brown externally. This vessel has resin all over its exterior and was clearly used as packaging for some kind of dry commodity. *c.* AD 60–120.

Fig. 14.12   Beaker of Marsh type 22 (1978) in grey LOMI-1247 fabric fired pink with external gilt mica dusting. *c.* AD 60–100.

Fig. 14.13   Beaker in black FMIC-1659 fabric (Davies *et al* 1994, fig 137, 847). *c.* AD 60–100.

Assemblage 6. From the first revetment in Ditch 1

Fig. 14.14   Bead-rim jar in black Highgate Wood B fabric. *c.* AD 40–100.

Fig. 14.15   Collared flagon of Frere type 112 (1972) in cream Verulamium Region Whiteware fabric with orange patches. Eight large, fresh sherds from this and another example fired reddish-brown were recovered. *c.* AD 60–75.

Assemblage 7. From pit [885] to the south of the road

Fig. 14.16   Jar with stubby, slightly everted rim in lumpy black Highgate Wood B fabric. 25 large fresh sherds from this vessel are present. *c.* AD 40–100.

Period 1, discussion

There is little to suggest any Roman activity on the site prior to the construction of the road, however the first twenty or so years of the road's creation witnessed a lot of activity, change and development. The first gravel extraction pits to be dug, although located beneath the earliest identified road surface, probably relate to the primary phases of road or road make-up, which was originally significantly narrower than its final width; this width and location being suggested by evidence from the Bonded Warehouse excavations (Graham 1978). These earliest pits contained pottery with an AD 50s date. Interestingly some of the wares were locally produced, indicating that the Roman town of *Londinium* was already in existence when the road was constructed. There is no reason why the earliest phase of road construction could not date to the middle, or even the first half of that decade. No definitive evidence

of this phase of road construction was found at Southwark Cathedral; although there are suggestions of an early road in the tip-lines of gravel make-ups for the earliest identified surface, and quarry pits beneath the first definite road surface are corroborating evidence for an earlier road, the two phases of early construction recognised by Graham (1978) at The Bonded Warehouse were not clearly evident here. Conceivably the construction of the road may have commenced at the bridgehead and progressed to the southwest, resulting in earlier construction and more frequent resurfacing of this road closer to the Thames crossing; and thus here while road make-up dumps may have been deposited, no actual surface was constructed.

If the tip lines recorded in section do represent an earlier phase of road it was thus apparently widened relatively soon after its original construction. Pottery recovered from the lowest gravels, including those on the 'new' northwest side of the road, suggests an AD 55–60 date, as does pottery from the systematically dug quarry pits to the southeast of the road. The roadside ditch, clearly a later addition as it cut through the backfilled early gravel extraction pits, produced pottery suggesting it was dug around AD 60–65.

Road 1, built in the very early AD 50s, was certainly Southwark's primary road. Early clay and timber buildings have been found fronting onto it at several sites on Southwark's north island; the Jubilee Line Extension excavations at Borough High Street revealed evidence for the destruction of buildings fronting the eastern side of Road 1, attributed to the Boudiccan revolt of around AD 60, indicating that the settlement was already well established at that time (Drummond-Murray *et al* 2002). Early buildings found fronting the other side of Road 1 during the District Heating Scheme works had also been destroyed by fire (Graham 1988). The Jubilee Line Extension excavations found no evidence for early buildings away from the road; nonetheless the pre-Boudiccan settlement probably extended along both sides of Road 1, possibly along the entire length of the road from the bridgehead to the southern edge of Southwark's north island (Drummond-Murray *et al* 2002, 49, 67). No buildings of this period were found along Road 2 nor was there evidence for the Boudiccan revolt on the site, although a 1st-century building excavated in Southwark Cathedral crypt may have burnt down (Hammerson 1978, 207). Further west, at Winchester Palace, evidence was found for a large, high status building, in the form of building materials recovered from waterfront reclamation dumps (Yule 2005, 21). Although not provably of local derivation (the material may have been deliberately imported to the site, perhaps by barge) it seems probable that this material represents a structure from the immediate vicinity. Whilst there was no indication of the alignment of this early structure, a metalled surface possibly representing a third road, Road 3, was constructed, dated to between AD 50 and 70–100, following approximately the same alignment as Road 1 (Yule 2005, 23–25).

The absence of buildings along Road 2 during the 1st century indicates that it was not a simple side-road built to extend the settlement area. Indeed the early date of its construction, and the fact that it was soon widened, presumably to allow the free flow of traffic in both directions, indicates that it was an important thoroughfare, linking the bridgehead with a focus of activity to the southwest. The road had a similar construction to Road 1 on the gravels of Southwark's north island, and it was of a comparable size; Road 1 measuring up to 1.5m thick by about 7m wide (Graham 1988; Drummond-Murray *et al* 2002, 15) while Road 2 was about 1.7m thick and 8m wide.

Despite its apparent importance, the destination of the road still remains a matter of some debate. One possibility is that it went to a crossing point of the Thames between Lambeth and Westminster as suggested, for example, by Sheldon (1978) although there is only limited evidence for this and to date no remains of Road 2 have been found southwest of Southwark Cathedral. If the road had gone as far as Lambeth it would have crossed two channels and would probably have been built on a timber raft, as was Road 1 at 106–112 Borough High Street where it approached the Southwark Street Channel (Graham 1988). It has been suggested that timbers exposed during the 19th century on the projected alignment of Road 2 at 51 Southwark Street may have been piles to carry the road over soft ground (Bird *et al* 1978, 525, site 85) but the possibility that timbers found during excavations at 51–53 Southwark Street were part of a bridge over the channel (Cowan 2003, 78) is not entertained by the excavator (Killock 2005). Dillon *et al* suggest that the road may turn south, crossing the channel further east (1991, 258) and it has also been suggested that it may not have extended beyond the island, being built to service the local settlement (eg Heard *et al* 1990, 611). There is limited evidence to support either of these alternatives; however what is clear is that to date there is a distinct lack of evidence for the road extending beyond modern-day Southwark Cathedral.

Had the road continued on the same alignment it would have passed within metres of excavations at the Courage Brewery site, but none of the buildings found on that site were on the known alignment of Road 2 (Cowan 2003, 78–79). This, however, does not disprove the continuation of the road on its projected alignment, as 1st-century buildings between Road 1 and Road 2 have been found aligned to Road 1 even when they are closer to Road 2; for example at the Cathedral crypt (Hammerson 1978, 207), Montague Chambers (Thompson *et al* 1998, 210) and the District Heating Scheme (Graham 1988). Further south, less reliable observations made on the south side of the Cathedral in the early 19th century describe a tessellated floor aligned northeast–southwest (Bird *et al* 1978, 524, site 79) which might just reflect the continuation of Road 2.

It is increasingly argued, as new road alignments and buildings are discovered in Southwark, that the settlement developed to make best use of the irregularly shaped land available which prohibited a regular grid system of roads being establishment (Cowan 2003, 78). However, the dominant influence on alignment seems to have remained that of Road 1.

PERIOD 2: AD 70–130 MAINTENANCE AND MODIFICATION OF THE ROAD

The road continued to be repaired with further layers of gravel and new surfaces being added. These developments are virtually impossible to date, as there was little or no finds evidence and little to relate the resurfacing events to activities on either side of the road. The third major phase of construction identified saw the road surface raised another 0.3m to 2.33m OD. Also associated with these works was the installation of a northwest–southeast orientated drain (Drain 1) cutting through the previous road surfaces but concealed below the new surface (Fig. 15, Fig. 16). The drain was 0.60m wide and 0.82m deep with vertical sides and a flat base, which drained to the northwest, presumably into the roadside ditch. The base of the drain was formed by a layer of flat compacted gravel and the impression of timbers and decayed wood along its sides suggested the road gravels had been supported by timber shuttering along the sides and roof of the drain. The fill of the drain produced pottery indicating an AD 100–120 date, although much 1st-century material was present as were a few small sherds of later wares suggesting material was still making its way into the drain as late as the 3rd century. Similar timber 'box drains' have been found channelling water beneath road surfaces in the City at Poultry and also beneath the surfaces of the arena at the

Fig. 15   Drain 1, looking north, showing traces of timber lining

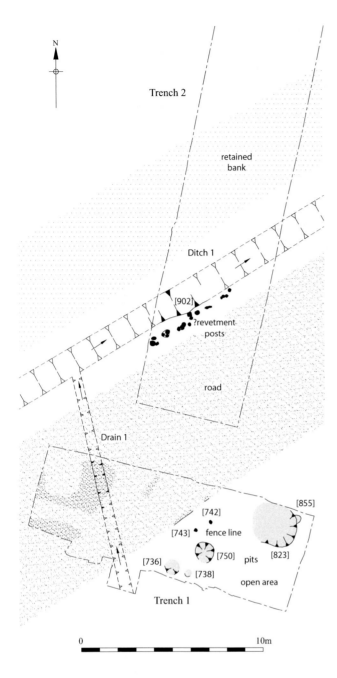

Fig. 16   Period 2 road showing Drain 1 and contracted Ditch 1 (scale 1:200)

Fig. 17   The road during excavation, showing the severe impact of later intrusions

Guildhall (Hill and Rowsome forthcoming, Bateman *et al* forthcoming).

The new road surface associated with the construction of the drain was frequently repaired with isolated areas receiving additional layers of gravel and new metalled surfaces (see Fig. 8). The next major resurfacing saw the road raised a further 0.25m and then by another 0.2m before its final major refurbishment raised its height another 0.25m to 3.06m OD with a total thickness of 1.7m (Fig. 17). The road therefore had six clearly identified main phases of construction and repair, with a possible further two inferred from excavations at The Bonded Warehouse to the northeast of the site. There was little dating evidence for

these various repairs and rebuilds, although a second large drain or ditch, Drain 2, added in the early–mid 2nd century (see below), presumably marked the disuse of Drain 1, but could not be directly related to any of the major phases of road construction.

Ditch 1

Maintenance of the ditch continued and it was apparently cleaned out from time to time, although following the last phase of revetment construction on its northwest side, it was left open and became infilled with a combination of natural silting, casual backfilling and refuse disposal. These infilling deposits produced finds indicating a Flavian date, AD 69–96 (Fig. 19.1–Fig. 19.4; Lyne 2003, Assemblage 8). Several fills post-dating the construction of the first revetment on the southeast side of the ditch were generally attributed to natural silting and occasional casual dumping. Remains of glass vessels were recovered from these infilling deposits, including fragments from a late 1st- to early 2nd-century pillar-moulded ribbed bowl (see Fig. 25.3), a fragment of late 1st- to mid 2nd-century jar (see Fig. 25.5) and the handle from a cylindrical bottle of late 1st- to early 2nd-century date (see Fig. 25.7).

Although the ditch was ultimately allowed to silt up, it may still have been necessary to maintain the revetment on its southeast side; this was apparently rebuilt, possibly on a larger scale due to the increasing thickness of the road (though it is possible that these timbers were associated with later construction of a roadside building, see Building 1, below). A series of posts, or piles, had been driven to depths of up to 1.5m, mostly through natural gravels and surviving postholes suggest the posts were arranged in groups of three. There was no evidence for planking, or other structural detail and none of the posts survived, having been driven from higher up the edge of the ditch than the timbers on the other side, and therefore being less waterlogged. Pottery associated with this revetment suggests a construction date of about AD 100 (see Fig. 19.5 – Fig. 19.7; Lyne 2003, Assemblage 9). Also recovered from

Fig. 18   Penannular brooch

these deposits was the femur of a black rat. This bone is the second earliest evidence yet for *Rattus rattus* in Britain, introduced to Britain by the Romans, the earliest being from a pre-Boudiccan level at Fenchurch Street (FEH 95) in the City of London (K. Rielly, *pers comm*). Although not the earliest example in London, it is of significance in being the earliest example in Southwark, indicating the rapid spread of this unwelcome rodent vermin, a subject previously discussed by Armitage (1984; 1994).

Decay and possible collapse of the revetments on the northwest side of the ditch had resulted in the clay bank partially slumping into the ditch. There was some evidence for the re-cutting [902] of the ditch during the late 1st or early 2nd century, possibly at the same time as the new revetment was constructed on the southeast side of the ditch. The re-cut ditch continued to become infilled, the various fills being interspersed with the insertion of piles and stakes for which no specific function could be attributed other than the possible repair of the roadside revetment. Early 2nd-century pottery produced from these later fills included fifteen sherds from a Verulamium Region Greyware jar indicating deposition after AD 120 (see Fig. 19.10; Lyne 2003, Assemblage 10); a late 2nd-century fragment of glass presumably being intrusive, possible falling down a void where a timber had rotted away. Also recovered from these deposits was a penannular brooch of Fowler Type A1 with its pin surviving and flattened faces to the knob terminals (Fig. 18).

Open areas to the northwest and southeast of the road

To the north of the road the absence of Flavian finds indicates that this area was little used during the later 1st century, whilst the area to the southeast of the road probably remained as general wasteland, again with little

evidence of any activity, except for two small pits, until later in the 1st century when sandy gravel layers up to 0.7m thick were dumped here to level the uneven ground, and to consolidate the relatively soft clay fills of the gravel extraction pits. These dumps were overlain by an organic-rich layer largely consisting of waterlogged hay; it is not clear if this material, which was up to 0.25m thick, had accumulated over a period of time or if it was dumped as a single event. It contained a quantity of residual early local wares but later pottery suggested a deposition date of around AD 70–100.

Further dumping occurred southeast of the road sometime around AD 120, possibly being contemporary with the backfilling of the roadside ditch to the north, extending across the entire excavation area south of the road. Five pits [750], [823], [855], [738] and [736] dug into these dumps ranged in size from 0.4 – 2.5m in diameter, the largest being about 0.7m deep, but there was little to indicate their function. As on the other side of the road, the latest dumps were also capped by a gravel surface at a maximum recorded level of 1.57m OD, although this had subsided to a level of 0.87m OD over the gravel extraction pits. Two large stakeholes [742] [743] may represent a fence line or other structure, running parallel with the side of the road

The pattern of alternate dumping and pit digging continued; the gravel surface was soon overlain by a series of dump layers, possibly laid down to compensate for the subsidence into the gravel pits and, ultimately, in preparation for construction. Several large rounded pits typically 1.5m–2.0m diameter and up to 0.7m deep were also dug (again to the south of the road, not illustrated here); one of these had the decayed remnants of a wooden, possible wattle, lining over its shallow concave base and sides. Several small pits, or possible postholes, and a possible cut linear feature about 1m wide were also recorded. Pottery from these deposits suggests a date not long after *c.* AD 120 for their infilling.

Open area to the west

To the west, in Trench 3, and overlying natural clay, was a series of deposits which appeared to have all been dumped sequentially from the southeast extending an area of dry 'reclaimed' ground away from the road. The dumps were generally composed of redeposited gravel, although some had a sandy or silty clay composition and collectively were about 0.4m thick, raising the ground level to *c.* 1.4m OD. The only finds from these dumps were a flint flake and a sherd from a prehistoric jar or cooking pot, both presumed to be residual. These were overlain by another layer mainly composed of gravel, which extended evenly throughout Trench 3 raising the ground by a further 0.15m.

Four small postholes and a small pit in Trench 3 and postholes in Trench 4 represent the earliest activity on this newly 'reclaimed' ground. There was not much dating evidence from the features themselves, and little to suggest what structure the postholes represented, although a further episode of dumping sealing these features produced AD 60–120 pottery; the activity therefore seems comparable to that occurring contemporaneously closer to the road to the east.

Period 2, catalogue of illustrated pottery

Assemblage 8. From the infilling of Ditch 1

Fig. 19.1   Tripolitanian amphora of Peacock and Williams Class 37 (1991) in very fine orange-pink fabric with rough greenish-cream outer skin. The neck and rim are complete but lack any sign of handles. It can therefore be assumed that the handles were attached to the body in the manner of Tripolitanian type II (Peacock and Williams, 1991). Amphorae of this type normally enjoyed a localised North African distribution during the 1st century AD and were only traded over the rest of the Roman Empire from the 2nd to the early 3rd century.

Fig. 19.2   Fragment from lamp in polished, very-fine-sanded deep-orange fabric similar to wares manufactured in Staines (Crouch and Shanks 1984 44).

Fig. 19.3   Reeded-rim bowl in grey ERSS fabric with profuse up to 0.50mm quartz (mainly silt-sized) and sparse-to-moderate up to 2.00mm. calcareous inclusions, fired smooth black. *c.* AD 50–120.

Fig. 19.4   Fragment from a white-slipped closed form in grey Highgate Wood C fabric with roller-stamping.

Assemblage 9. From revetment in Period 2 ditch

Fig. 19.5   Large part of necked jar (16 fresh sherds) in leaden-grey ERMS fabric with burnished vertical lines on the body (Davies *et al* 1994, fig. 77, 467). *c.* AD 50–100.

Fig. 19.6   Top half of flagon of Frere type 238 (1972) in pink Verulamium Region Whiteware fired cream with orange streaks. *c.* AD 60–100 .

Fig. 19.7   Much of fine cordoned bowl of Monaghan (1987) type 4J1–1 in polished black Upchurch NKFW fabric with pink

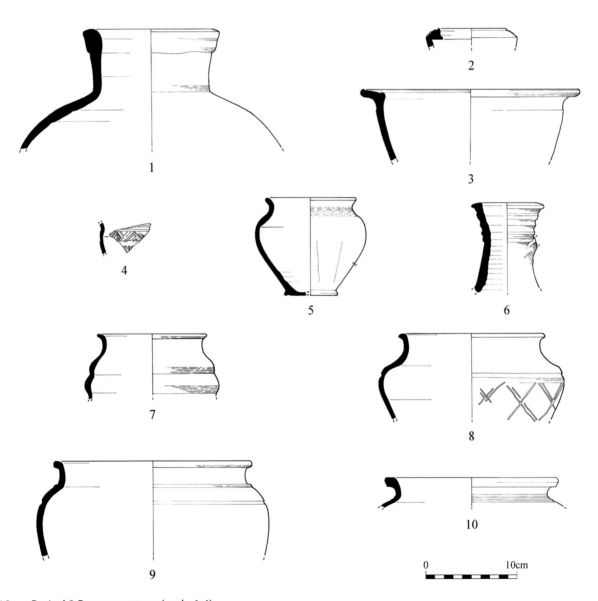

Fig. 19   Period 2 Roman pottery (scale 1:4)

margins. This type is dated to *c.* AD 43–120 in Kent but only appears to reach London in any quantity during the period *c.* AD 100–120.

Assemblage 10. From the infilling of the recut ditch

Fig. 19.8   Jar in black ERSB fabric with girth groove and burnished latticing on the lower part of its body. Three large fresh sherds from this vessel are present.

Fig. 19.9   Jar in polished black ERSB fabric with cordoned neck and shoulder.

Fig. 19.10   Cordoned and necked jar of Frere type 2218 (1984) in reddish-grey Verulamium Region Greyware fired grey. *c.* AD 120–135. Fifteen large fresh sherds from this vessel are present.

Period 2, discussion

The Flavian expansion of Southwark and London north of the Thames is well recognized. Excavations at Borough High Street suggest that renewal of the buildings destroyed by Boudicca occurred around AD 70 with settlement expanding to the east of Road 1 onto lower-lying marginal land, demonstrating that prime areas had all been built upon (Drummond-Murray 2002, 67). This, however, does not appear to be the case on the western side of the road. Here, the buildings fronting Road 1 were rebuilt and extended back from the road, accounting for 1st-century buildings on adjacent sites (eg Thompson *et al* 1998, 210; Hammerson 1978; Graham 1988) but there is little to suggest buildings occupied the Millennium site during the 1st century; the only evidence for this period adjacent to the road being dump layers and pits.

The area to the southeast of Road 2, to the rear of properties fronting onto Road 1 may have been used as a backyard for various activities. Environmental evidence suggests the area was damp waste ground, while an abundance of chickweed indicates it was often disturbed but also nutrient-rich perhaps suggesting exploitation by locally reared animals, a possibility supported by the bones of suckling piglets recovered from contemporary ditch fills. An organic-rich dump deposit contained significant quantities of compacted plant matter, and the abundance of grassland species including buttercups, common chickweed, lesser stitchwort and fat hen clearly suggest the presence of hay.

Drainage of this low-lying area would have been problematic as it would attract run-off water from the road and presumably from the roofs of buildings to the east, and probably other waste from the buildings' occupants. This may have provided the motivation for the construction of Drain 1, which was culverted beneath the road, presumably draining into the roadside ditch. If Drain 1 were built to service buildings fronting onto Road 1, it would have had to be elevated as it crossed the relatively low area adjacent to the road where the partially filled gravel pits would still be apparent. The elevated section of drain may have been

supported on timbers or possibly an earth bank running to the south of the excavation area.

The roadside ditch was sporadically maintained throughout this period and, between episodes of cleaning, material was allowed to accumulate, presumably through a process of silting and casual refuse disposal. Plant remains indicate that a semi-permanent if not permanent stream of water still ran through the ditch, which was colonised by common spike-rush and pondweed with buttercups and dock along its sides. Hazelnuts, wild strawberry and brambles were probably deposited from surrounding hedgerows, while sloes and imported figs are more likely to be food waste. The occurrence of herbs such as coriander and cabbage/mustard seeds may suggest their cultivation in local gardens. Crops such as barley were also indicated, along with large seeds of the corncockle weed but the absence of chaff suggests it was cultivated and processed some distance away, as has been concluded on other sites in the area (Gray 2002, 249). A black rat femur from a ditch fill associated with the construction of the revetment in about AD 100, and certainly no later than *c.* AD 120, makes this specimen the second earliest archaeological record of *Rattus rattus* in Britain found to date. The black rat, an introduced exotic (southern Asian) commensal rodent, is now believed to be virtually extinct in Britain.

The lack of evidence from this period to the northwest of the roadside ditch may also indicate that this area remained wasteland at this time, although the absence of pits or other deep cut features may be due to late 1st-century buildings occupying the area. The remains of the later 1st-century ground surface, and consequently any shallow, or above-ground feature would have been removed during the Victorian period.

Certainly during the early 2nd century attempts were made to make more use of the land. On the southeast side of the road, the ground was raised and levelled and on the northeast, the ditch was backfilled; there appear to have been deliberate attempts made to reclaim a damp and marshy area. Gravel surfaces were laid on both sides of the road around AD 120 and further back from the road in Trench 3 postholes indicated some structural activity.

PERIOD 3: C. AD 130–200 LANDSCAPE REORGANISATION AND BUILDINGS

Roadside ditch

During the 2nd century the roadside ditch (Ditch 1) was deliberately backfilled with dumps, which produced mainly residual pottery; contemporary sherds suggesting a date shortly after AD 120 for their deposition. A thin compacted silty clay layer with frequent stones formed an external surface in this area, probably laid down soon after the backfilling of the ditch. It only survived where it had slumped due to subsidence of the poorly-consolidated ditch fills.

Building activity

Around AD 130, buildings of clay and timber were constructed. Their remains were fragmentary, surviving patchily on both sides of the road and leaving only a hint of the buildings' layouts, their occupants and the activities conducted here. The buildings on the northwest side of the road only survived where they had slumped into the underlying soft ditch fills, thus avoiding destruction during the construction of Victorian warehouses. On the southeast side of the road a more extensive sequence of Roman buildings survived, but only as isolated islands between areas of truncation caused by later interventions, including those which resulted from previous archaeological excavations. All the buildings on the northwest side of the road appeared to be influenced by the alignment of Road 2 (Fig. 20), while as far as could be ascertained some fragmentary remains on the southeast side were aligned with Road 1, some with Road 2.

Building 1

Several make-up layers were dumped onto the gravel surface north of the road, raising the ground level by approximately 0.1m for the construction of a clay and timber building. All that survived of this first building (Building 1.1) was a row of stakeholes parallel to the line of the road with an internal compacted brickearth floor to the southeast (Fig. 20). The stakeholes were initially thought to have contained the upright posts of a wall but it is also possible that they represent the locations of piles that supported the wall, built over the soft ditch fill. The relatively small appearance of the 'stakeholes' may be a misleading consequence of the soft ditch fills becoming compressed, thus reducing their size and they may have originally contained larger timbers such as those recorded on the same alignment in the base of the ditch, the upper parts having decayed. It is possible that the putative revetment posts alongside the road to the south of the building (discussed under Period 2, Ditch 1, above), may in fact have functioned as piles supporting the southern, external, wall of the building. The floor was found at a maximum level of 1.17m OD but sloped steeply down towards the wall due to subsidence of the unconsolidated ditch fills. Pottery from these deposits indicates a construction date for this building in the second quarter of the 2nd century, around AD 130 (Fig. 23.1 – Fig. 23.3; Lyne 2003, Assemblage 11).

Building 1.1 was demolished or fell into disrepair and was ultimately rebuilt. Overlying the brickearth floor were deposits of painted wall plaster, indicating that the building had had plastered walls decorated with a panel-type scheme in pink, red and black on white ground, a relatively common design during the 2nd century. Some yellow and green pigment was also present on the plaster.

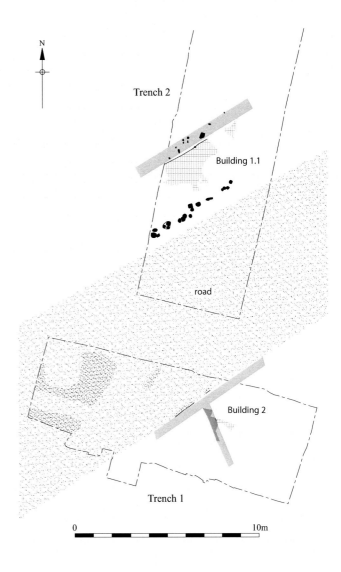

Fig. 20   Period 3 road and adjacent buildings c. AD 130 (scale 1:200)

Building 2

To the south a beamslot and at least two phases of brickearth floors have been interpreted as representing the remains of a second structure, Building 2. Very little of this survived and it is not possible to reconstruct much of its original form with any certainty. The fragmentary remains of wall that did survive suggest that it respected the alignment of Road 2.

Drain 2

Cutting the road from southwest to northeast was a substantial drain (Drain 2) approximately 0.9m wide and at least 1m deep (see Fig. 21). This marked the disuse of Drain 1 and cut through all earlier road surfaces. It appeared, from the vertical nature of its sides and the impression of a timber bearer in its base, to have had a timber lining and may have been similar in construction, though obviously wider and deeper, than Drain 1. It could not be determined whether later road surfaces sealed the drain or not due to later truncation; no surfaces survived that may have sealed the drain. The severity of subsequent truncation renders any attempts to connect this drain with features either side of the road difficult and no evidence for the drain was seen beyond the limits of the road. Infilling dumps incorporated pottery dated to the period AD 120–170, with the drain apparently fully infilled by AD 170 at the latest (Lyne 2003, Assemblage 15). The pottery recovered was typical of an urban domestic assemblage, with cooking pots and flagons alongside smaller quantities of open forms and beakers.

This substantial drain seems likely to have been associated with a major reorganisation of the landscape, perhaps reflecting a need for serious drainage measures, and indicating a continuation of the activity which resulted in the reclamation dumps seen in the previous phase. The course that the drain followed is also curious as it runs parallel to Road 1, some 46m to the east, replacing the earlier Drain 1 and Ditch 1.

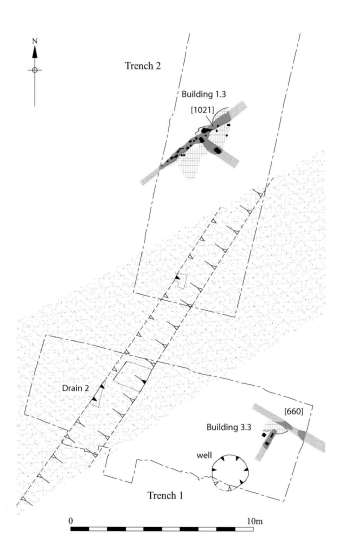

Fig. 21   Mid 2nd-century buildings and Drain 2 in relation to the road (scale 1:200)

Building 1.2 and 1.3

Following the collapse or demolition of Building 1.1, the second building to occupy the same site, perhaps using some elements of the original structure, (Building 1.2), comprised a northeast–southwest orientated beamslot set parallel, but slightly to the southeast of the previous building's wall, with internal compacted brickearth floors surviving to 1.19m OD to the southeast of the wall. This may simply represent a repair to the previous structure; no stakeholes or postholes were found associated with this building's main walls but two stakeholes in the floor may suggest internal modifications to the building.

Dumps up to 0.1m thick overlay the remains of Building 1.2, representing preparation for the third phase of construction in this location. Building 1.3 again comprised a northeast–southwest orientated wall in the same position as its predecessor, represented by a slot with postholes and stakeholes in its base. This building also had a northwest–southeast orientated internal wall represented by a beamslot and posthole (Fig. 21). An internal brickearth floor was found to the south of the beamslots and also an internal clay floor was found beyond the northeast–southwest aligned wall to the northwest, possibly suggesting an expansion of the building at this time. The highest recorded level on the floor was 1.27m OD but, as with the earlier phases of this building, the floor and structural elements that survived later truncation were only those that had slumped into the subsiding ditch fills; the building may well have extended beyond these limits. Most of the pottery from Building 1.3 was residual and those few sherds that may have been contemporary provided little conclusive dating evidence other than to suggest that this building might date to the third quarter of the 2nd century (Lyne 2003, Assemblage 13). A fragment of late 1st- or early 2nd-century jug (Isings 1957, form 55a/b) in thin natural blue-green glass was recovered from a posthole of this building (see Fig. 25.6).

The partial skeleton of a lamb/kid recovered from beamslot [1021] of this building was presumably once a complete carcass placed in the foundations during construction, as a votive offering to help ensure success and good fortune to the occupants.

Building 3

A beamslot and three stakeholes, associated with a brickearth floor at 1.57m OD, represent the remains of a second building to the southeast of the road (Building 3.1). The floor height is probably a relatively accurate indication of the true mid 2nd-century floor level, as the surviving remains of this building did not appear to have suffered much subsidence. The building followed roughly the same alignment as Drain 2 and Road 1. The building probably post-dates the initial construction of Building 1 and must have replaced Building 2, pottery from the beamslot suggesting an AD 160 date for its abandonment (Fig. 23.4 – Fig. 23.5; Lyne 2003, Assemblage 12).

The original surviving wall of the building was rebuilt, a new beamslot being cut seemingly on a slightly different alignment and a new brickearth floor at 1.71m OD was laid on new make-up deposits overlying the old floor. A third phase of construction (Building 3.3) left more substantial remains (Fig. 21). Two beamslots were recorded, one on the same alignment as the original Building 3.1 wall, though slightly further south, with a second perpendicular to it and two associated postholes representing the construction of a new internal wall, though no associated floor surfaces survived. The partial remains of an articulated dog skeleton, comparable in size to a modern Fox terrier, from beamslot [660] may represent a propitiatory offering.

A circular well was located to the south of Building 3.3. Lined with vertical timber planks, the silty fill and backfill produced large fresh early Antonine pottery sherds (Fig. 23.6 – Fig. 23.10; Lyne 2003, Assemblage 14) suggesting infilling around the middle of the 2nd century.

External surface and Ditch 2

To the west, a compacted gravel surface recorded in Trench 3 at 1.91m OD was dated by pottery in its make-up to AD 120–150 indicating the demise of the possible Period 2 structures. Burnt daub and charcoal recovered from a layer overlying this surface may indicate the destruction of a nearby building at this time. Subsequent structural activity was suggested by two more postholes sealed by another gravel surface at 2.0m OD. Contemporary deposits in Trench 4 comprised dump layers and a large but shallow circular pit.

A northwest–southeast orientated ditch (Ditch 2), 1.8m wide and 1.22m deep, cut through the gravel surfaces in Trench 3 (Fig. 22). Its lower fills produced early 2nd-century pottery, which may have been residual, while its upper fills produced a mid 2nd-century assemblage including material from the BB2-producing kilns of North Kent, and from the Highgate Wood and Verulamium

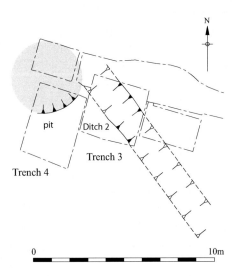

Fig. 22   Ditch 2 and associated pitting (scale 1:200)

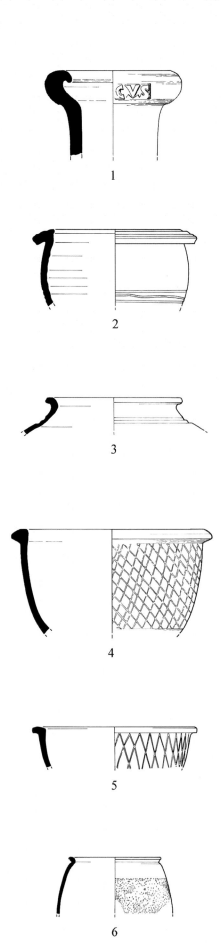

Fig. 23   Period 3 Roman pottery (scale 1:4)

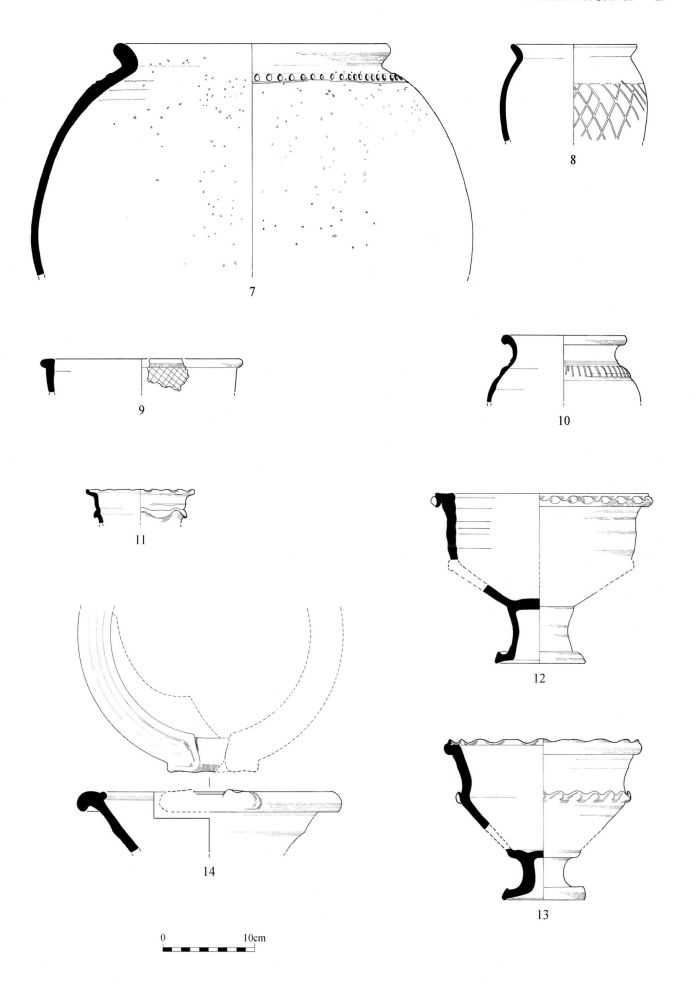

0   10cm

Region Whiteware industries, but did not include anything deposited later than *c.* AD 150/70 (Fig. 23.11 – Fig. 23.14; Lyne 2003, Assemblage 16). The form breakdown of the pottery recovered from this ditch is rather unusual in that there are comparatively few cooking-pots, no flagons and abnormal numbers of tazzae which all have evidence for use in the form of internal sooting. This does not seem to be a typical domestic assemblage and the tazzae suggest the close proximity of a shrine.

Three moderate-sized pits were excavated cutting into the fill of Ditch 2. The fills of these pits produced pottery assemblages from the first half of the 2nd century, except for one possible late 4th-century sherd and a single sherd of 3rd-century pottery, which could have been intrusive.

Period 3, catalogue of illustrated pottery

Assemblage 11. From the construction of Building 1.1

Fig. 23.1   Complete rim of Dressel 20 olive oil amphora of Martin-Kilcher (1983) type 14 in early Baetican fabric with CV.S stamp on rim (not in Funari 1996). *c.* AD 50–70.

Fig. 23.2   Reeded-rim bowl in off-white VRG fabric fired patchy blue-black/white. *c.* AD 100–140. Seven fresh sherds from this vessel are present.

Fig. 23.3   Neck cordoned jar in similar fabric fired rough blue-grey. *c.* AD 130–150.

Assemblage 12. From Building 3

Fig. 23.4   Deep 'pie-dish' of Monaghan (1987) type 5D1.2 in Cliffe BB2-1462 fabric from North Kent. *c.* AD 110–180.

Fig. 23.5   Flanged-bowl in BB2-2759 fabric (Davies *et al* 1994, fig.100–600). *c.* AD 120–160.

Assemblage 14. From the well associated with Building 3

Fig. 23.6   Large cornice rimmed bag-beaker sherd in CGBL 1658 fabric with sand rough-casting below black colour-coat. *c.* AD 70–120.

Fig. 23.7   Large part of handmade storage-jar in NKSH fabric with jabbed shoulder cordon and traces of resin sealant over the rim. 27 fresh sherds from this vessel and a second example are present. *c.* AD 50–170.

Fig. 23.8   Everted-rim cooking-pot of Monaghan (1987) type 3J1 in black BB2 fabric with acute-latticing on the body. *c.* AD 110–190.

Fig. 23.9   Flanged bowl of Monaghan (1987) type 5D3 in similar fabric. *c.* AD 120–190.

Fig. 23.10 Class 2E jar with burnished vertical lines on its shoulder in Highgate Wood C fabric (Davies *et al* 1994, fig.178–1107). *c.* AD 140–160.

Assemblage 16. From Ditch 2

Fig. 23.11 Tazza of Frere type 309 (1972) in pinkish-brown Verulamium Region Whiteware fabric. *c.* AD 75–105.

Fig. 23.12 Another, much larger, example in similar fabric fired pink with cream surfaces.

Fig. 23.13 Another example in grey VCWS fabric fired buff-brown with orange margins.

Fig. 23.14 Mortarium in the hard cream Rhenish fabric characteristic of the Verecundus workshop with sparse quartz and red ironstone trituration grits. *c.* AD 150–250.

Period 3, discussion

The alignment of Building 3 suggests that during the first half of the 2nd century settlement expansion was influenced more by the alignment of Road 1 than by that of Road 2. Although several phases of road resurfacing were identified which may have been associated with this period of activity no dating evidence was forthcoming, a similar situation to that found at the Bonded Warehouse site (Graham 1988, 243) and it is thus not possible confidently to establish for how long the road was maintained. The construction of a substantial drain (Drain 2) cutting the road on the same alignment as Road 1 may even mark the demise of the road; there was no evidence for the drain having been sealed by road surfacing deposits. However, even if Road 2 did continue to be used the evidence suggests that Road 1 was more influential in determining settlement layout. The digging of this major drain and subsequent building activity reflects settlement expansion during this period and reflects an increased need for drainage.

Whether the drain's construction reflects a diminishing of the importance of the road or not, its function and course remains problematic. It might initially have been associated with the narrowed roadside ditch (Ditch 1) but, by the time Building 1 was constructed, the ditch was infilled. So where did this drain flow to once buildings were constructed, if it continued to function at all? Unfortunately any evidence for the course of the drain, beyond the limited area excavated, had been destroyed by later truncation. That it continued to function throughout the life of the buildings might be inferred from the pottery assemblage recovered from its fills. This large assemblage had a date-range spanning the first three quarters of the 2nd century therefore contemporary with the building activity identified and comprised vessels typical of an urban domestic assemblage: cooking-pots and flagons make up nearly 60% of the assemblage with considerably smaller quantities of open forms and beakers, suggesting the vessels may have been thrown into the drain from nearby domestic properties.

The construction of buildings on the site follows a similar pattern to those excavated elsewhere along the length of Road 2. Those on the northwest side of the road were built over the backfilled ditch on the same alignment as the road. Excavations at Hibernia Wharf, immediately to the northeast of the site, revealed similar evidence with 2nd-century clay and timber buildings partially built over the backfilled ditch, timbers found in the ditch being interpreted as piles for the building. On this site however, the ditch was re-cut to form a narrow revetted drain (Thomson *et al* 1998, 208). To the northeast, at the Bonded Warehouse site, upright timbers driven into the gravels were thought perhaps to support a roadside structure over the ditch, although there was little evidence to support this idea (Graham 1978, 242). On that site however, an undated stone building was found overlying the backfilled ditch on the same alignment as the road (Graham 1978, 245).

Little can be said of the buildings' functions although the street front location might suggest they were built as both workshop and housing, typically having a workshop or shop on the street frontage with domestic quarters to the rear. There was however, no indication as to which trades, if any were conducted in the buildings.

Building 3, on the southeast side of the road, was not aligned with Road 2. Although there was some variation in the precise alignment of the three phases of Building 3, they were all generally aligned with Road 1, despite being almost adjacent to the line of Road 2 and about 35m from Road 1. This may suggest that these were the rear part of buildings, which fronted on to Road 1, or outbuildings associated with them, or that Road 1 had a dominating influence on settlement layout, or that Road 2 was no longer in use. Buildings on the southeast side of Road 2 at nearby sites, such as District Heating Scheme (Graham 1988), Southwark Cathedral crypt (Hammerson 1978) and Montague Chambers (Thompson *et al* 1998, 210), are generally on the same alignment as Road 1, despite their proximity to Road 2, although evidence for a timber-framed building on the same alignment as Road 2 was found at the Bonded Warehouse (Graham 1978, 247).

This building was probably served by the well. Building 2 may also have been but its proximity suggests this is unlikely; there would have been little space for the building to occupy. An apparent wall line running parallel to Road 1 just to the east of the well is shown in Graham Dawson's publication (1976) but it contains little other information to help relate this wall, or any other Roman stratigraphy to the buildings found during the Millennium excavations. The well was abandoned by the middle of the 2nd century although five 2nd-century wells excavated at Hibernia Wharf (Thompson *et al* 1998, 208) indicate the apparent frequency of wells, possibly reflecting the density of settlement in the area.

PERIOD 4: AD 200–400 LATER ROMAN DECLINE

Building 4

The remains of Building 3.3 were sealed by a greenish silty dump layer, which produced AD 180–250 pottery. Structural features found cutting into this dump included a beamslot along the same general wall line of the earlier building phases; a second beamslot represented an internal feature, possibly associated with what appeared to be a clay-lined hearth, whilst a thin mortar spread to the south may represent a contemporary floor or surface (not illustrated). The internal slot produced late 2nd- to early 3rd-century pottery while the hearth produced pottery indicating the continued use of the building into the late 3rd century (Lyne 2003, Assemblage 18). Curiously, a sample taken from the hearth produced an assemblage of mineralised plant remains, generally characteristic of cesspit fills, although this feature was far too small to have been used for such a function. The mineralised remains from the hearth in Building 4 suggest a phosphate rich environment. The assemblage is mainly composed of edible and medicinal plants: poppy seeds (*Papaver* sp.) and peas are edible, whilst sheep's sorrel and selfheal are both used in traditional healing.

Pits and external activity

Elsewhere, the earlier Roman occupation deposits were overlain by dark, predominantly sandy silt deposits in Trenches 1, 3, 4 and 5, although equivalent deposits in Trench 2 had been truncated by the Victorian warehouse basements. These deposits were initially thought to represent 'dark earth' which is frequently found sealing Roman occupation sites. However, excavation in Trench 1 revealed a sequence of intercutting pits, which had removed virtually all traces of the 'dark earth' layers. The fills of these pits may be largely composed of redeposited 'dark earth,' which was seen to survive in Trench 3 as several sandy clayey silt layers, which produced late 2nd- and 3rd-century pottery (Fig. 24.1 – Fig. 24.5; Lyne 2003, Assemblage 17), presumably increasingly residual towards the top of this sequence. Corresponding deposits in Trench 5 were up to 0.5m thick and contained similarly-dated pottery along with 2nd- and 3rd-century ceramic building material, perhaps deriving from a nearby building. The uppermost dark earth deposit in this trench produced 3rd-or 4th-century wares.

The late Roman pits in Trench 1 were generally cut into the 2nd-century occupation deposits and much of the material recovered from these pits proved to be residual. The pits were generally small, measuring less than 1.0m across and less than 0.2–0.3m deep, although a few relatively large examples were present. One larger pit, about 1.5m across and over 1.6m deep, produced 3rd- and early 4th-century pottery while another produced a small, late 3rd-century assemblage (Lyne 2003, Assemblage 19) contemporary with the finds from Building 4 (Lyne 2003, Assemblage 18).

Several deep, near vertical, irregular cracks [572] were recorded in the Roman road. These were typically orientated along the length of the road and measured *c.* 30mm wide by up to 1.0m deep. They were certainly not deliberately dug but perhaps a result of contraction of the strong but brittle and inflexible fabric of the road after its abandonment and, possibly, its burial. The cracks were filled with a dark sandy silt that had presumably fallen into these voids.

There was a dearth of 4th-century pottery from across the entire site and many of the few sherds that could be

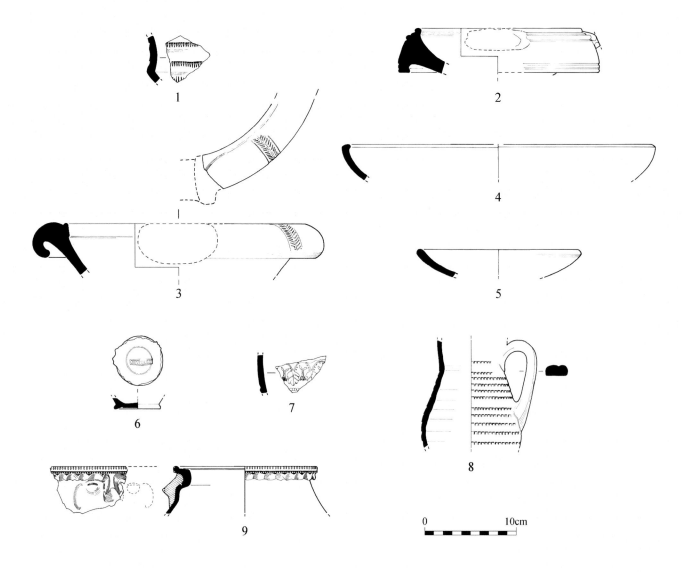

Fig. 24   Period 4 Roman pottery (scale 1:4)

attributed to the 4th century were residual finds from Saxo-Norman pits or other later deposits. The overall impression is that the area excavated was peripheral to human activity for the last hundred years or so of Roman occupation.

Period 4, catalogue of illustrated Roman pottery

Assemblage 17: from the fills of intercutting pits in Trench 1

Fig. 24.1   Part of tazza in Verulamium Region Whiteware with square-toothed rouletting.

Fig. 24.2   Wall-sided mortarium of CAM 501A form in pink-cored cream Colchester fabric. *c.* AD 170–250.

Fig. 24.3   Mortarium of CAM 497 form in sand-free greenish-cream Colchester fabric with flint and ironstone trituration grits and a herringbone stamp. This mortarium is closely paralleled at Colchester (Hull 1963, fig. 66,7). *c.* AD 130–170.

Fig. 24.4   Platter with in-turned rim of Gose type 232 (1975) in Cologne colour-coated whiteware. *c.* AD 180–250.

Fig. 24.5   Platter of Dubois *et al* form A1a (1994) in late terra-nigra fabric from Picardy. *c.* AD 160–270.

Miscellaneous

Fig. 24.6   Base of cup in Early Roman Micaceous Sandy ware with internal herringbone stamp. *c.* AD 50–90.

Fig. 24.7   Two sherds from Central Gaulish green-glazed bowl of Greene Form 5 (1978) with moulded decoration. Decorative motifs include Greene's C15 leaf. *c.* AD 43–80.

Fig. 24.8   Large sherd from flagon in grey FINE-2866 fabric with square-toothed rouletting on its shoulder. *c.* AD 70–120

Fig. 24.9   Fragment from face-pot in cream VRW fabric with orange-brown patches. Similar to Davies *et al* 1994, fig. 47, 266. *c.* AD 150–200.

ROMAN DISCUSSION

The earliest known Roman features in Southwark are the two main roads, which approach the bridge, or at least the crossing point of the Thames, to *Londinium* on the north bank. Both roads and the bridge were constructed in about AD 50, or shortly afterwards. Major construction projects such as these would generally be undertaken by the military and it has been suggested that this is the case in Southwark. Although the Millennium excavations have not been able to confirm this, neither is there any contradictory evidence. The motivation behind the construction of Road 2 remains a matter for debate, as does its course and final destination to the southwest of the site.

Beyond establishing this initial infrastructure, the Millennium excavations have produced no fresh evidence to suggest that further development of the settlement south of the Thames was anything other than organic growth of domestic housing and workshops. The excavations have helped to confirm that the settlement was initially focused along Road 1 during the 1st century, and later extending along Road 2 in the second quarter of the 2nd century. In the latter half of the 1st and early 2nd centuries the area of Southwark Cathedral either side of Road 2 appears to have been largely wasteland or the backyards of properties fronting Road 1. The abundance of chickweed seeds along with elder (*Sambucus nigra*), mallow and nettle in a Phase 2 dump deposit in the open area to the south of the road indicates that it was a nutrient-rich environment. The species present are indicative of meadowland, and the whole deposit may therefore have contained hay (herb-rich grass fodder or bedding). Greig (1984) suggests, however, that the absence of ribwort plantain (*Plantago lanceolata*) in plant assemblages is indicative of plant material other than hay. However, Greig's classification is not supported by the data presented here, with the presence of abundant, unambiguous grassland indicator species including buttercups, common chickweed, lesser stitchwort and fat hen clearly suggesting the presence of hay.

The generally wet nature of the area is attested by examination of the plant macrofossil assemblage from Ditch 1, which indicates that it acted as a drainage ditch probably for both the road it lined as well as the surrounding land. The assemblage of both common spike-rush, which requires shallow water, and pondweed, which colonises habitats with standing or slow-flowing water (Stace 1997), indicates that a semi-permanent if not permanent stream of water ran through the ditch. The damp-habitat species like buttercups and docks would have lined the ditch, taking advantage of the more marshy land. Occasional trees are likely to have been scattered in rough ground alongside the banks. The presence of hazelnuts and fruits like wild strawberry and brambles probably derived from local hedgerows as may have the sloe, and although these may reflect human consumption or at least use (sloes, being very bitter, are more likely to have been used in preserves than consumed directly). Nevertheless they are likely to reflect the local environment, even if humanly deposited along with the fig seeds.

Clay and timber buildings were constructed alongside the road in the second quarter of the 2nd century. The exact function and form of the buildings remains difficult to ascertain, due to the fragmentary nature of the remains, which had been largely destroyed during construction of the Victorian warehouses and by the construction of 17th-century pottery kilns. In addition, those remains that had survived were partially removed during archaeological investigations in the early 1970s.

Evidence from the site indicates a contraction of settlement towards the end of the 2nd century with only slight evidence for buildings continuing into the late 3rd century. However the data may be skewed by the lack of survival of later structures due to extensive truncation. Dawson identified several phases of building during his excavations in the late 1960s and early 1970s (Dawson 1976), but in the absence of published dating evidence the longevity of this sequence remains unknown. As noted elsewhere in north Southwark the accumulation of 'dark earth' deposits, associated with extensive pitting, appears to mark the end of Roman settlement.

Diet and environment

Examination of faunal remains and plant macrofossils provides an indication of the inhabitants' diets and some insight into the use of plants in traditional medicinal remedies.

The bulk of the animal bone from the Roman assemblages is recognized as food debris from all stages of meat preparation and consumption, including the unwanted by-products of primary and secondary butchering, as well as kitchen and table waste. Based on the relative bone-element (NISP) frequencies of the main meat-yielding species, cattle are recognised as the principle contributor to the diet (56% of the total), and sheep (and goats?) and pig provide 27.8% and 16.2% respectively. It should be noted that the value for the sheep/goats is inflated owing to the inclusion of a partial articulated lamb/kid skeleton (comprising 18 bone elements) from Building 1.3. This particular animal may represent a votive offering (see below) and it was not possible to determine if its flesh had been eaten. Lamb/kid however does appear to have featured in the diet as evidenced by the presence in the food debris of immature sheep jawbones and immature sheep/goat long-bones. Of special interest is the neonate (lamb/kid) metacarpus, also from Building 1.3, as this suggests livestock (backyard) farming in the immediate vicinity of the site, an interpretation supported by the presence of skeletal elements of neonate/sucking piglets and at least one immature hen.

Apart from the consumption of lambs/kids, sucking piglets and a pullet, there is no evidence in the food debris to indicate that the Roman inhabitants of the area had an especially rich diet. Beef, mutton and pork formed the staple meats, supplemented by poultry. Surprisingly there is no evidence for the exploitation of wild game (other than the occasional roe deer) or of wildfowl. On the available archaeological evidence, consumption of fish was apparently restricted to the single marine species identified (cod) although nearby excavations have produced bones from several marine species during the Roman period (Ainsley 2002, 268).

Butchering patterns in the cattle, sheep and pig bones follow those already documented at other Romano-British sites. Special mention should be made however of the ten articulated thoracic vertebrae of an ox, found in a Period 1 gravel extraction pit, in which the right and left transverse processes have been removed together with the attached ribs; a similar example (dated not later than AD 140) being recorded by Armitage in the City of London (Jones 1980, Plate 4).

Charred waterlogged and mineralised plant remains provided further indicators of diet. Amongst the mineralised remains from the probable hearth in Building 4 were some edible plant species, such as those from the pea family (Fabaceae sp.). Unfortunately their mineralised state prevented further identification. Charred remains recovered from the same sample included the occasional seeds of arable / grassland habitats with sheep's sorrel (*Rumex acetosella*) and pulses (Fabaceae indet.), whilst a sample from a Period 2 fill of Ditch 1 contained just a single charred grain of barley (*Hordeum* sp.). Waterlogged plant remains recovered from Ditch 1 included a range of edible fruits, both local and exotic. The seeds of fig (*Ficus carica*) were abundant and grape pips (*Vitis vinifera*) were occasional, along with sloe stones (*Prunus spinosa*), wild strawberry (*Fragaria vesca*), and fragments of hazelnut shells (*Corylus avellana*).

Fig seeds are one of the most common food remains on Roman sites, having been found for example at 64–70 and 199 Borough High Street, Finck Street (Tyers 1988), Jubilee Line extension (Gray 2002) and 5–27 Long Lane (Carruthers 1999) in Southwark. They produce a high density of seeds per fruit, so abundant remains do not imply vast quantities of the fruit itself. It is highly unlikely that they were indigenous, and they are commonly believed to have been imported as a dried fruit (Willcox 1977; Tyers 1988). This assemblage has some parallels with those at Hunts House in Southwark (Carruthers 2002), which recorded the food remains of fig, strawberry and plum along with plants species indicative of waste or marshy ground.

The components of this assemblage also have a number of traditional and medicinal properties worth mentioning. Sloe for example was commonly used to flavour spirits (Wilson 1975); hazelnuts can be ground into flour for baking; and the leaves of common sorrel can be used as a herb in cooking (Grieve 1995). The seeds of selfheal, which were fairly promiscuous in this sample, are poisonous, but under correct preparation can help maladies such as a sore throat, ulcers, whooping cough and epilepsy (Kruger 1992), while ribwort plantain can be used to stiffen linen fabrics. Given that the depositional context was a ditch, and the fact that many of these plants are common in the wild, the presence of their seeds in the ditch may simply have been the result of aeolian processes. However, this clearly does

not exclude their possible use by the local population. The occasional charred items would have been preserved as a consequence of domestic activities (eg cooking or tinder for a fire), and could have been deposited at any point along the length of the ditch and subsequently transported (redeposited).

The occurrence of herbs such as coriander (*Coriandrum sativum*), plus cabbage/mustard seeds, although scarce, suggests their cultivation and use, if only in local gardens. The possibility that they grew wild cannot be discounted, although this would not have excluded their use in cooking. The presence of barley (*Hordeum*) and corncockle (*Agrostemma githago*) indicates the presence of cereal cultivation. Corncockle was a common and irritating weed in ancient arable fields until the introduction of herbicides (Greig 1981). However, the absence of the by-products of cereal cultivation in the samples (eg chaff) suggests that the crop was unlikely to have been cultivated and processed in close proximity to the site; an interpretation supported by the presence of corncockle. As a large weed seed, corncockle is one of the last contaminants to be separated from grain, often requiring hand sorting because it is a similar size. Consequently, corncockle often indicates poorly cleaned grain stores or that the final hand sorting was left until the cereal was needed. Previous archaeobotanical studies in London also support this interpretation, with evidence for predominantly clean or semi-clean grain assemblages, indicating that grain was probably stored and consumed in the area, rather than being cultivated locally. The area of Borough High Street in particular provides some of the best evidence, implying that it may have been a centre for the storage of both plant and animal food (Gray 2002). Although this is a tentative interpretation of the remains from Southwark Cathedral, based upon a poor plant assemblage, there is probably enough evidence to provide general support for the model proposed by Gray.

Glass imports and possible evidence for manufacture

The fragments of glass that can be assigned to the Roman period are all, in the main, small and only a few can be identified by form and date (see Carter and Shepherd 2004). These come from well-attested forms and can easily be paralleled elsewhere in London and beyond. Of interest, however, is the presence of glass that attests to a supply during the second half of the 2nd century. Such assemblages are not common in London where the main supply on many sites appears to diminish dramatically by the middle of the 2nd century.

Ten identifiable fragments of colourless glass were recorded. All, except one, come from drinking vessels; the exception being a fragment from the neck of a flask or unguent bottle, in very thin, bubbled colourless glass with a greenish tint, which can be dated to the 2nd to 4th century. Three examples (eg Fig. 25.1) come from the distinctive range of late 1st-century conical bodied cups with facet-cut decoration (Isings 1957, form 21; see Oliver 1984 for a detailed discussion of such vessels and Price and Cottam 1998, 80–83 for lists of examples from Romano-British sites). These vessels, manufactured in good quality colourless glass with good wheel-cutting, can be interpreted as high quality imports, perhaps from as far afield as glasshouses south of the Alps. Six examples, most of which can be dated to the 2nd to 3rd centuries, come from thinner walled vessels, decorated with fine horizontal wheel cut lines, datable from the 2nd and 3rd century (eg Price and Cottam 1998, 88–89 and 91–92 for the cups with a separately blown foot). These too should be interpreted as high quality items but it is likely that their manufacture was closer to London, perhaps in the Rhenish glasshouses.

Fourteen vessels come from pillar-moulded bowls (Isings 1957 form 3; Price and Cottam 1998, 44–46) (eg Fig. 25.2 – Fig. 25.3). These vessels, in naturally coloured glass, probably date from the last half of the 1st century AD with an emphasis on the last quarter of the century. They were not blown but were fashioned by sagging, a technique commonplace before the introduction of blowing in the middle of the 1st century BC. The form is very common throughout the northern provinces, but whether they were products of the glasshouses north of the Alps or not is debatable. Their presence here, along with the late 1st-century conical beakers above, are the best evidence for glass supply to this site during the late 1st century AD. Although they appear in early 2nd-century contexts, their numbers are diminishing rapidly. Note that in the large cullet dump at Guildhall Yard, dated to the second quarter of the 2nd century (GYE92 – Perez-Sala and Shepherd

forthcoming) pillar-moulded bowl fragments were comparatively scarce.

All of the other fragments come from vessels which are first made during the late 1st century but whose peak period of manufacture and use continues into the 2nd century. Among these are fragments of globular and conical bodied jugs (mainly Isings 1957, forms 52 and 55; Price and Cottam 1998, 150–157) and their associated open jar form (Isings 1957, form 67c; Price and Cottam 1998, 137–138) (eg Fig. 25.4 – Fig. 25.6). These vessels appear to have been the products of glasshouses, primarily in the Seine-Rhine region and again should be regarded as imports into Britain during the late 1st and early 2nd century.

Amongst the glass recovered from site was a small fragment of a very thin glass rod in colourless glass with a green tint and surface patina and two fragments of badly weathered glass fused to a piece of soil, which may be evidence of manufacture.

Catalogue of illustrated glass

Fig. 25.1   From the fill of Period 3 Ditch 2: Fragment from the rim and body of a conical beaker with a cracked off and ground smooth rim, decorated with a horizontal cordon beneath which are horizontal rows of ground oval facets set closely in a quincunx form (Isings 1957. form 21). Colourless glass. Late 1st or early 2nd century.

Fig. 25.2   From Period 1 road make-up gravels: Two fragments from the base of a pillar-moulded ribbed bowl (Isings 1957. form 3). Natural pale blue-green glass. Late 1st century.

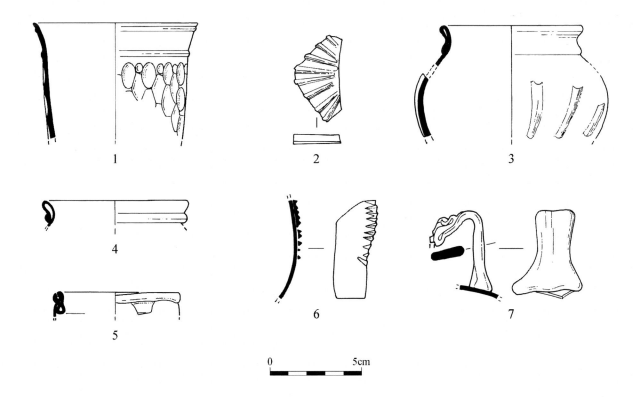

Fig. 25   Roman glass (scale 1:2)

Fig. 25.3   From Period 2 infilling of Ditch 1:Two fragments from a pillar-moulded ribbed bowl (Isings 1957. form 3). Natural pale blue-green glass. Late 1st or early 2nd century.

Fig. 25.4   From a Period 2 pit fill: Fragment from the tubular rim of a jar with the edge rolled in and then bent out and down to from a double fold. (Isings 1957. form 67c). Natural blue-green glass. Late 1st or early 2nd century.

Fig. 25.5   From Period 2 infilling of Ditch : Two fragments from the tubular rim of a jar with a multiple rolled edge (probably Isings 67c). Natural blue-green glass. Late 1st to mid 2nd century.

Fig. 25.6   From Period 3 Building 1.3: Fragment from a jug (Isings 1957. form 55a/b) with pinched decorative projections which would have continued down the vessel from the base of the handle. Thin natural blue-green glass. Late 1st or 2nd century.

Fig. 25.7   From Period 2 infilling of Ditch : The handle from a cylindrical bottle (Isings 1957. form 51). Natural blue-green glass. Late 1st or early 2nd century.

Ritual, religion and foundation deposits

There can be no doubt that the lamb/kid skeleton from the beamslot [1021] of Building 1.3 (see Fig. 21) had originally been placed in as a complete carcass, presumably as a votive (sacrificial) offering in a foundation rite (to confer/ensure good fortune on the building and household). The complete pelvis and three lumbar vertebrae, from the fill of beamslot [660] of Building 3.3 represent the part skeletal remains of another adult dog, and again may represent a foundation offering. Archaeological evidence of such rituals have been widely documented at other contemporary sites; for example pottery vessels were found placed under the floors of three buildings at the nearby Courage Brewery site and a cattle head was placed below the timber floor of the warehouse (Cowan 2003, 85),

More problematical is the interpretation of the isolated dog skull in Ditch 1 and the isolated horse skull in the small Period 1 pit [1448]. The dog skull from Ditch

1, was identified as male with a prominent, ridge-like sagittal crest, as seen in the skulls of modern terriers. Craniometrical analysis identified the form of the skull as Mesaticephalic: i.e. of intermediate form between Brachycephalic (broad, short skull with blunt nose) and Dolicephalic (long, narrow skull with long nose). The horse skull was that of a male aged 8 to 9 years. Its stature could not be established, in the absence of associated skeletal elements, but withers heights in two other horses from the site were reconstructed as 139.3cm [881] (from Period 1 gravel extraction pit [882]) and 130.0cm (from a Period 2 ground raising dump) which put both horses into the upper size range for Romano-British horses.

Either of these specimens could be explained as 'normal rubbish', the dog skull deriving from a disturbed burial of a pet and the horse skull as the discarded processing debris of a knacker's yard. Alternatively (and somewhat speculatively) it might be suggested that one or both these skulls represent heads placed as votive/propitious offerings either in association with construction works (erection of the revetment as in the case of the dog) or in a ritual pit (as in the case of the horse). Examples of Romano-British votive horse skull burials are reviewed in Luff (1982, 188–189).

The pottery assemblage recovered from Ditch 2, towards the west of the site, contained numerous tazzae fragments with internal sooting, indicative of a shrine in the vicinity. Notably previous investigations in the crypt beneath Southwark Cathedral revealed the presence of numerous Roman sculptures in the backfill of a well, probably constructed in the late 3rd century, deposited with dumps of mid 4th-century material. The four statues spanned a date range from the 1st or 2nd century to the early to mid 3rd century and were associated with fragments of a votive altar and tombstone (Hammerson 1978). Hammerson concludes that the majority of the pieces are more likely to derive from a rich family mausoleum than from a temple, being predominantly funerary in nature. Remains of a dog and a cat were found in the base of the well, although Hammerson attaches no ritual significance to this (Hammerson 1978, 209).

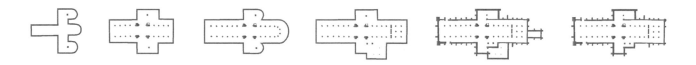

Chapter 3   The Medieval Priory

Nathalie Cohen and Chris Mayo

with Philip Armitage, Natasha Dodwell, Chris Jarrett, Gustav Milne,

Simon Roffey, Ken Sabel, Kathelen Sayer and Alys Vaughan-Williams

A SAXO-NORMAN *MONASTERIUM* IN SOUTHWARK? AD 950–1106

John Stow's Survey of London, written towards the end of the 16th century, preserves legends surrounding the earliest ecclesiastical activity on the site of the Cathedral; traditions suggesting that a nunnery was founded here during the 7th century, which was later replaced by a college of priests established by St Swithun, the Bishop of Winchester from AD 852 to 862 (Stow 1994, 52). Given the location of the site near the 'fortified bridgehead' of Southwark it seems highly probable that some form of settlement originally grew up around a ferry point prior to the reconstruction of the bridge, and this suggests that there may have been activity in the area of the site from at least the mid 9th century onwards (Carlin 1996, 9).

However, while archaeological investigations have demonstrated Roman settlement in the area, little tangible evidence for occupation during the Anglo-Saxon period has yet been discovered. Hammerson's (1978) discoveries in the Cathedral crypt raise the intriguing possibility that there had been a building of some religious significance on the site during the Roman period and thus that the presence of the Cathedral in this location may not be without precedent. However there is a large time-gap between the deposition of the sculpted figures in the well in the 4th century and the possible resumption of activity in the 9th century and thus any continuity is difficult to prove, although this need not necessarily preclude the possibility that the location of the Cathedral respects an earlier Roman building with religious associations.

To realise the full potential of the Saxo-Norman activity at Southwark Cathedral, it needs to be considered against the current state of information about the period in Southwark. The romantic origins of Southwark Cathedral, as perpetuated by Stow, make clear the connections to the river crossing:

'A ferry being kept in place where now the bridge is built, at length the ferryman and his wife deceasing, left the same ferry to their only daughter, a maiden named Mary, which with the goods left by her parents, and also with the profits arising of the said ferry, built a house of Sisters, in place where now standeth the east part of St Mary Overies Church, above the choir, where she was buried, unto which house she gave the oversight and profits of the ferry.' (Stow 1994, 52)

Exactly when medieval London Bridge was built is uncertain, but it was probably in existence by *c*. AD 1000 (Watson 1999, 17) and the area around the bridgehead in Southwark appears to have been fortified and 'a vital part of London's defences' (Watson *et al* 2001, 53), protecting London from attack, both from down river and from the south. These defences are described in the great saga of St Olaf, written in *c*. 1220 by Snorri Sturluson, a description based on the *Vikingarvisur* compiled in the early 11th century, which describes Southwark as 'a great trading place' being surrounded by 'large ditches', with a sizeable army stationed there. It is possible, however, that a degree of poetic licence was applied in the compilation of the 13th-century saga (Watson *et al* 2001, 53). It is thought that a substantial 10th-century ditch excavated at New Hibernia Wharf to the north of the Cathedral may represent part of the defending ditch (Thompson *et al* 1998, 208), yet this makes the enclosed area small in size, with the early church outside it (Watson *et al* 2001, 53). Southwark is listed amongst the holdings of Odo, Bishop of Bayeux in Kingston Hundred and is linked to a 'tideway' (*aque fluctu[s]*) (Morris 1975, fol. 32a). In the pre-Conquest period, the dues for the tideway were divided between the King and Earl Godwin (Higham 1955, 24).

Domesday Book (AD 1086) records a *monasterium* on the site of the Cathedral during the reign of Edward the Confessor (AD 1042–1066). The position immediately to the west of the bridgehead would thus have been dominated by the early church; that structure itself was probably set back from the river owing to the problems of foreshore erosion which resulted in reclamation and revetments through the late 11th and 12th centuries (Watson *et al* 2001, 63). The other land around the route to the crossing point may have contained timber structures such as were found at Fennings Wharf, immediately to the east of new London Bridge, there associated with multi-functional pits for the disposal of rubbish and cess. The small amount of evidence that has been found has

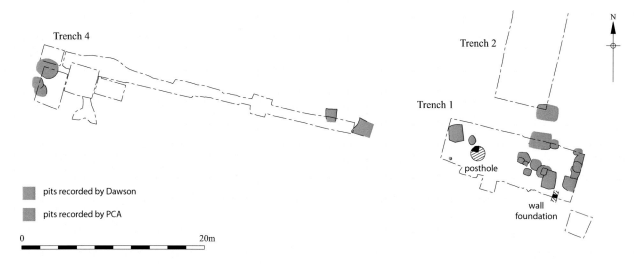

Fig. 26   Saxo-Norman pitting and structural remains (scale 1:400)

prompted the conclusion that there was a 'considerably lower density of settlement around the southern bridgehead during the Saxo-Norman period' (Watson *et al* 2001, 56) than on the northern side.

Saxo-Norman activity

Possible Saxo-Norman structural remains

The *monasterium* has always been an enigmatic structure, its existence only suggested by historical references and writings. No remains have been found that can be attributed to the building with any certainty, although given the widespread tradition of rebuilding churches on the sites of earlier ones, due to the status attached to them, this is perhaps unsurprising. Saxo-Norman churches and monasteries could be timber or masonry structures, or a combination of both (Rodwell and Bentley 1984, 56) and the likelihood is that any structure pre-dating the priory church had either been robbed for the new building or severely truncated by it.

A linear feature found in Trench 1 contained a large concentration of flint nodules in its base and could have been a wall foundation plinth. Five sherds of early medieval sandy ware were found in its fill, dating from AD 970 to 1100, as was a residual Roman bone implement. A posthole was found approximately 8.5m to the west that contained large stones as packing material; no dating evidence was recovered from this, but it cut the road and was stratigraphically earlier than the masonry remains of the priory (Fig. 26). These two features represent the only possible evidence for a timber-framed building on the north side of the Cathedral, although any possibility that they relate to the *monasterium* is speculation. Dawson's excavations identified two elements of chalk wall foundation, which he interpreted as being of probable Saxon date and therefore possibly part of the *monasterium* (Dawson 1976, figs. 4 and 5).

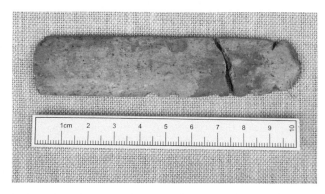

Fig. 27   Bone textile implement (10cm scale)

A bone object was recovered residually from the foundation trench; this is a flat and highly polished implement 103mm in length and 24mm wide with a decorative oval terminal created by a small notch on either side (Fig. 27). Several further notches down one side may have had a practical function. Similar polished bone strips are known from Roman sites in England and on the Continent, where they date from the 1st and 2nd centuries AD. It has been suggested that they may be textile implements, associated with the production of woven fabrics either used as shuttles or as weaving bats to beat the weft tight (Price 2000, 100 and fig. 6.2 no.83).

Saxo-Norman pitting

Pitting, contemporary with the structural remains, was found in Trenches 1 and 2; domestic pottery recovered dated from AD 970 to the 12th century. A number of the pits were generally larger (for example 2.10m by at least 0.85m), deeper (for example 1.4m) and better defined than others, several being sub-rectangular in shape. One example had a layer of compacted gravel in its base, possibly to allow it to be more easily emptied; that such a process occurred was also suggested by evidence for re-cut edges to the pit. Another pit in the group revealed evidence for a timber lining and base. Of particular interest is that the pottery recovered and their stratigraphic sequence reveals phases within the Saxo-Norman period. Three contained sherds of early medieval sandy ware, dating from AD 970 to 1050. Sixty-three sherds from another pit date give a date from AD 1000 to 1150, while a re-cut of the same pit contained sherds dating from AD 1050 to after 1100. A further ten pits contained pottery of the same date. Four others produced pottery dating from after AD 1080 and from one of these came two sherds of sandy shelly ware indicating the filling of the pit in the mid-12th century. Such distinct date ranges show fairly intense and continued use of the area to the north of the Cathedral in the Saxo-Norman period and into the life of the first priory church. The 1970s excavation work (Dawson 1976, 45–47) uncovered comparable features of late Saxon to early medieval date (see Fig. 26): seven pit cuts were also large in size (for example 1.9m by 1.5m), deep and square or rectangular in shape and one revealed traces of timber or wattle lining.

Analysis of environmental samples taken from the pits suggests that they are likely to have been multi-functional but predominantly used for rubbish disposal because they contained a lower concentration of seeds than would be expected from cesspits, and those seeds that were found were either casually discarded or windblown. That some of the pits were lined and re-cut shows that waste disposal was ongoing and, to some extent, managed. This is further suggested by animal bones within the pits that show no evidence of either weathering or degradation; in other words, waste was disposed of efficiently. Four indeterminate fish vertebrae from one of the later pits show distortion and partial destruction consistent with digestion, possibly human, and therefore present further evidence for the multi-functional nature of the pits and indicate that some cess was being disposed of.

In Trench 4 a further three pits were excavated, at a distance of over 40m from the main group in Trench 1, one of which contained two sherds of early medieval sand- and shell-tempered ware, dating from AD 1000 to 1150. This provides evidence that not only was waste disposal ongoing and managed, but it was also widespread across the area to the north of the later church.

The presence of mineralised bran within three of the pits, dating from the 11th to 12th centuries, is of interest as elsewhere it has been suggested that bran was a staple food in the medieval period, being attested at sites in York (Hall *et al* 1983) and Worcester (Greig 1981, 271). Other cereals represented within the pits include wheat, barley and pulses.

Examination of the assemblage of animal bones from the pits showed that in order of prevalence, cattle, sheep and pig were eaten. Poultry, freshwater fish and cod were also being consumed. The withers height of a horse, whose metacarpus was recovered from a pit at the later end of the sequence, can be calculated at 1.5m, or 14.8 hands; when compared against other late Saxon and high medieval

Fig. 28   Iron padlock slide key (5cm scale)

horses this is an unusually tall example, which can be seen as a development of the improvements in harnesses in the 10th century that allowed the more efficient use of the horse as a draught animal (van Bath 1966, 64). Furthermore, with the increasing importance of the horse through the high medieval period for war, agriculture and transport, larger horses became more common (Audoin-Rouzeau 1994, 3).

An iron padlock slide key and copper-alloy pin or handle were recovered from one of these pits (Egan 1998, 99–100). Measuring 114mm in length, the key had a rectangular-section shank, widening to a flat, near-triangular plate towards the head with a circular bit and a looped terminal for suspension (Fig. 28). The pin or handle was U-shaped, *c.* 50mm in length, with both ends broken, but one flattened with horizontal ribs and the other slightly thickened with traces of possible hole for suspension at the break (Fig. 28).

The Saxo-Norman pottery

The pottery assemblage from the Saxo-Norman pits has proved a vital tool in understanding a relatively under-represented period in the history of Southwark Cathedral. That is to say that the pits offer a window into what is known to have been a much wider and busier environment, one which incorporated the contemporary settlement around the bridgehead of London Bridge and the possible site of the Saxo-Norman *monasterium* itself. Comparatively little of this activity has been found archaeologically, and therefore the phased pottery assemblage is valuable evidence of not only the ceramic forms and functions, but trade and influence as well.

The assemblage included Late Saxon shelly ware, dating from AD 900 to 1050, as jar-shaped forms (Fig. 29.1–Fig. 29.2) with characteristic rims, one of which bore sooting indicating its use as a cooking vessel. This type of pottery was produced in the Oxfordshire region but within the area of the Danelaw (Vince and Jenner 1991; Mellor 1994; Blackmore 1999), and forms one of the most common pottery types in London in the 10th and early 11th centuries.

The paucity of Late Saxon shelly ware within the pits indicates that 10th-century activity in the area was

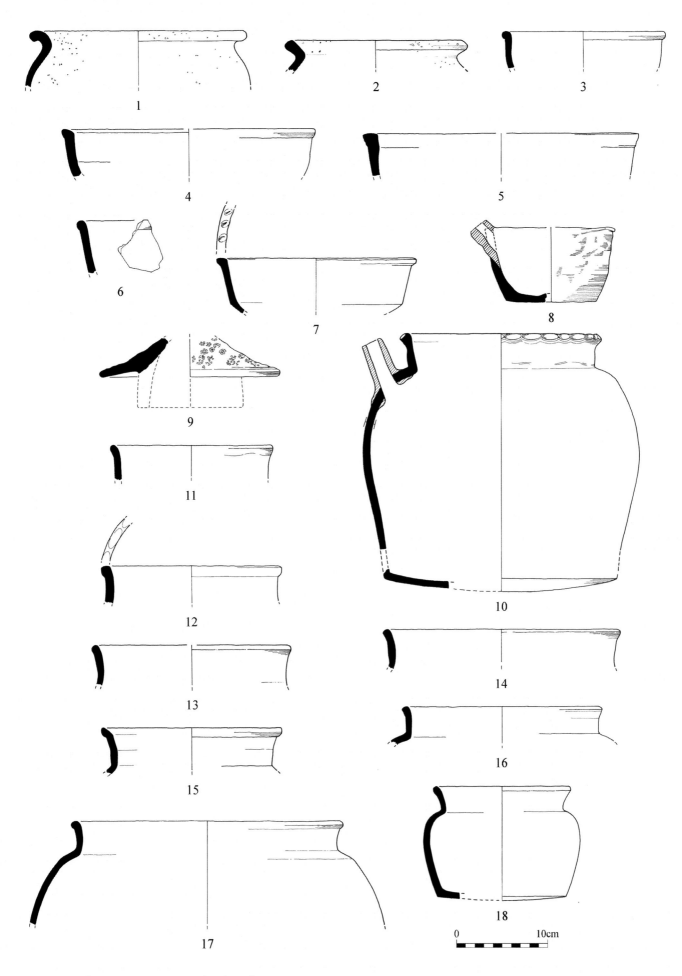

Fig. 29   Saxo-Norman pottery (scale 1:4)

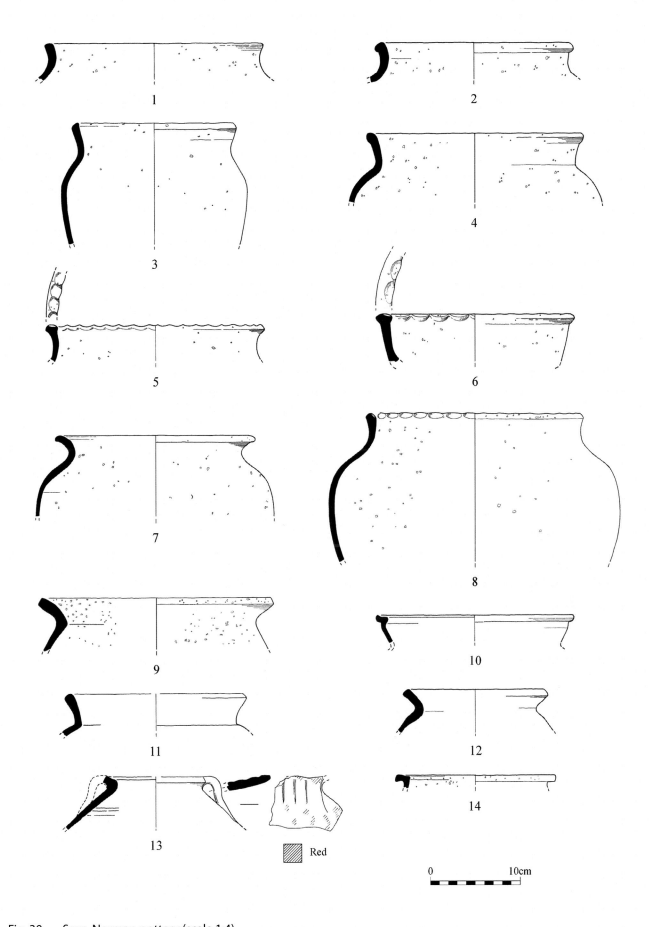

Fig. 30   Saxo-Norman pottery (scale 1:4)

relatively low-level, however the increased occurrence of early medieval sandy ware (Fig. 29.3–Fig. 29.18), the most common type from the assemblage, with a date range of AD 970 to 1000 suggests an increase in activity at this time. This fabric is derived from London Clay, most likely a tertiary deposit in the Thames Valley (Vince and Jenner 1991, 57–58). The forms represented are bowls (Fig. 29.3–Fig. 29.8), a lid (Fig. 29.9), spouted pitchers (Fig. 29.10) and jars (Fig. 29.11–Fig. 29.18), some of which also bear sooting and internal carbonised deposits as evidence of their use in cooking. Although damaged, it can be seen that the lid (Fig. 29.9) is a flanged type with wheel-stamp decoration and is a rare find from this period, with perhaps only two other examples known, although these are in non-local and imported wares (Vince and Jenner 1991, fig. 2.115.290 and fig. 2.101.244). One of the spouted pitchers (Fig. 29.10) is testament to a skilled potter, having a tubular spout attached by being mortised through a circular hole on the shoulder, with fillets of clay used on the inside and outside of the join to secure it.

Early medieval sand- and shell-tempered wares were also present in the assemblage (Fig. 30.1–Fig. 30.8). The fossil-shell tempering within the pot suggests a local origin, possibly between Greenwich and Southwark, for the clay (Vince and Jenner 1991, 63–64) with a date range from c. AD 1000 to 1050. The forms represented are jars (Fig. 30.1–Fig. 30.5, Fig. 30.7–Fig. 30.8) and a bowl (Fig. 30.6), which again bear signs of their use in cooking. Early medieval shell-tempered ware is also present (Fig. 30.9), the shell-temper of which most probably originated from the Woolwich Beds in northwest Kent, where such pottery has also been found on early medieval sites (Vince and Jenner 1991, 64). Early Surrey ware was also present as jar-shaped cooking pots, one of which had an internally lid-seated rim (Fig. 30.10), paralleled at Westminster Abbey (Goffin 1995, 81, fig. 9.6).

Sherds of early medieval flint-tempered ware (Fig. 30.11), and early medieval grog-tempered ware, as recovered from the pits, are rare in London, and thus are assumed to have originated elsewhere (Vince and Jenner 1991, 69). Four sherds of early medieval chalk-tempered ware (Fig. 30.12), which has been sourced, by its distribution, to the northwest of London around St Albans and Buckinghamshire, were also found.

Whilst the above pottery types are all considered to be 'local', the Saxo-Norman pits also contained pottery, such as Stamford ware and Ipswich-Thetford type ware, from further afield as well as continental pottery, represented by sherds from Germany and France as Badorf ware, North French earthenware and red-painted ware (Fig. 30.13).

Saxo-Norman discussion

Dawson concludes that the lack of rubbish recovered from the pits he excavated implies their use for something other than waste-disposal. On the basis of this and their large size and regular shape he argues that these may have been post-pits for substantial timbers (Dawson 1976, 45) and

thus possibly the remains of a large wooden church, the *monasterium* referred to in Domesday Book. However, the pits were heavily inter-cut and bear remarkable similarity to the pits found in Trench 1, and thus alternatives are proposed here.

Bearing in mind the apparently low density of settlement around the southern bridgehead and evidence for timber structures and multi-functional pits for the disposal of rubbish and cess such as were found at Fennings Wharf (Watson *et al* 2001, 56), the Saxo-Norman pits at Southwark Cathedral conform to what is known about the area archaeologically, although additionally they are linked to the historical site of the *monasterium* and the early priory church. Covering a date range from AD 970 to the 12th century, they have revealed their use for the disposal of domestic waste. Most of the pits were dated from c. 1050 to 1100, suggesting that this was the period of most intense activity, and their closeness in date to the foundation of the priory church in 1106 cannot be ignored, implying that this may not have been a sudden and decisive act but rather the climax of a continued period of expansion. Despite this, the north–south alignment of the plinth, the roughly east–west alignment of the rubbish pits, and the overlapping date ranges for these features, do imply managed waste disposal in the Saxo-Norman period, related to some form of structure, and associated with domestic activity as indicated by the pottery.

The evidence from the pits is frustrating because, whilst providing information for the Saxo-Norman period at Southwark Cathedral, they cannot be directly associated with any other activity which might help to elucidate their function. However, the concentration of pits in Trench 1 are aligned roughly east–west: this could suggest that the *monasterium* was sited in the same place, and on the same orientation, as the later church, and furthermore that the pits were being used, for waste disposal, by the resident priests during the 11th century. There were more pits dating from c. 1050 to 1100 than the other phases represented, suggesting that this was the period of greatest activity, and the pottery implies that this activity largely related to kitchens; perhaps therefore reflecting proximity to the Saxo-Norman refectory which was sited in this area in the 12th century. The sandy shelly ware from the later pits (Fig. 30.14), indicating their use in the 12th century, shows that the use of this area for waste disposal continued until well beyond the building of the first priory church; evidence again of a link between the *monasterium* and priory church.

Considering the location of the site so close to the river, and also the probable links that the Augustinian community would have had with Europe, the size of the imported element of the pottery assemblage is surprisingly small, comprising twelve sherds from approximately eight vessels, 1.3% by sherd count and 2% by MNVs (minimum number of vessels). The preliminary analysis of pottery from ongoing archaeological work by Pre-Construct Archaeology at the nearby Cluniac and later Benedictine monastery at Bermondsey Abbey, shows a very similar range of early medieval pottery types to that from Southwark Cathedral with, however, a wider range of imported wares, some glazed, notably from Normandy. At Bermondsey Abbey Early and Middle Saxon pottery (perhaps from a secular settlement or the Minster) is also represented, while medieval pottery is much more abundant than at Southwark Cathedral. Elsewhere, comparable assemblages have been recovered in Southwark from contemporary sites without monastic connections, for example at Tabard Square (B. Sudds, *pers comm*), and therefore the presence of this pottery may be attributable to the site's position close to the main thoroughfare and bridgehead area north into the city, rather than any ecclesiastical links.

In summary, the structural evidence for a *monasterium* is disappointingly inconclusive. Only a short length of foundation trench was revealed and, if projected much further north than its surviving extent, it makes an unsatisfactory building element; pits line the wall to east and west. However what is clear is that that there is good evidence for intensive occupation from the late 10th into the early 12th century in the area immediately north of the church and that whatever alignments influenced this activity they were reflected in the later church construction.

THE MEDIEVAL PRIORY OF ST MARY OVERIE

The priory of St Mary, founded in 1106, is believed to be London's first Augustinian house (Luard 1866, 430). On the opposite bank of the Thames, the houses of Holy Trinity and St Bartholomew were founded in 1107–8 and 1123 respectively (Schofield and Lea 2005; Weinreb and Hibbert 1995, 715). However, the exact circumstances and nature of the foundation of St Mary's are somewhat shrouded in mystery. Three men are associated with the priory's early history: William Giffard, Bishop of Winchester, William Pont de l'Arche, Sheriff of Hampshire and Royal Treasurer and William Dauncey. The earliest documentary references claim Giffard as the founder, while the other Williams are not mentioned (Tyson 1925, 33). Giffard was King William II's chancellor from 1094 but upon the death of William in the New Forest, and the accession of Henry I, he was exiled (Dickinson 1950, 120). He did not return from exile until 1107 (Newman 1988, 184), so his part in the foundation of a priory in 1106 appears unlikely. It has been suggested that Giffard received the Minster church or *monasterium* at Southwark while he was the Chancellor, and refounded it as a secular college during this period (Blair 1991, 102). Regularisation of the priory and the establishment of formal Augustine rule seems to have followed at a later date (possibly only a few decades later), and this accords well both with what is known about the lives of the founders of the priory and with the wider pattern of the foundation and development of early Augustinian houses.

The collapse of the tower at Winchester Cathedral in the first years of the 12th century may have occupied much of Giffard's time during the early part of his bishopric (1107–1129) and meant that his priorities lay closer to home. However, it seems likely that his possible early association with the Southwark *monasterium*, his role as Bishop of Winchester and the fact that his London residence was next door to the priory, encouraged his involvement with regularisation of the monastic rule. As will be discussed below, this may also have had an impact on the construction of parts of the priory buildings.

William Pont de l'Arche was one of Henry I's 'new men' who become increasingly influential from the late 1120s onwards (Newman 1988, 96). He was Sheriff of Hampshire and Royal Treasurer during the later parts of Henry's reign, and therefore had close associations with Giffard. He seems to have been more prolific during the second and third decades of the 12th century and certainly he features as a major witness for royal charters from 1127 onwards (Newman 1988, 187). The role of William Dauncey is more enigmatic. He is claimed to have had some part in the foundation of the priory in 1106 with Pont de l'Arche, but unlike the latter, he appears to have figured little in the political events of the early 12th century.

Finally, it is worth noting that the first Augustinian house at Colchester, founded only a few years earlier than St Mary's, was originally a secular foundation. From the 1120s onwards many former religious houses were re-founded as houses for regular canons, such as Portchester (Greene 1992); Haughmond, Salop (West 1980, 240); and St Frideswide's, Oxford (Blair 1990). Both Giffard and Pont de l'Arche are known to have founded, or re-founded other Augustinian houses, during the second quarter of the 12th century. Pont de l'Arche founded the Augustinian priory at Portchester in 1133 (Greene 1992, 224), and the priory at Taunton, Somerset, was regularised a few years earlier by Giffard (Dickinson 1950, 118).

The original structure was apparently a cruciform and aisled building (Smith 1958, 176), although its precise size is unknown. Analysis of the surviving medieval fabric suggests that the regularisation of the priory during the second quarter of the 12th century led to a campaign of building which included the construction of the cloister to the north, and extensive rebuilding of parts of the church, namely extensions at both the eastern and western ends. It is thought that the original western wall was in alignment with the second set of piers from the current west end of the Cathedral, and that the extension added the existing two westernmost bays. This accords well with the documentary evidence showing that the priory was well patronised during the period up to 1200 and:

'owed its prosperity to the accretion of modest grants from a wide range of the land-holding class…only a few of the numerous small grants….suggest lord-tenant relationships; other motives must be sought for what must often have been free genuinely pious offerings made under no duress. Surely here we trace the strong popular appeal of the Augustinian canons, in close touch with everyday life and attractive objects of spiritual investment for those of limited means' (Blair 1991, 143 and 147).

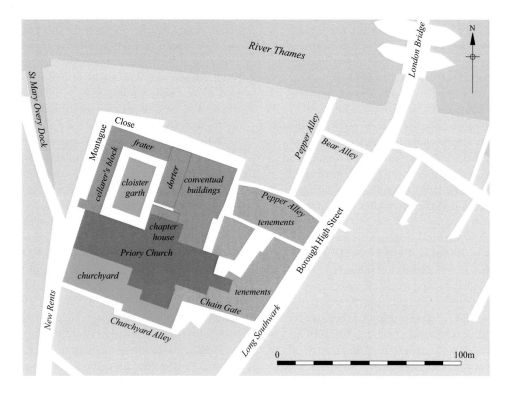

Fig. 31   The layout of the medieval priory church and precinct, based on Carlin (1996) (scale 1:2,000)

Interestingly, many of the grants made to the Priory are concentrated in clusters around the settlements at Mitcham, Banstead, Addington, Reigate and Southwark itself, suggesting the canons tended to win local support after gaining a foothold in the area (Blair 1991, 147).

The buildings that accompanied the church of the Priory of St Mary were positioned on the north side of the church to allow convenient access to the River Thames (Fig. 31). Although not typical of the normal claustral arrangement, there are comparable examples of such positioning to allow water access, be it for sanitation or transport (Thomas *et al* 1997, 100; Coppack 1990, 66).

In 1207, or 1212, a disastrous fire destroyed much of this new work (Malden 1967, 107–112), leading to a further, prolonged building campaign, which was still incomplete at the end of the 13th century. In 1273, the Archbishop of York granted an indulgence to all those who would assist in the completion of the church of St Mary, (Stevens 1931, 44) while in 1303 the church was called 'for thirty years a ruin' (Cherry and Pevsner 1983, 564) suggesting that the canons experienced some difficulties during the rebuilding. The 13th century also saw the construction of the parochial chapel of St Mary Magdalene on the south side of the priory church, a foundation of Peter des Roches, Bishop of Winchester from 1205 to 1243 (Daniell 1897, 208). In addition to the destruction of parts of the priory by fire, its riverside location rendered the priory buildings vulnerable to encroachments by the Thames. The structure as it survives today shows evidence of subsidence in several places, and Dawson's excavations in Montague Close revealed traces of flood damage from two separate inundations in the early and later 13th

century respectively (Dawson 1976, 50). It may be that the construction of embankments on the City side of the Thames and London Bridge affected the flow of the river and increased the risk of flooding.

It was during the 14th century that the priory became known as St Mary Overie ('over the river'), encapsulating its relationship to the City of London. Disaster struck again in the 1390s when fire damaged the south transept and parts of the choir. This was repaired under the direct supervision of Cardinal Henry Beaufort, Bishop of Winchester (Carlin 1996, 70–72), whose arms are preserved on the eastern side of the south transept of the Cathedral; their presence reflects the cardinal's involvement. In 1469 the nave roof collapsed and was rebuilt in timber. During the early 16th century, Bishop Fox erected the stone screen, or reredos, in the choir and inserted a window in the gable above it (Higham 1955, 97).

Remains of the priory church

As described in detail above (Methodology, Chapter 1) the description of the Cathedral below brings together two disciplines: one archaeological, dealing with below-ground remains and the other standing building recording dealing with visible remains above ground. Given the piecemeal nature of the evidence brought together through the two independent projects, combined with the problems of accurately dating what remains of the church, the description below takes the form of a 'tour' examining the strands of evidence for each area of the building and its environs independently. The nave is discussed first,

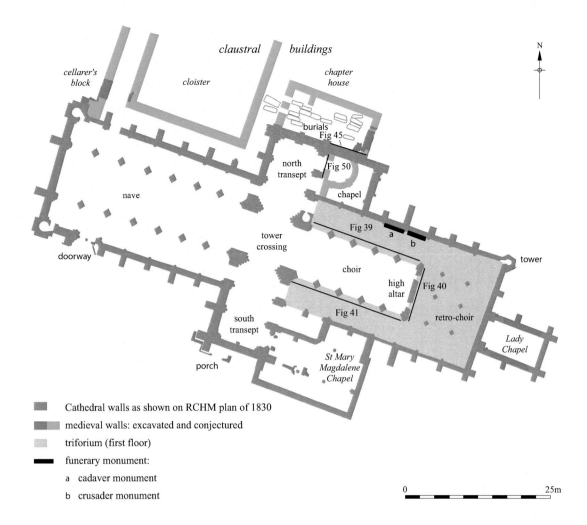

Fig. 32   Elements of medieval Cathedral fabric identified during archaeological investigation (scale 1:625)

followed by the tower crossing, tower and triforium, the transepts and their chapels, retro-choir, Lady Chapel and claustral buildings (Fig. 32).

The nave

Building remains were found during excavations on the external sides of the north and south aisles in Trenches 4 and 18. To the north the remains are most probably attributable to the proposed late 12th-century extension to the church, whilst the remains of the foundations of a doorway in the south probably reflect early 13th-century modifications.

In Trench 4 a north–south aligned Reigate stone, ragstone and chalk wall survived to a maximum height of 2.12m OD [3022] (Fig. 33). The northern corner of the wall was seen projecting from beneath the north aisle, and it was truncated on its eastern side. A further wall had been built against its west face, of the same material [3016]. This relationship was implied because traces of the mortar used in the former were seen on re-used stones within the latter. Only the corner of the later wall was exposed, the feature

running both south under the north aisle and west beyond the edge of the trench. Both wall elements were to the west of the current doorway on that side.

In Trench 18, on the southern side of the church, irregularly coursed masonry was exposed on either side of the existing door, in the form of the foundations of a buttress and a doorway. This masonry was built with Kentish ragstone and chalk, and was faced with Reigate stone. The nature of these foundations indicates that the doorway was framed by a series of recessed arches, similar to the current design of the doorway.

Dating these remains with any refinement is difficult because of the often-similar nature of medieval stonework; thus they have been considered with the known, and conjectured, histories of the church's development. On the north side, the earlier wall in Trench 4 appears to have been added to or extended, which could be attributed to a reconfiguration of the church in the 12th century. The remains at the southwest door, considering their similarity in composition, may relate to either the Norman church or its 13th-century repair. An engraving of 1818 and a 19th-century drawing showing the external elevation of the nave's south aisle, both indicate that the nave and aisles

Fig. 33   Details of remains of cellarer's block and southwest doorway (scale 1:200)

Fig. 34   The easternmost five bays of the timber ceiling *in situ*

from a 19th-century journal which says that 'About this time a magnificent south porch … was added to the nave' (The Building News 1879, 51), the quote referring to the time of Peter de Rupibus, Bishop of Winchester from 1208 to 1243 (Dollman 1881, 5). Although the dating could not be fixed with any precision, it seems likely that the remains are of this, early 13th-century, date.

The 15th-century timber vaulted ceiling

Many major medieval building projects suffered structural problems, sometimes caused by differential settlement or by the inaccurate calculation of loads, or following fire damage. In contrast to most current thinking on church restoration, the repair or refurbishment that followed such events in the medieval period would often be taken as an opportunity to rebuild in a more contemporary fashion, rather than faithfully replicating the old design. This pattern is seen at the priory church in Southwark when, for example, the masonry roof of the nave partially collapsed in 1469. During the stewardship of Prior Henry Burton (1462–1486), the vault was replaced with a highly decorated ribbed and embossed timber ceiling. Unfortunately this remarkable structure was itself dismantled in 1831 and all that survives today are some 50 of the bosses (of which

were built in the Gothic style with two centred arched openings, and it is therefore possible that the foundations revealed in Trench 18 were those of post-Norman Gothic work. The foundation was faced with Reigate stone and had a rubble stone core, so there is a possibility that the re-facing was contemporary with the Gothic work and that the rubblestone represented the original late 12th-century facing material. That these medieval remains survived, untruncated, to dictate the same angled-alignment of the 19th-century and modern doorway shows that the entrance has been maintained, in terms of position, since the 12th century. One clue to the date of the southwest door comes

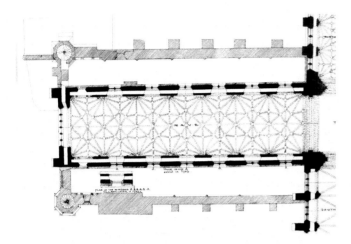

Fig. 35   Plan of the nave ceiling (from Dollman 1881)

Reproduced by kind permission of Southwark Local
Studies Library

29 have been gilded and re-set in the ceiling of the central
tower) and three important 19th-century illustrations,
reproduced here as Fig. 34, Fig. 35, Fig. 36. Research on
the 15th-century ceiling was undertaken by Rachel Foster
(2000); what follows is broadly a summary of some of her
conclusions.

Fig 34 shows the easternmost five bays of the timber
ceiling *in situ*, presumably drawn up before demolition. The
vaulting can be seen springing from corbels carved with
heraldic motifs; although it is possible that these corbels
represent the remnants of the original masonry structure,
they do not seem to relate to the truncated vaulting shafts
rising from the body of the arcade wall, and may therefore
be of late 15th century date, and an integral part of the 1469
design.

Fig. 35 is a plan of the nave ceiling reproduced in
Dollman's study of the priory published in 1881, and clearly
shows the complex way the ribs and bosses interlocked.
This was an ornate seven-bay structure comprising wall-
ribs from which transverse and diagonal ribs run towards
the main ridge-rib, with intermediate tiercerons and
additional lierne ribs completing the complex design,
all held together by some 117 elaborately-carved bosses
(Dollman 1881, Plate 4).

Fig. 36, also originally published in the same volume,
shows illustrations based on detailed, measured records
made by Charles Edwin Gwilt, presumably during the early
19th-century demolition of the ceiling. These include a
cross-section of one of the moulded ribs some 0.15m wide
and 0.20m deep, although there is no record of the form
that the web of the vault took. The rest of the drawings
show 21 different designs carved on the faces of the bosses,
several of which can be readily identified with the surviving
examples currently displayed in Southwark Cathedral.

Foster's study included an examination of these
surviving bosses. Each one comprised a wide head with
the ornately carved face pointing downwards, set below a
narrower neck of square or hexagonal section into which
mortises had been cut to accommodate the tenons on the

Fig. 36   Designs of the 15th-century roof bosses,
from a figure entitled: 'Oak bosses from the
roof of the Old Nave and north transept and
stone capitals from the aisles of the old nave'
(Dollman 1881)

Reproduced by kind permission of Southwark Local
Studies Library

Fig. 37   The Devil swallowing Judas: one of the roof bosses on display in Southwark Cathedral

ends of the ribs. Study of the tree-ring pattern evident on the base of the bosses showed that they had been cut from the centre of the bole of the parent log. Clearly several boss-sized blocks could have been cut from one single timber, and these rough-outs would then have been carved to shape, with the required motif on the face and the necessary mortises in the neck. Assembly marks were also incised on the neck, to indicate in which part of which bay the boss should be fitted, confirming the assumption that the vault was prefabricated: indeed it could hardly have been otherwise.

As is clear (from Fig. 35) the number of ribs that articulated with the boss relates to the location of the boss to the complex framework. Thus some bosses set on the wall-ribs would only have three mortises, whereas others had up to nine: those occupying more central positions would have at least four, five or up to eight mortises, all cut at the appropriate angles to accommodate the disposition

of the interlocking ribs. Several different configurations were identified of which two types (classified by Foster as Type A and B) had eight symmetrically-disposed mortises. From the published plan (see Fig. 35, Dollman 1881, plate 4) these bosses can only have come from the central ridge-rib. It is therefore of some interest to note that the designs in this key location included the coat of arms of the priory, (in which traces of paint survived suggesting the rose and cross were painted red, the shield gold) and both versions of the rebus of Prior Henry de Burton (three rough hairs or 'burrs' issuing out of a cask or 'tun'). These designs were interspersed with others including two intertwining beasts, a pelican and a dragon. Other motifs cut on the faces of bosses elsewhere in the vault included a man wearing a crown, the Devil swallowing Judas (Fig. 37), flowers, shields, and a monogram incised MR, thought to refer to Maria Regina (Mary Queen of Heaven) to whom the priory was dedicated.

Cave's study of English medieval roof bosses (1948) suggests that figurative designs, rather than the simpler foliate designs, became increasingly common by the 15th century. This trend is certainly borne out by the design of Southwark's late medieval timber ceiling, reflecting as it does a colourful and varied display of contemporary iconography. Its relative inaccessibility preserved it from the destructive zeal of later reformers, intent on establishing a more austere interior. As a consequence, the records of the ceiling and surviving bosses serve as an all too rare example of the vibrancy of medieval ecclesiastical embellishment. This can now be appreciated, at least in part, by a modern audience seeing the ground-level display of the bosses in the Cathedral. However, it is worth recorded that few of these intricately carved motifs when set high up in the roof would have been readily identifiable by anyone standing in the nave in the late 15th century. Such mortal matters were not, of course, the prime concern

Fig. 38   Recording masonry on the north side of the triforium
©SCARP

of the medieval craftsmen, whose artistry was dedicated to a higher cause.

Five bosses also survive in the vaulting of the choir; it has been suggested that these bosses belong to the original choir roof and were incorporated during the early 19th-century rebuilding. C. P. Cave noted that the four eastern bosses 'have very unusual foliage….and none of it conforms in the least to the conventional trefoil foliage; some of these bosses have angle heads which are not common in this country'. Comparable foliage designs are however found at Canterbury, dating to post 1180 (Cave 1948, 7). The fifth boss is in a different style, and is believed to have come from the masonry vaulting of the mid 13th-century nave roof which, as discussed above, collapsed in 1469 (Cave 1948, 77)

The tower and crossing

The tower piers may incorporate early masonry, possibly of the pre-priory *monasterium* (Smith 1958, 177), but more likely to be from the 1106 foundation. Cherry and Pevsner (1983) note that the crossing is odd in its detail, and their observations are worth quoting at length:

'The crossing piers towards the nave and E arm are completely unmoulded, as if they were the remaining parts of a plain wall. The outer orders of the E and W arches die into this wall, the middle order (with flat soffit and angle rolls, a Canterbury Gothic type) rests on corbels supported by crocket capitals (E) or by carved heads (W). These crossing arches perhaps pre-date the fire (of the early 13th century); if so, they must have dictated the height of the new choir. The later N and S arches rest on grouped shafts which on the S side run nearly down to the ground, and on the N side stop some way above it' (Cherry and Pevsner 1983, 568).

It has been suggested that the north transept may have served some special purpose, and that gates were attached to the piers at this position (Stevens 1931, 45).

Above the internal arcade of the tower is a large room with early 14th-century Y-tracery windows, which may once have been glazed. They are now blocked and whitewashed and form a blind arcade. It seems likely that this stage of the tower, with its large windows, originally functioned as a 'lantern' throwing light into the crossing and the body of the priory. Two further floors were added during the early 16th century, before the Dissolution of the priory.

The choir and triforium

The construction of the five bay choir, (also referred to as the quire or presbytery) with triforium, clerestory and ploughshare vaulting, is dated by most authors to the 13th century, after the destructive fire of 1207 or 1212. The ornate screen or reredos behind the high altar was constructed during the early 16th century, necessitating the removal of the triforium arches (Stevens 1931, 31). The roof, vaulting and clerestory were largely reconstructed during the early 19th century (RCHM 1930, 60). However, structural and decorative details at ground and triforium level suggest the survival of pre-13th-century fabric. The choir arcade has alternating circular and octagonal piers, a style paralleled at Canterbury and earlier English Romanesque buildings (Cherry and Pevsner 1983, 567). Stevens notes a series of differences between the north and south sides of the choir: on the south side the inner order of the moulding in the main arcade is supported by brackets or corbels but on the north side, stone shafts are used. Again on the south side, the outer order of the moulding ends in a carved termination, with nothing on the north side. The capitals of the triforium shafts differ and the bases on which the shafts stand are not alike. On the north side there is some dogtooth decoration at triforium level, however such decoration is not found on the south side. There are small apertures at triforium level, which are not set at regular intervals; additionally some have round and some pointed arches (Stevens 1931, 30). The choir aisles form an ambulatory with the retro-choir.

Archaeological investigation in the choir triforium, aisles and retro-choir recorded a wide variety of construction techniques and materials demonstrating periods of renovation and repair over hundreds of years, from the 12th century to the present day. Elevations were drawn of the walls of the triforium (Fig. 38) and are reproduced here (Fig. 39, Fig. 40, Fig. 41 and see Fig. 32 for locations); for the purposes of the description the north and south elevations have been split into a series of bays. This recording work identified seven separate building phases, four of which are interpreted as medieval and are described in detail below, two post-Reformation phases (described in Chapter 4 below) and one modern. The phases identified have been defined through examination of the triforia masonry combined with information relating to construction and rebuilding in other parts of the church.

Phase 1: 1106

The earliest surviving masonry remains are to be found on the north side of the church, at the westernmost end of the choir (described during the project as 'Bay 1'), and in the eastern wall of the north transept. The masonry recorded in these areas is very different in style and makeup to the fabric to its east (Fig. 39). In Bay 1, pieces of Caen and ragstone rubble are visible in areas of repair (2 and 3), beneath the ashlar (of Reigate and Mertsham sandstone, where visible) of the main body of the wall 8. The ashlar work is heavily coated with limewash and a Reigate stone moulding 1 has been set slightly off-centre relative to the bay. The construction of this moulding is different to that of those in Bays 2 to 5 and the courses of ashlar work do not align on either side of the aperture. It seems likely that this is a window inserted into pre-existing masonry, or possibly into an earlier, smaller window aperture. The

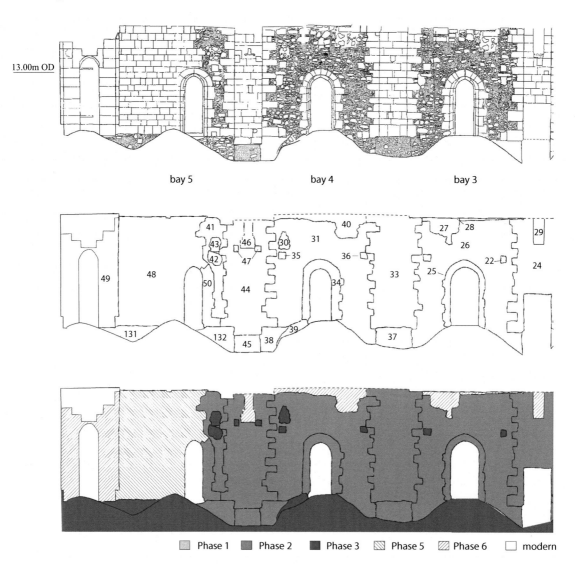

Fig. 39   Elevation of the north choir wall at triforium level (scale 1:100)
©SCARP

courses of the ashlar also do not line up with that of the buttress immediately to the east 13, and there are no keystones, further indicating that the masonry of Bay 1 is of a different, and probably, earlier build.

Context 4 consists of two corbels, which have probably been inserted in 8. These corbels are set at the same height as those in Bay 2 (17 and 18) and must relate to the roof over the north choir aisle and transept chapel, constructed during the 13th-century rebuilding of the east end and are discussed further below. Other context numbers assigned to this elevation (5–9), relate to later, probably modern, modifications including holes for electricity cables and a wooden partition wall erected to create the present storage room.

Phase 2: 1150s –1190s

The next phase of construction is well represented at triforium level. This includes masonry in Bays 2, 3, 4, 5 and at the east end (Fig. 40, Fig. 41). The walls (12, 26, 31, 41, 52 and 54) are built of a mixture of different stone types and, (with the exception of context 54 which contains squared blocks of Reigate and Caen stone), consist of small, roughly hewn pieces of Reigate, Caen, Ragstone, Mertsham, flint, chalk, with some tile and slate. Fragments of re-used moulded stonework are also visible in places. The masonry is randomly coursed and bonded with a pale pink/buff mortar of variable consistency with frequent chalk and gravel inclusions. On the north side, each bay has a round-headed, single splayed opening (contexts 11, 25, 34 and the remains of the opening in Bay 5 50). Two round-headed apertures are present in the east wall (55 and 58). The mouldings are all of Reigate stone, finely dressed and bonded with a fine white mortar, as are the buttresses

W

13.00m OD

bay 2   bay 1

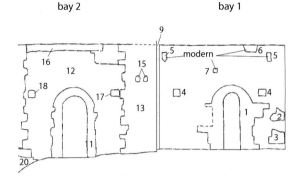

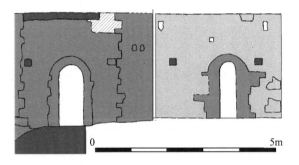

0   5m

and keystones, which define the 'bays' (13, 24, 33 and 44). The use of ashlar blocks for quoins and buttresses with roughly coursed materials making up the remainder of the face, and a poured rubble and mortar core (together with the presence of putlog holes in the rough rubble masonry) gives an indication of the building techniques used to construct the walls, and suggests a date of construction in the middle of the 12th century. This period saw a refinement in the quality of ashlar work, (Tatton-Brown 1989, 55) compared with that found in Norman buildings of the first generation (i.e. of the late 11th century).

Most of the masonry of the north choir aisle and the lowest courses of the easternmost bays of the south choir aisle can also be assigned to this phase. A similar range of stone types is evidenced, bonded with a friable yellow mortar with frequent gravel pebble inclusions. This suggests that the aisle walls were built contemporaneously, or soon after the construction of the choir walls.

Thus, it appears that from the mid 12th century the east end of the priory church was the scene of a building programme. While it seems clear that the choir was extended and provided with aisles, the plan form of the extreme east end could be reconstructed in two ways. If the dating and sequence of the suggested conversion of the northeast transept chapel from an apsidal to a square ended structure is accepted (see Roffey 1998b), then the east end could have been converted from a single bay apsidal structure to a square ended building of five bays in *c.* 1130 to mirror the changes in the transept chapel (see Fig. 74b). This development may have included a stair at the north east corner, as represented by context 60. However, the redevelopment of the northeast transept chapel at this date is predicated on an acceptance of the evidence presented by the re-use of a single piece of decorative stone in the east wall of the square end and the suggestion that Bishop Giffard, influenced by Cistercian ideals, was involved in the reorganisation of the layout of the building (see Discussion below).

There is a series of intriguing clues within the masonry of the triforium that suggest an alternative (and more likely) building sequence. The location of the round headed triforium windows is key to this hypothesis: the surviving *in situ* windows of Bays 2 to 4 are evenly spaced, while that of Bay 5 and the (reconstructed) window of Bay 6 are set to the west of their bays. At the east end, the two windows are set less than 3m apart. The layout of these windows could represent the remains of a short-lived extended apsidal end, possibly with an ambulatory (see Fig. 74c), constructed *c.* 1150–1190, and destroyed by the fire of 1207 or 1212. The aisles were groin vaulted and may have been of a single storey only, with the round-headed triforia windows above the roof line. It is also possible that a clerestory stage was constructed during this period (meaning the triforia openings are internal features) but no evidence of this was recorded. At ground level, antiquarian observations noted: 'a round arch covered with plaster and whitewash. This is Norman work, disguised by 'restoration'', (Thompson 1904, 130) in the southeast corner of the northeast transept chapel. This supports the suggestion that a north aisle was constructed during this period, and access was created from the northeast transept chapel. It is also possible that the ambulatory was ringed with subsidiary apses, similar to those postulated at Lichfield (Rodwell 1993, 21) and St Paul's Cathedral (Gem 1990, 53–54). The structural weaknesses inherent in the east elevation, as evidenced by considerable subsidence (Fig. 42) and repeated rebuilding of both the north and south ends of the wall during the post-medieval period, could be the result of the conversion from an apsidal to a square end at this location. In this context, the offset walls visible at the base of the easternmost elevations (context 66, Fig. 41; contexts 131, 132, Fig. 39) are the extensions of the choir walls to create a right angle, (replacing the pre-existing curving apsidal wall) while the remains of context 60 may represent part of a buttress emplaced to support this new junction. As discussed below, it is suggested that this construction of a

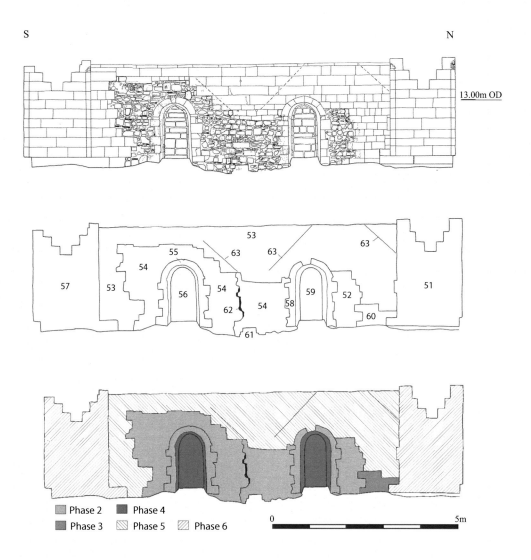

Fig. 40   Elevation of the east end wall at triforium level (scale 1:100)
©SCARP

square choir form took place during the 13th century, as part of the rebuilding after the fire.

Phase 3: 13th century

The evidence from the existing vaulting of the aisles supports the latter hypothesis, and the destructive nature of the early 13th-century fire is clearly demonstrated. It appears that the building was most severely damaged on the south side, and it is suggested that the path of the fire can be traced from the south to the north of the building. On the north side, as discussed above, 12th-century fabric survives to a considerable height. It is apparent that the fire caused the original groin vaulting to collapse and the new pointed vaults that replaced it rose to a higher apex, necessitating the removal of the bases of the surviving round headed windows, in order to incorporate the new vaulting structure. The vaulting, where examined, contained considerable quantities of re-used moulded stone (Fig. 43). It is possible that the corbels (including 4, 17, 18, 21, 22, 35, 36 and 42) were inserted at this time

on the north side of the triforium in order to support a timber roof structure and allow for the construction of the clerestory above (as represented by 16). The central vault structure of the choir is of ploughshare or stilted vaulting 'in which the wall ribs, in order to increase the light from a clerestory window, are sprung from a higher level than the diagonal ribs, thus producing a warped, twisting surface of web resembling a ploughshare' (Lever and Harris 1993, 42). This development is dated to the first half of the 13th century, and this accords well with the dating of the roof bosses of the choir (see below).

On the south side rebuilding of the main choir walls was required up to the full height of the triforium level, including the construction of new windows, this time using a pointed style, indicative of a later date (94, 102). Some elements of 12th-century masonry may have survived (for example the keystones and buttresses of 87, 89 and 105), however the walls of Bays 9 and 10 were largely reconstructed (90, 106, 147 and 148). In Bay 9, the reconstruction was apparently undertaken by reusing the pre-existing masonry, including fragments of moulded stonework, largely un-coursed and bonded with an orange mortar with flint pebble inclusions. The range of stone types used here mirrors that found on the north side of the triforium and it is likely that the masonry of Bay 9, (and that to its east, in Bays 8, 7 and 6, where the medieval fabric is masked by later cladding), was reconstructed first (reusing the material to hand) later followed by the westernmost bay of the choir.

The post-fire rebuilding began during the episcopate of Peter des Roches and also included the construction of the chapel of St Mary Magdalene. The chapel was located to the south of the choir and was accessed via the south choir aisle. Surviving masonry of the aisle at triforium level is fragmentary but again suggests the damage caused by the fire was concentrated at the southwestern corner of the choir, with 12th-century masonry surviving further east. The lengthy period of reconstruction (which continued with the rebuilding of the north transept in *c.* 1280, when much of the surviving 12th-century fabric was encased within the later masonry) and the re-use of earlier material accords well with the documentary evidence, which suggests that the post-fire rebuilding proceeded both slowly and suffering from a lack of funding. The repeated 13th-century flooding events attested by excavated archaeological evidence may also have hampered rebuilding efforts.

Phase 4: 14th–16th centuries

The construction of Bay 10 consists of largely squared blocks of stone, built to courses and using a different range of materials including Mertsham stone, possibly Ardingly and Wealden stone. These contexts (106, 147 and 148) are bonded with a creamy white mortar of a powdery consistency. The very different construction of Bay 10 and of the south transept wall to its west must represent the building work of the 14th century when the south transept was rebuilt.

In the triforium the round-headed windows of the east wall were blocked with regular courses of squared stone (of chalk, Caen stone and occasional Reigate and ragstone, contexts 56 and 59). The stone types of the blocking suggest a 13th-century date, and the east end window of the new clerestory would have provided light from this angle, replacing that once cast by the triforium-level windows. At ground level, the triforium arches are believed to have survived until the early 16th-century installation of the reredos (Stevens 1931, 31). Finally the RCHM plan of 1930 shows that during the 14th century large buttresses were added to the north and south choir walls. The necessity of additional support for the choir aisle walls provides further evidence of the subsidence of the east end masonry, which may have been exacerbated by the change in plan form during the previous phase of building works.

There is no evidence for any major structural changes to the east end during the 15th and 16th centuries, although alterations and rebuilding in the south transept, the tower and the nave of the church continued during this time.

The north transept and chapel

The remodelling of the north transept has been dated to *c.* 1280 (RCHM 1930, 61) but the thickness of the north and west walls indicates the presence of earlier masonry concealed by the blank pointed recesses. Purbeck marble has been widely used for both the column and vaulting shafts (Cherry and Pevsner 1983, 569).

Part of the masonry of the eastern wall of the north transept was recorded at triforium level (Fig. 44). The lower part of the stonework stands proud of the rest of the north transept wall, and this fabric (203) is constructed of largely square, well dressed blocks of Reigate, ragstone, Caen stone and tile bonded with a pale pink/buff mortar with occasional chalk flecks and angular gravel pebbles. Intriguingly, this masonry appears to have been blackened or damaged through contact with fire. It is possible that this represents a later exposure to smoke (for example, during the period when the triforium was used as a fire watchers' station during World War II, a stove could have been located in this area). However, the masonry fragment is located right next to the access trap door to the roof and this would tend to argue against a stove being sited here. Additionally, the softer stones show signs of weathering after the fire damage has occurred, suggesting that this masonry was originally part of an external wall. It is suggested here that context 203 represents the surviving fragment of a blank wall between choir and transept, prior to the construction of aisle, and that the damaged stones represent direct evidence for the early 13th-century fire. Contexts 204 and 206 to the south and north of the 'burnt fragment' are entirely of squared blocks of Reigate stone and represent the 13th-century rebuild of the north transept wall. Above all of this masonry are the sandstone blocks of Gwilt's 1822 rebuild 205, with incised graffiti dated 1907.

At the base of the elevation is roughly hewn ragstone (207). This represents a rebuild to 203, either during the (re)construction of the vaulting in the 13th century or associated with the construction of a stair from the tower turret to the triforium area. This masonry butts up against the north aisle wall 112 (unlike 203), suggesting it is a later addition (i.e. post 13th century).

It is suggested here that the ashlar masonry of 'Bay 1' and the north transept wall represents the fragmentary remains of the original 1106 foundation, and should be viewed in context with the early masonry of the northeast transept chapel, as described below. The nature of the build would seem to indicate that these walls were originally external. Thus, the form of the first priory church can be reconstructed as a cruciform building with north and south transepts and a central tower. The plan of the nave is unclear, however it is probable that there were no aisles to the choir. The suggested reconstruction of the east end (see Fig. 74a) shows apsidal ends to the north and south transept chapels, mirrored by a single bay apsidal end for the choir itself.

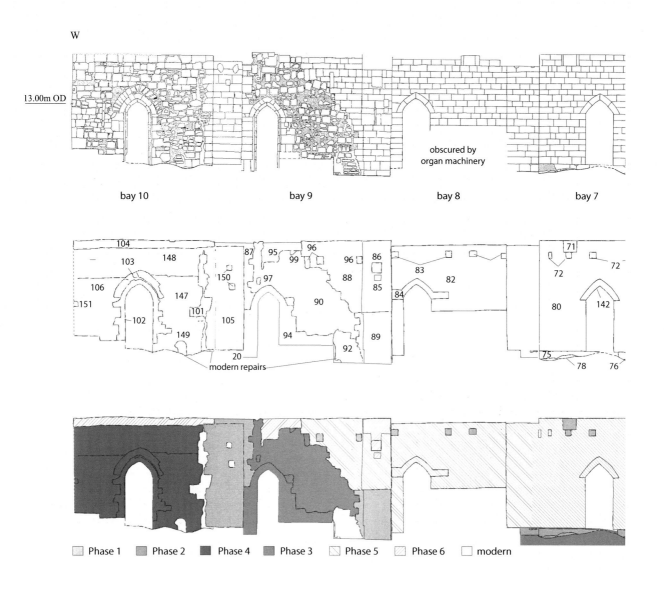

Fig. 41   Elevation of the south choir wall at triforium level (scale 1:100)
©SCARP

The northeast transept chapel

The northeast transept chapel, or Harvard Chapel, formerly known as the chapel of St John the Evangelist, is situated to the east of the north transept of the Cathedral. It was one of several chapels within the priory church including that of St Peter in the north transept (for which the medieval aumbry survives) and the chapel of St John the Baptist in the north aisle, which later became the chantry chapel of the poet John Gower (Hines *et al* 2004). The results of standing building survey in the chapel have previously been described (see Roffey 1998b, 255–262; 1999, 45–47); an extended and edited version is presented below.

Architectural elements of the chapel have been said to be among the most ancient parts of the surviving church (RCHM 1930, 58; Cherry and Pevsner 1983, 566). The present interior of the chapel was restored in the 'Gothic' style, so beloved by Victorian 'restorers', in 1907 by A. Blomfield, the Cathedral Architect. The cost was borne by

Harvard University whose benefactor, John Harvard, was baptised in the church in 1607. External restoration of the structure was carried out in 1847 under George Gwilt.

Observations by antiquarians of the interior and exterior of the chapel during renovation recorded the foundations and parts of the superstructure of an apsidal terminus (Dollman 1881, 22; Taylor 1833, 37; Benson 1885, 2) while structural features including arches in the west wall and southeast corner were also noted (Thompson 1904, 130).

Exterior fabric

The apsidal chapel

Investigation of the exterior fabric of the north chapel wall revealed several related features. These included an apsidal feature, an associated buttress, and part of a shaft with the spring of an arch or wall rib (Fig. 45, Fig. 46). The lower

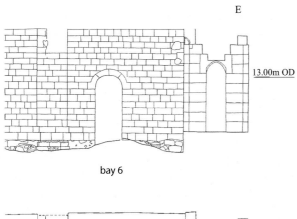

E

13.00m OD

bay 6

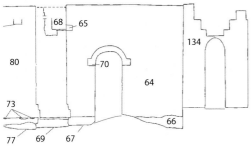

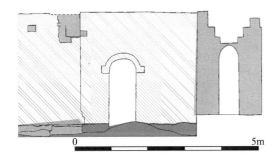

0   5m

Fig. 42   Evidence for subsidence at the east end (1m scale)
©SCARP

Fig. 43   Masonry at the base of the Bay 5 elevation, showing offset wall and re-use of moulded stones in vaulting (1m scale)
©SCARP

[204]

[203]

[206]

[205]

Fig. 44   The 'burnt' fragment of masonry in the north transept (1m scale)

©SCARP

parts of this elevation were inaccessible during the time the building recording was undertaken.

The earliest features of the elevation consist of part of the eastern apse of the original chapel and an associated buttress constructed immediately to its west. The apse is constructed of randomly coursed ragstone rubble. On the lower part of the wall, the remains of a string course of Reigate stone are visible. One chip-carved moulded stone (of the same design as that found within the chapel's east wall) survives in this course, although it is now badly eroded. A line of Caen quoins marks the eastern edge of the buttress, the western edge is now masked by later re-facing, added when the chapel was extended in length by *c.* 4m and a square end was built. Where some of this randomly coursed ragstone rubble facing has been removed, evidence for the buttress's chalk rubble core can be seen.

The existence of comparable fragments of chip-carved moulded stones on both the apsidal feature and embedded within the east wall of the extended chapel suggests that the construction dates of the apsidal chapel and its later extension are not far apart. Although it is possible that the string course fragment within the east wall was simply re-used as a structural element, it could be conjectured that this style was still in fashion, and it was re-used as a decorative item, as has been found with re-used masonry in other parts of the Cathedral. Also, the use of similar building materials and techniques in the construction of both the original apsidal chapel and the later square end

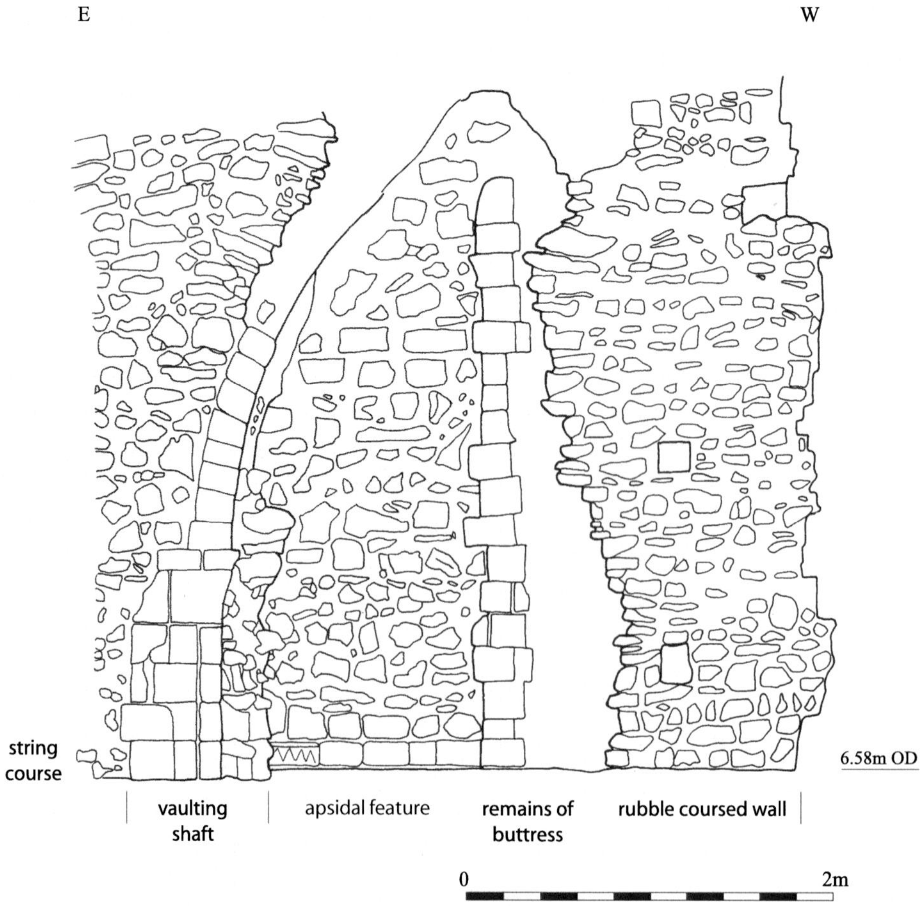

E   W

string
course

6.58m OD

	vaulting	apsidal feature	remains of	rubble coursed wall
	shaft		buttress	

0   2m

Fig. 45   Elevation of the external north wall of the northern transept chapel showing medieval features (scale 1:40)

©SCARP

extension suggests a closely contemporaneous construction date

A foundation wall [267] exposed during excavations in Trench 1 was a buttress to this apsidal structure (Fig. 47). The wall, aligned approximately north–south, was built of chalk and ragstone with a substantial width of 1.2m and an exposed length of *c.* 0.5m. The later rebuild which added the square-ended extension to the apsidal chapel is starkly visible in the north-facing section of the chapel's exterior, and may correspond to an additional wall [123] built on the northern edge of the buttress from the apsidal chapel in order to give further support. This masonry extended the buttress northwards by 0.4m.

It is interesting to note that the construction of this buttress as evidenced from the interior of the chapel (see above) shows continuing problems with subsidence of the north wall and it is possible that underlying Roman cut features may have had an early impact on the stability of this wall.

An incomplete Roman stone mould for pewter vessels was recovered re-used as building stone within the extension [123] to the buttress wall. The mould was of igneous rock, probably basalt, carved on two sides, both with outer moulds (Fig. 48). One mould is for a shallow bowl, *c.* 250mm in diameter and *c.* 45mm deep, the other mould is for a plate, *c.* 190mm in diameter and *c.* 18mm deep. Moulds of this type are known from several Roman sites in Britain, demonstrating the importance of pewter production (Beagrie 1989; cf. Blagg 1980, 103–105). The bowls would have been cast; late 3rd- or 4th-century examples were recovered from excavations at St Just, Penwith in Cornwall. Here two examples of moulds were found, carved from greisen, a granitic rock, representing the upper and lower parts of the mould, with a casting

Fig. 46   Medieval elements visible in the external north wall of the Chapel, looking southeast

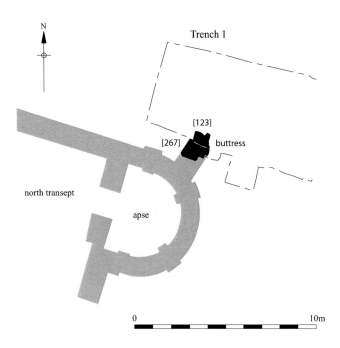

Fig. 47   The buttress against the apse on the north transept chapel (scale 1:200)

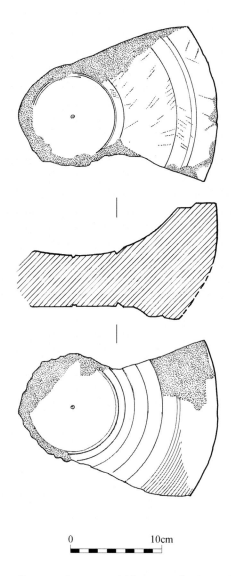

Fig. 48   Roman stone mould for manufacture of pewter vessels, found incorporated into the extension to the buttress on the apse (scale 1:4)

channel, through which molten pewter was poured, on the upper mould (Hartley *et al* 2006).

Interior fabric

Nook-shaft in the northeast corner of the chapel

The remains of a nook-shaft (or angle shaft) are to be found in the northeast corner encased in the fabric of 19th-century restorative work. Constructed of Caen stone, this exists to a height of 2.91m and is compound in form, with a central circular shaft with double roll-moulded base set within a diagonally placed square plinth (Fig. 49).

The wall to the north of the pier has been dated to the early 12th century (RCHM 1930, 62) whilst that to the east of it is modern, though a chip carved moulding, also datable to the early 12th century, can be seen to run behind it. Although no evidence of the capital or spring for a vaulting component survives, it seems likely due to its position and with regard to evidence for the position of the apsidal terminus on the north elevation, that this feature formed part of an original vaulting shaft for the later 12th-century rectangular chapel.

Interior fabric: Elevation of the west side of the chapel

The piers of the open arcade, which formed the original entrance to the chapel from the north transept, were also examined (Fig. 50).

The northernmost pier leans decidedly to the north and has been encased within the later fabric of the chapel wall. The northern edge of the central pier also appears to lean slightly to the north, although its southern edge, in comparison, is relatively vertical. This slight difference in

vertical alignment and the fact that the both the masonry and coursing of the northern edge is different from that of the rest of the pier (as described below), would suggest that the major part of the central pier was reconstructed during the general restoration of the 19th century, or during the chapel's restoration of 1907.

Architecturally the two piers are of 'square type' and although there are similarities to piers of Anglo-Saxon date (examples of comparative designs of pier and arch can be seen at Worth, Sussex; Skipworth, Yorks; Breamore, Hants and St Mary's Stoke d'Abernon in Surrey: Taylor and Taylor 1965), the abaci of both piers of the northeast chapel at Southwark date to the Norman period. Both bear a simple hatchet design (although that on the central pier has been restored), and examples of this particular type of moulding have also been recorded at Winchester Cathedral and in London, on the square piers of the choir of St Bartholomew the Great, which was founded in 1123.

Fig. 49   Nook-shaft in the northeast corner of the northeast transept chapel (2m scale)

©SCARP

S   N

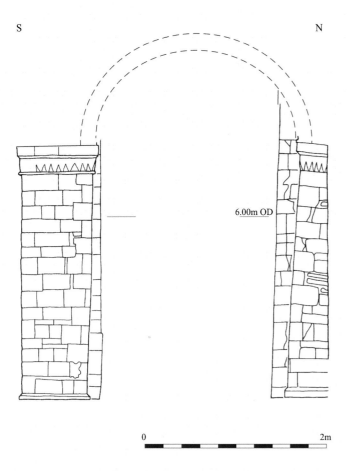

6.00m OD

0   2m

Fig. 50   Elevation of early 12th-century piers in the
           west wall of northeast transept chapel (scale
           1:40)

©SCARP

Thus the arches show both Anglo-Saxon and Norman
elements in their design. It is possible that the hatchet
ornament was inserted at a later date, and thus that the arch
dates from before the Augustinian foundation of 1106 and
represents the remains of the Anglo-Saxon *monasterium*.
However, it is more likely that they demonstrate the work of
local masons still influenced by pre-Conquest architectural
tradition.

The leaning of the piers could be due to either damage
caused by the fires of *c.* 1212, or the 1390s, or general land
subsidence caused by flooding. The Annals of Bermondsey
relate the regular occurrence of floods from the 1090s
onwards which eventually led to the canons petitioning
the king against 'the violence of the river' (Graham 1978,
102). Excavations in the 1970s revealed evidence for a 'very
destructive flood ' at the end of the 13th century, although
admittedly over an area north of the dormitory and some
30m north of the chapter house (Dawson 1976, 39).

The south transept and St Mary Magdalene Chapel

The north and south transepts are very different. It has
been suggested that a chapel of similar size and shape
to the northeast transept chapel originally occupied a
symmetrical position by the south transept (Thompson
1894, 102), although any such structure would have been
removed or obscured by the construction of the St Mary
Magdalene Chapel.

Construction of the south transept

Historical references indicate that the south transept
has had an eventful history. Initially constructed in the
early 12th century, it was damaged by fire in the early
13th century and not rebuilt until around 1310. This
reconstruction of the south transept after the fire of 1212
has been variously dated to c. 1310 (RCHM 1930, 58), and
c. 1350, from the tracery designs of the windows (VCH
1914, 456). Another fire in the 1390s led to a rebuild
by Henry Beaufort, Bishop of Winchester, around 1420
(Carlin 1996, 68–70). Elements of the south transept
foundations were seen in excavations in Trench 18
(Fig. 51) where both core and face were contemporary
as demonstrated by mortar from the former being
present on the latter. The core was rubble-built, with a
high proportion of mortar, and faced with better-laid
stonework that was brought into courses in the usual
medieval fashion. The material used was Kentish ragstone
and Reigate stone, with some flint and occasional re-used
worked Caen stone. The foundations were revealed in
elevation around the southern and eastern exterior of the
transept and in places projected from it. The irregular
form of the foundations is due to the modification of the
transept in the 19th century when the existing façade
was built. The internal elevations of the south and west
walls of the transept show evidence for this 19th-century
rebuilding and renovation reusing medieval masonry
as well as new material. The later masons re-used the
medieval foundations and clad the transept with new
stonework. This also applies to the east side of the south
transept where medieval foundations were found below
the later façade. The presence of fragments of faced
Caen stone in one of these foundations implies that they
incorporated re-used facing stone from the Norman
church fabric. The remains may therefore date from the
second or third rebuilds. This, and the contemporary
construction of both core and face, indicates that one or
both of these rebuilds involved the complete replacement
of the earlier foundations.

The internal elevations of the south and west walls of
the transept show evidence for rebuilding and renovation
dating to the 19th century, reusing medieval masonry as
well as new material. In several places the lower courses
of the walls have been rebuilt, possibly indicating areas
damaged by damp.

The secure dating of the elements of the transept
foundations is a problematic one. The remains showed

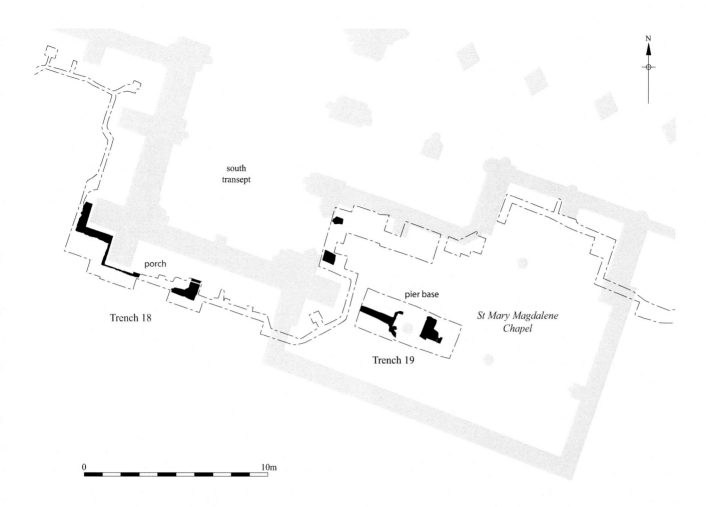

south
transept

porch

Trench 18

pier base

St Mary Magdalene
Chapel

Trench 19

0   10m

Fig. 51   Remains of the St Mary Magdalene Chapel, south transept and porch (scale 1:200)

no sign of heat damage to indicate that they pre-dated either fire, yet this is perhaps unsurprising as a high intensity of heat would need to be generated to impact on the foundation level. As such it cannot be said from the evidence whether the foundations of the second build were re-used or newly built. For the third build of the structure, at least, this could only be seen by the comparison of construction styles and mortar between the foundations and the upper walls, which is impossible owing to the 19th-century façade. The façade also prevents the realising of firm stratigraphic relationships between elements of the early walls, a problem that persisted around the Cathedral.

Remains of a porch by the south transept

Evidence for a rebuilt porch was found in excavations on the south side of the south transept in Trench 18. Masonry remains formed the southern and eastern extents of the structure that would have granted access to the church through a doorway in the transept, the arch of which can still be seen inside the Cathedral.

The remains comprised the lower courses of two distinct sections of wall (Fig. 52). Only 0.1m of the north–south length of the earlier build was exposed, built of randomly coursed Kentish ragstone. The southern extent of this wall was squared rather than truncated, but there was no evidence that this represented the edge of a smaller porch, as there were no signs of a truncated return to the wall. A gap of approximately 70mm separated it from a southerly extension. This later addition continued for 0.9m and then returned to the west for 1.32m, where it was truncated. No surviving remains were seen for the opposing west side of the porch, yet there was no reason why such remains should not have survived. Therefore it is probable that the porch was built into the buttressed corner of the south transept, and the buttress itself formed the western side of the structure. This would give the porch external dimensions of at least 3.1m east–west by 1.8m north–south. The additional section of wall was randomly coursed and built with a variety of materials including Caen stone and bricks. The bricks are likely to date from between 1450 and 1480 at the earliest, which conflicts with historical sources dating the third phase of the south transept construction to around 1420 (Carlin 1996, 70).

The area interior to these walls contained make-up material and a mortar layer at 4.01m OD, possibly a bedding for a floor surface some 0.24m below the surviving 19th-century floor level within the south transept, at 4.25m OD. The porch structure can be seen

Fig. 52   Remains of the porch during excavation (1m and 2m scales)

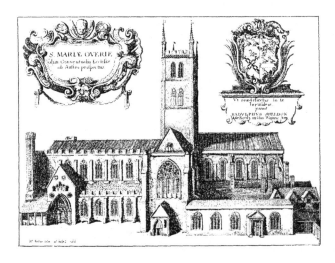

Fig. 53   The southeast elevation of the church as shown by Hollar (1661), showing the porch on the south transept
Reproduced by kind permission of Southwark Local Studies Library

on an impression of the church dating from 1661 (Stevens 1931, 34; Fig. 53) but had been removed by 1818 as indicated on Dollman's engraving of the south elevation of the church at that date (Dollman 1818, fig. 6).

The St Mary Magdalene Chapel

The St Mary Magdalene Chapel was built during the reign of Bishop Peter des Roches of Winchester 1212–1239 (Malden 1967, 153) as the parochial church of the priory. Historically there does not appear to have been any further building or repair of this structure throughout the medieval period despite the extensive reworking of the adjacent south transept. Post-Dissolution it is likely that the church would have fallen into disrepair, because the parishes of St Mary Magdalene and St Margaret-at-Hill were incorporated under that of St Saviour after 1540 (The Building News 1879, 51), rendering the chapel superfluous and 'used simply as a vestibule' (Dollman 1881, 11).

Elements of the chapel were found in Trenches 18 and 19 in the form of masonry foundations, built mostly with chalk, Kentish ragstone and Reigate stone rubble (Fig. 51, Fig. 54). These could date to the 13th century or later, thereby concurring with the documented construction date. It is

Fig. 54   Excavations in the St Mary Magdalene Chapel

from east to west and were supported on four clustered piers producing a three bay by three bay arrangement. Two depictions of the chapel, dating to the 17th and early 19th century, are contradictory, showing a classical façade applied to a low Gothic building. The Gothic windows in the 19th-century engraving (Moss and Nightingale 1818; Fig. 55) definitely post-date the mid 13th-century structure, appearing to be Decorated or even Perpendicular in style, thus possibly dating to as late as the 16th century.

The retro-choir

The retro-choir is believed to have been constructed during the middle of the 13th century. The windows in the retro-choir are all modern restorations along original lines, and together with the windows of the choir aisles represent different periods of construction, ranging from the 14th-century lancet windows through to windows with early 14th-century reticulated tracery (VCH 1914). The vaulting is quadripartite, with moulded ribs, and appears to have been largely reconstructed. A solid wall replaced the two arches formerly opening into the choir on the west (RCHM 1930, 58); the decorative detail of the blind tracery at the top of this elevation suggests that this development took place *c.* 1340. Access to the high altar is possible from the retro-choir through later doors cut through the wall at the north and south.

Detailed examination of the east end by Cherry and Pevsner suggested a construction in slowly proceeding stages and a possible chronology was defined: the initial building works consisted of the lower walls of the choir aisles and north arcade, followed by the retro-choir and south arcade (and the upper part of the north arcade). That the vaulting ribs of the north aisle have more varied profiles than those of the retro-choir and south aisle may also suggest an earlier construction date (Cherry and Pevsner 1983, 568).

Further building work was undertaken in the retro-choir during the early 14th century when the ground floor open arcade behind the high altar was replaced with ashlar masonry and blind tracery.

At the northeast corner of the retro-choir, beneath a polygonal turret was a masonry foundation, the lower level of which comprised uncoursed rubble, sealed by coursed Reigate stone and Caen stone (Fig. 56). The distinctly sandy mortar in each of these strongly implies a medieval date, as does the fact that the turret is not mirrored at the southeast corner of the retro-choir, indicative of Gothic style (K. Sabel, *pers comm*). A plan of the Cathedral in Malden (1967, opp. 156) shows the turret as being of 15th-century date, although the basis for this is not clear. It may have functioned as a staircase (Taylor 1833, 71), the steps of which are now gone.

The construction of the retro-choir is dated to the mid 13th century on stylistic grounds (see Fig. 74d), and evidence from the ground floor windows and the west wall suggests cosmetic and internal alterations of the structure into the early 14th century. Having noted the influence of

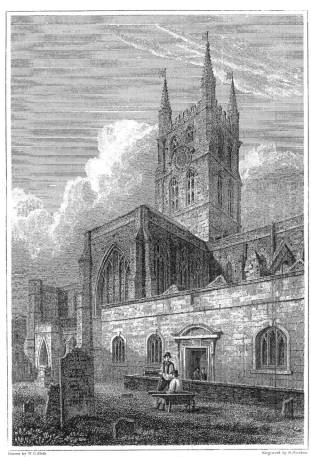

Fig. 55   View from the southeast of the Cathedral by W. Moss (1881)

Reproduced by kind permission of Southwark Local Studies Library

considered that it would have been possible to rebuild the south transept in the 14th century without having to rebuild the chapel (K. Sabel *pers comm*). It is therefore feasible that a pier base found in Trench 19 represents the only evidence of the chapel's interior arcading.

The foundations exposed in Trench 18 (one incorporating re-used Norman facing stone) extended some distance from the line of the east wall of the south transept. Rather than relating to the foundations of the east wall of the second or third phase of that structure, they may represent buttresses relating to the transept or even pier bases relating to the St Mary Magdalene Chapel. If they are pier bases, the fact that they do not align with another pier base and sleeper wall of the final phase of the St Mary Magdalene Chapel, found to the southwest in Trench 19, may indicate that the chapel was rebuilt in the 14th or 15th century with the south transept, and that the positions of the arcades were moved.

Historic plans and illustrations of the chapel show that its roof was considerably lower than the adjacent chancel and transept and that the arcades within the chapel ran the Bishops of Winchester upon building programmes at St Mary's Priory, it is probably not coincidence that the retro-choir construction followed on immediately after the completion of Winchester's own retro-choir (built between 1200–1238). Very little medieval masonry survives above the vaulting of the retro-choir. The vaulting itself appears to have been largely reconstructed, together with the east wall of the retro-choir, probably during the 19th century. The surviving 13th-century wall fabric demonstrates the continued use of Reigate and Kentish ragstone, with some chalk and flint, bonded with a creamy white lime mortar. Greater proportions of squared and dressed stone were used during construction, compared to the earlier masonry.

The Lady Chapel

Throughout the late medieval and post-medieval periods the area to the east of the retro-choir was occupied by a Lady Chapel. The chapel was entered via two steps (The Mirror of Literature, Amusement, and Instruction 1832) through a doorway in the second bay from the south wall

of the retro-choir. Substantial remains of the medieval structure were excavated, revealing detailed information relating to the construction and types of stone used.

Two walls of the Lady Chapel were exposed in Trench 14, forming the north and south sides and incorporating a *c.* 1.37m long buttress on each [3385], [3384] (Fig. 56, Fig. 57). The eastern wall of the chapel had been demolished in the 19th century. Both the north and south walls were seen to continue westwards to abut the wall of the retro-choir in Trench 20 [3895], [3893]. These showed that the internal east–west dimension of the Lady Chapel was at least 9.25m, while the internal north–south dimension was 5.25m.

The walls of the 14th-century chapel were built on slightly battered masonry plinths approximately 0.74m thick. The stone was mostly Kentish ragstone with some Reigate stone and small quantities of Caen stone, Barnack stone, Hassock sandstone and septaria. The Caen and Barnack stone were mostly re-used and worked, and presumably derived from elements of the church that were demolished during the church's expansion, or were obtained from other demolished buildings. Reigate stone was used for the plinth's chamfer. This stone type was, by the late 14th century, known to weather badly (K. Sabel, *pers comm*) and its use in such an exposed location was unusual by this date, indicating that the chapel either pre-dated the late 14th century or that the stone was re-used, as such a soft stone is unlikely to have been quarried specifically for the relatively exposed plinth chamfer from the late 14th century onwards.

Although the chapel was demolished in 1830, drawings dating to 1880 (Dollman 1881; Fig. 58) portray the tracery of the windows of the chapel as being built in the Decorated style, dating it to the period between *c.* 1250 and the mid 14th century. If these drawings are accurate the stylistic evidence, combined with the fact that Reigate stone was chosen for the exposed plinth chamfer, suggest a chapel in the Decorated style and accord with the accepted late 13th- to mid 14th-century date of construction. That the plinth is omitted from the drawing of the chapel's south elevation suggests that the plinth was below the external ground level when drawn. The base of the walls of the

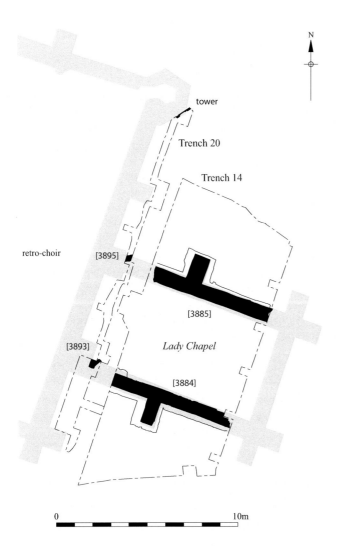

Fig. 56   Remains of the Lady Chapel and the northeast tower (scale 1:200)

Fig. 57   Recording the Lady Chapel, looking northwest

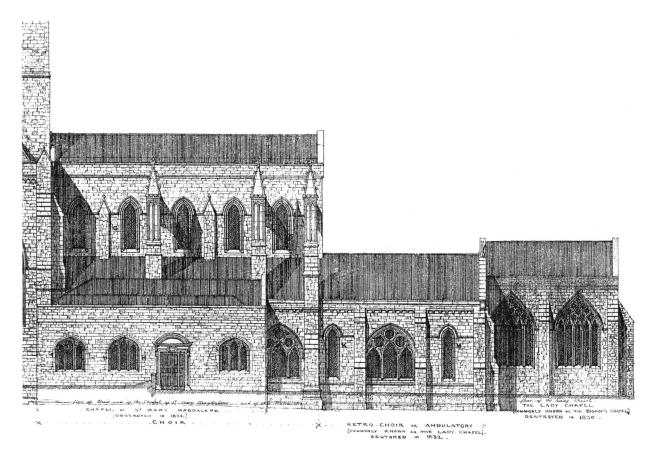

Fig. 58 Dollman's (1881) engraving of the southeast elevation of the Cathedral
Reproduced by kind permission of Southwark Local Studies Library

chapel are depicted on the drawings as higher than those of the retro-choir, and, except for a shadow that shows that the chapel is set back from the line of the south wall of the retro-choir, the drawings are architectural in character and do not show walls on different planes with any perspective. The base of the chapel's wall is shown at or above the level of the plinth of the retro-choir. The later chapel's plinth would most probably have been built at the same height as that of the adjoining structure.

The thickness of the chapel's walls (0.74m) is also indicative of their 14th-century date and architectural style. The 19th-century historic plans and elevations of the church show that the walls of the retro-choir (which was not as high as the chapel) were much thicker. This solid construction is characteristic of early Gothic building (Coldstream 1994, 18) and indeed the retro-choir walls are confirmed to date to before 1290 by their Early English fenestration. The relative thinness of the walls of the Lady Chapel compared with those of the retro-choir therefore reflect the general trend in the development of Gothic architecture towards thinner, lighter walls and larger areas of fenestration.

Worked stones within the chapel walls included a re-used fragment of Reigate stone mullion with the same moulding as those that survive between the 20th-century grouped lancet windows at the east end of the retro-choir. The east wall of the retro-choir is Early English in style and it is likely that it was rebuilt to match the original work.

This is confirmed by an engraving showing the east end of the retro-choir after the demolition of the Bishop's Chapel (Taylor 1833) but before its rebuilding in flint, with similar grouped lancet windows. The re-used mullion, which remains *in situ* in the wall, has a flat face. It most likely derived from the windows of the second bay from the south at the east end of the retro-choir, which was cut through to create the arch between the retro-choir and the chapel.

The internal face of the southern wall of the Lady Chapel bore a coating of painted plaster, surviving fragmentarily below a later render. This may represent the original decoration of the building.

The claustral buildings

Elements of the buildings that accompanied the Priory of St Mary on the north side of the church were recorded by antiquarians in the 19th century (Dollman 1881), and seen archaeologically in works in the 1970s following the demolition of the Bonded Warehouse (Dawson 1976). These elements were tantalisingly small, restricted to areas that had been undisturbed by the construction of the warehouse, which itself was complete by 1835 (Raymond 1999, 26). The only area that has been subjected to modern archaeological investigation, in the 1970s and during the Millennium excavations, is along a small corridor adjacent to the north of the choir and retro-choir.

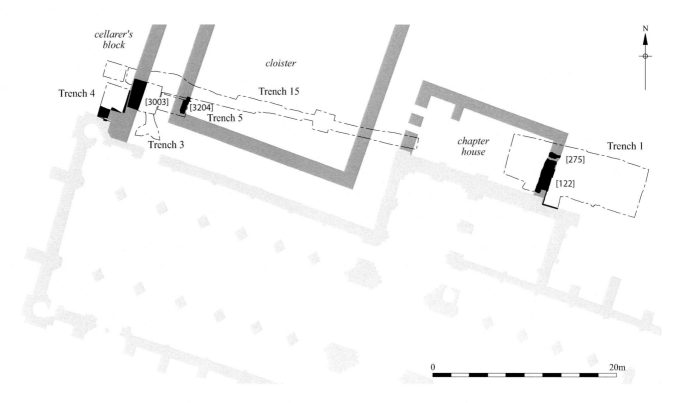

Fig. 59   Remains of the cloister, chapter house and cellarer's block (scale 1:400)

Layers of material observed in Trench 15 served to raise the ground level by 0.6m to 3.52m OD; one of these contained a sherd of 16th- to 17th-century pottery. Given the position of this deposit in Trench 15 (seen east–west across the position of the cloister garth) and its date, it may represent evidence of landscaping within the former priory buildings. If this is the case then the two undated layers stratigraphically below, at an upper height of 3.34m OD, may be close to the ground level of the cloister garth.

The west range

To the northwest of the Cathedral, investigations revealed further elements of the priory buildings. A north–south aligned wall [3204] exposed in Trench 5 consisted of roughly coursed Kentish ragstone and Reigate stone blocks, built on a crude foundation (Fig. 59). The wall had a visible width of *c.* 1.5m, and extended through the trench for *c.* 1.75m. Its western side was partly built of dressed Reigate stone, found in good condition and not weathered, indicating that this was the internal aspect of the wall. At a distance of *c.* 3.5m to the west of this wall, and running parallel to it, a robber cut was excavated [3003]. This had removed all traces of a wall that would have had a maximum width of 1.5m. The cut was recorded throughout Trenches 3 and 4, a north–south distance of *c.* 4.0m. The robber cut was 19th-century in date, and may have resulted from demolition of the cloisters and the construction of the warehouses to the north of the church. The northern extents of both the robber cut and the wall in Trench 5 had

been truncated by modern activity recorded in Trench 15. Given that both the wall and the robber cut had the same width, and were parallel, it is reasonable to suppose that they marked either side of the cloister walk, with a width of 3.5m. The area to the west of robber cut [3003] in Trench 3 roughly corresponds to the suggested position of the cellarer's block, the westernmost of the priory buildings (Dollman 1881).

The east range

A substantial wall was seen in Trench 1 extending northwards for 4.5m from the squared end of the northeast transept chapel, indicating that it was either contemporary or post-dated the build of that structure in the late 12th century. The wall was made of Kentish ragstone, with a width of 1.4m, and a surviving height of 1.3m in a construction cut which had truncated the upper levels of the Roman road. Its position roughly corresponds to the eastern extent of the chapter house as suggested in 19th-century illustrations (Dollman 1881). These show that a north–south wall extending from the squared end of the northeast transept chapel formed the eastern external wall of the chapter house. To the west of the wall the fragmentary remains of mortar layers were found at *c.* 3.1m OD, interpreted as internal floor surfaces or the bedding for such surfaces, potentially of the chapter house itself. The only place in which the floor height of the 12th-century church can be approximated is at the doorway between the north aisle and vestry (see Fig. 122). The level

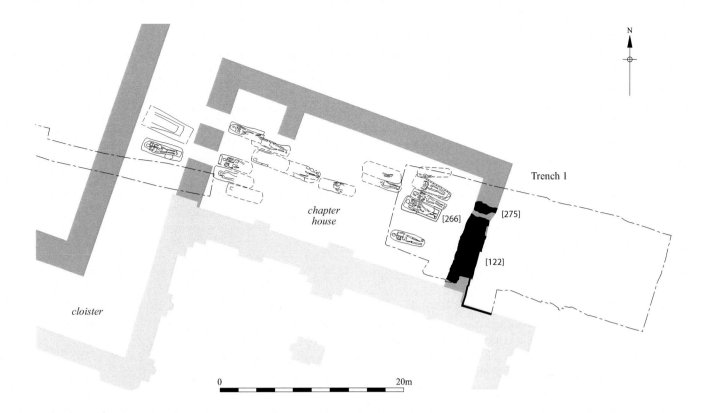

Fig. 60   Burials within the chapter house (scale 1:200)

After Dawson 1976b, fig. 5

is not precise because of modern rendering of the lower section, yet it provides a maximum height for the early floor, at 3.47m OD. The 0.37m difference between the two heights is substantial, but can be made more plausible if it is presumed that the chapter house layers were bedding for a tiled floor, and that the modern rendering in the 12th-century doorway is of some thickness.

The external face of the north wall of the north transept and chapel reveals a compound nook-shaft and its three shafts, constructed largely from Reigate stone, although the abacus of the capital could be made from Caen stone (T. Tatton-Brown, *pers comm*). The circular shafts are formed in orders, and a simple roll moulding rounds off the outer edges of the respective abaci. These features could point to a late 12th-century or early 13th-century date (Fletcher 1967, 452), and comparative types can be seen at Winchester, and on the base of the 12th-century door at Sempringham in Lincolnshire (Fletcher 1987, 386).

Drawings of the shafts in the 19th century (Dollman 1881) also suggests slightly flattened roll-moulded bases, now lost, or encased in the lower brickwork. This is a type introduced in some Cistercian churches and also in the second rebuilding of the later 12th century at Canterbury (Clapham 1934, 120). This might also correspond with a suggested rebuilding of the nave at Southwark in the architectural style of the Canterbury school during the later half of the 12th century (Lethaby 1914, 158–159). The design of the shafts is also comparable to the door jambs of the elaborate 'Prior's entrance' within the north wall of the nave, datable to the second half of the 12th century.

Examination of the column capital and spring shows that part of it would have projected northwards (this part having been broken off at some stage) and must be related to the remains of an off-set of an east wall. The column and shafts must have provided the corner support, or jamb, for a vaulting shaft of an adjoining building. The remains of the voussoirs, or stone segments, within the wall must be from an arch or vault 'frame' providing one of the bays of the chapter house. Dollman refers to similar 'jambs' within the former refectory 'where no opening exists' (Dollman 1881, 27).

Burials in the chapter house and cloisters

Excavation work by Dawson in the 1970s revealed nineteen graves, seventeen within the chapter house and two within the eastern alley of the cloister (Fig. 60). Of these, sixteen produced skeletal remains that Dawson concludes are probably those of the Priors who served within the church, as it was 'customary for the heads of monastic houses to be buried within the chapter house' (Dawson 1976, 48).

Gilchrist and Sloane (2005) discuss spatial hierarchies in the medieval world in relation to the location of burials with monastic cemeteries. The chapter house, the site of monastic discipline, was a favoured burial place for monastic superiors, certainly until the 13th century, but they might also be found buried within the cemetery and to a lesser extent the cloister. Nor were burials within the chapter house confined exclusively to members of the monastic community; monasteries were also places of burial for certain members of the lay community. Founding families, patrons or wealthy benefactors were often buried within monastic precincts and, although the church itself was the preferred place of burial, such individuals might also be found buried in the entrance to, or within, the chapter house. It is also worth noting that preferences appear to have changed over time, as is demonstrated at Bury St Edmunds where, between 1148 and 1234, all six Abbots were buried within the chapter house, whilst formerly they had been interred within the infirmary chapel and presbytery and subsequently favoured the Lady Chapel, north aisle and again the presbytery for burial (Gilchrist and Sloane 2005, 60). The cloister was closely associated with the burial of the dead although the central garth was rarely used, the alleys were used more commonly and Gilchrist and Sloane suggest that burial in the cloister was highly structured (2005, 57).

Dawson's investigations identified nine simple graves, some apparently containing no evidence for a coffin, six within stone cists, i.e. the grave was lined with mortared stonework, two burials within lead coffins and also two within stone sarcophagi carved from a type of Oolitic Limestone. The Millennium excavations uncovered the unexcavated remains of half of one of these stone coffins, containing the lower half of a skeleton [266], in Trench 1. The coffin was within a grave, cut from at least 2.8m OD, thereby indicating a minimum height for the contemporary ground level, which compares well with a possible internal height of the chapter house of c. 3.1m OD. Such coffins have been excavated elsewhere in prominent positions, for example at the Old Minster in Winchester (Kjølbye-Biddle 1992, 228). Whilst being far less elaborate than earlier and more decorative Anglo-Saxon examples (Hadley 2001, 104), stone coffins become far more common in the later medieval period. Excavations at the Gilbertine Priory of St Andrew in York found six 13th- or early 14th-century burials in the north chapel, four of which were in stone coffins, where their prominent position and form led to the conclusion that the individuals were of high status (Hadley 2001, 115–116). Burials within stone coffins are also discussed by Gilchrist and Sloane who note that in religious houses they seem to have been far more common in buildings than in cemeteries, and they conclude that they must have been the privilege of the elite, whether members of religious orders or the laity (Gilchrist and Sloane 2005, 150), unsurprisingly given the significant investment, both financially and in terms of labour, needed in order to obtain such a burial. Thus we can conclude that the stone coffins from Southwark Cathedral, of which several can be seen placed around the Cathedral precincts, are likely to have held similarly important persons, either within the religious community, or wealthy lay individuals with an interest and investment in the church (Fig. 61).

A pathological assessment of the skeletal remains from the chapter house and cloister for the Millennium excavations has shown a number of diseases to be present as outlined below. These include degenerative joint disease and diffuse idiopathic skeletal hyperostosis (DISH), a

Fig. 61   One of the stone coffins visible within the Cathedral precinct (1m and 0.5m scales)

condition often associated with older men, obesity and diabetes. Examples of this condition have been found at medieval monastic sites including Merton Priory in Surrey (Waldron 1985), Guisborough Priory in North Yorkshire (Anderson 2000) and Marmont Priory in Norfolk (Anderson 1998). Such occurrences have led to the theory that DISH is linked to a wealthy lifestyle, combining rich food and alcohol, providing an insight into the lifestyle of those buried at the Priory of St Mary.

The remains from the 1969–73 excavations were very fragmentary and in poor condition with bone flaking away from many of the surfaces. Unfortunately no skulls were available for analysis. As a result many of the areas used in ageing and sexing were not present or were too fragmentary to use.

There was no skeletal report available for the remains recovered from the 1969–73 excavations therefore a brief analysis was undertaken to ascertain the age and sex of the individuals and any pathology present. It should be noted that this was in no way intended to be a full osteological analysis of these remains. Where applicable the methodology used was that outlined above (see methodology, Chapter 1).

Demography

Of the sixteen burials thirteen were adults, the four remaining could not be aged. Only three could be sexed as ?male and one ?female. Stature was estimated for one individual as 1.76m – 1.77m. In addition to the burials, disarticulated remains were identified from one grave fill.

Pathology

Degenerative joint disease was identified in six individuals. This affected the vertebrae in four individuals (3 of these with Schmorl's nodes) medial clavicles and a calcaneus. Periostitis was recorded on the lateral aspect of a tibia. A possible case of diffuse idiopathic skeletal hyperostosis (DISH) in its early stages was identified within the thoracic and lumbar vertebrae of an adult ?male. Although the aetiology of DISH is unknown it is often associated with older men, obesity and diabetes.

Ossified costal cartilage, usually found within older people, was present in two individuals. Pronounced deltoid tuberosities were observed on two individuals, these could be activity-related, with a possible increased use of the shoulder muscles.

Dental pathology

Although no skulls were present 5 loose teeth were included with one individual. Calculus was recorded on the 1st upper premolar and the 3rd lower left molar.

Medieval funerary monuments

The 14th-century ledger slab

During the recording work a medieval slab was examined in the southeast corner of the retro-choir (see Fig. 86 [L438] for location). The Purbeck marble slab has a series of cracks and breaks across the surface and the inscription is badly eroded and largely illegible. However, antiquarian examination of the monuments within the church meant that the identity of the deceased had been recorded. The stone was first discovered by workmen at the nearby site of St Margaret's and was removed and reset into the floor at St Saviour's during the 19th century. Whether the rest of the tomb, including any mortal remains, was also moved is unknown, but it is recorded that in 1930 the floor level of the retro-choir was lowered by several inches, suggesting that the ledger slab, along with others in the area, was re-laid at the time (Stevens 1931, 60).

The inscription was in old Lombardic characters and stated that 'Aleyn Ferthyng lies here, may God have mercy upon his soul. Amen' (Thompson 1904, 85). Ferthyng was a Member of Parliament for Southwark five times between 1337 and 1348. The latter date coincides with the outbreak of the Black Death and perhaps Ferthyng was an early victim, being consigned to a church burial and not a plague pit.

The case of the 'Ferthyng slab' highlights one of the problems associated with these types of monument. Apparently still readable in the early 20th century its inscription has since been almost completely obliterated, and that is why there is an urgent need for the preservation and recording of such monuments.

The Cadaver memorial

The 15th-century cadaver monument (Fig. 62, top; and see Fig. 32a for location) situated on the north choir aisle is strangely different to other, more elaborate and perhaps more comforting, monuments within the Cathedral. The use of the naked decomposing corpse as a monument is not exclusive to Southwark; in his survey of the church, Taylor noted that a similar example existed in Clerkenwell church (Taylor 1833, 113). Most are dated to the same period, and this figure is believed to represent one of the Augustinian canons from the former priory.

This monument is not *in situ* (as is also the case with the wooden effigy described below); during the early 19th century it was to be found in the retro-choir, alongside the remains of medieval stone coffins (Taylor 1833, 110), while in the latter part of the century it was located in the north transept (Daniell 1897, 220).

The wooden crusader effigy

Dated to around 1280, by its armour type and conical helmet design, the life-sized wooden crusader effigy is in a remarkable state of preservation (Fig. 62, bottom, Fig. 63), especially as during its long life it has had several uses,

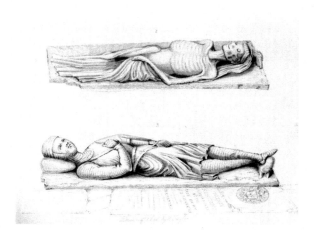

Fig. 62   Medieval funerary monuments within the Cathedral: top, 15th-century stone cadaver effigy; bottom, late 13th-century wooden effigy (from Taylor 1833)
Reproduced by kind permission of Southwark Local Studies Library

Fig. 63   The wooden crusader effigy

Fig. 64   Moulded stone fragment <M4> (15cm scale)

©SCARP

including being used as a prop to support part of a stair case (Thompson 1904, 111).

Though the identity of the knight is uncertain, it is commonly held that he was a member of the De Warenne family (Taylor 1833, 88–92), who were among the earliest benefactors to the priory. It has been suggested that the wooden effigy represents a crusader, as the legs crossed at the ankle are believed to symbolise participation on one crusade, while the extent to which the sword is drawn may mean that the deceased was a member of the Knights Templar (Thompson 1904, 111–112).

Moulded stone fragments

Twenty-five fragments of worked stone were recorded, collected from several locations around the Cathedral, and an assessment of this collection made (Quevillon 1999). Of the fragments catalogued, several are significant in a discussion of the medieval priory:

Moulded stone <M4> represents a 'springer' of 12th-century date and may be the only surviving fragment of a now destroyed door, or arcade, of the earliest priory church (Fig. 64). This fragment was also recorded by Taylor (Fig. 65) and was noted to have been found 'worked in with the materials of the north wall' (Taylor 1833, 44). The most ancient parts of the standing building survive on the north side of the church and the fact that <M4> appeared to have been found re-used here lends further weight to the hypothesis that it is a remainder of one of the earliest buildings on the site.

Fragments <M5>, <M6> and <M7> (Fig. 66) are voussoirs from a door; it has been suggested that they represent the remains of the original canons' doorway, located at the west end of the north nave aisle (Quevillon 1999, 52), although this seems doubtful as the door now in this position is believed to be the original. The chevron design, while not closely dateable, suggests a construction date in the late 12th century, and thus the fragments may represent the remains of a door of the priory (location unknown) from the period of regularisation.

Fig. 65   Moulded stone fragment 3, as recorded by Taylor (1833)

Reproduced by kind permission of Southwark Local Studies Library

Fig. 66   Moulded stone fragment <M7> (15cm scale)
©SCARP

Fig. 67   Moulded stone fragment <M8> (15cm scale)
©SCARP

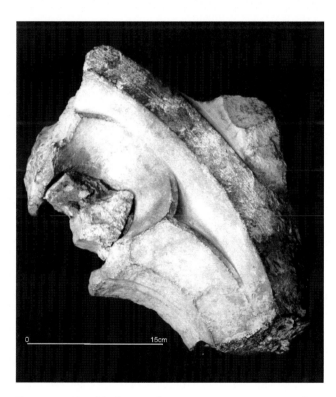

Fig. 68   Moulded stone fragment <M14> (15cm scale)
©SCARP

Fig. 69   Moulded stone fragment <M15> (15cm scale)
©SCARP

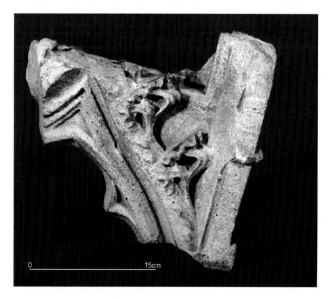

Fig. 70   Moulded stone fragment <M18> (15cm scale)
©SCARP

Fig. 71   Architectural fragment (7) recorded during
demolition (from Taylor 1833)

Reproduced by kind permission of Southwark Local
Studies Library

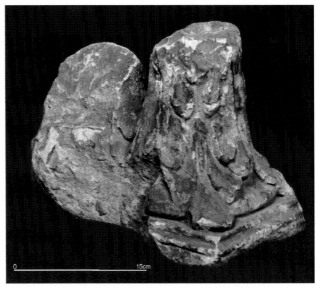

Fig. 72   Moulded stone fragment <M20> (15cm scale)
©SCARP

Fragment <M8> is part of a Purbeck marble grave
cover. The fragment is very small and only three letters
of the text survive, together with incised lines above and
below the lettering (Fig. 67). It has been suggested that the
fragment represents part of a grave cover ornamented with
an incised cross (Quevillon 1999, 47). Examples of Purbeck
marble grave slabs have also been found at St Bride's church
(see Milne 1997, 83–84) and nearby at 18–20 London
Bridge Street (LNB97). Two fragments were found at St
Bride's, both with cross motif designs in relief and were
dated to the late 12th/early 13th century and the 13th/14th
century respectively. The remains of the two grave slabs
from London Bridge Street were found re-used in a 15th-
century cellar or cesspit and are believed to have come from
the nearby hospital chapel of St Thomas. The first (dated *c.*
1270–1330) is decorated with a semi-circular base of a relief
cross, while the second has part of a French inscription,
possibly indicating the commemoration of a member of
the laity. This piece has been dated to *c.* 1305–1338 (Askew
1998, 15–16). A further example of a Purbeck marble grave
slab has been found at the Cathedral (see [L438] above)
and has been dated to the mid 14th century. Although the
language of the inscription on <M8> is not known, the style
compares well with both the example from London Bridge
Street and [L438], and suggests a 14th-century origin.

Fragment <M14> is a fragment of tracery, closely
comparable to that found on the blind tracery at the back
of the reredos, dated to *c.* 1340 (VCH 1914, 457). The piece
seems unfinished and may represent an unused part of the
tracery (Fig. 68), which was rejected due to an error in the
carving (Quevillon 1999, 53).

Moulded stone <M15> is a piece of a scalloped capital,
which may have formed part of a cluster of capitals from
a compound pier (Fig. 69). The decoration compares
closely with that found on the column capitals of the nave
at Peterborough Cathedral, dating to the first quarter
of the 12th century. A similar scalloped capital has also

from the north aisle

from the south aisle

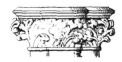

Fig. 73   Column capitals from the north and south aisles of the old nave, as illustrated by Dollman (1881)

Reproduced by kind permission of Southwark Local Studies Library

been recorded on the west door at Mickleham Church, Surrey, dated to *c.* 1120 (VCH 1914, 447). However, a further example of a scalloped capital from the site of St Mary Spital in London has been dated to the late 12th century (Thomas *et al* 1997, 25). Thus, the fragment from Southwark could have come from the nave or choir arcade of either the first or second priory church on the site.

Fragment <M18> is an intriguing piece (Fig. 70). The fragment is finely carved and unweathered, suggesting it derives from an internal location and the fan vaulting on the interior face demonstrates that this is not a piece of window mullion. It could represent part of either an altar piece, similar to that shown as surviving in the nave prior to its rebuilding as part of the Gower chantry (Fig. 71), or as a part of a funerary monument. The decorative details suggest a date of construction in the late 14th or early 15th century.

Fragments <M20> and <M25> are two double headed capitals believed to come from the cloister. <M25> is in good condition but <M20> is very eroded and the details are difficult to see (Fig. 72). However, the foliate decoration is discernible. These fragments appear to be two of those examined during the early 20th century (see Lethaby 1914, 155–160) and dated to about 1190. Lethaby also examined fragments of column bases from the cloister, which have now disappeared. These fragments are closely comparable to examples from Canterbury and must be part of the building of the cloister during the late 12th century. Dollman (1881) illustrates a series of column capitals from the north and south aisles of the old nave, which also show use of Corinthian decorative order (Fig. 73).

MEDIEVAL DISCUSSION

The elements of the medieval priory that were revealed during the Millennium excavations were tantalisingly small due to the 'keyhole' nature of the investigated trenches required by the works, and in many ways this has limited the conclusions that can made purely from the archaeological evidence (see Fig. 32). Yet, when this is considered in tandem with the known history of the priory, it can be seen to illustrate various phases of construction. These phases were necessitated by expansion, as the priory grew in stature, and disaster, such as the 13th-century inundations of the Thames and fires that occurred in the 13th and 14th centuries.

The detailed building recording of the east end of the priory, together with observations from the main body of the church, examination of the *ex situ* architectural fragments, and the evidence from documentary and antiquarian sources demonstrates that the layout and method of the construction of the church was influenced by a variety of factors. These included the cost and supply of raw materials as well as the wider issues of liturgical topography, religious reform and prevailing architectural styles.

Smith (1958) highlights similarities between the suggested plan forms of Southwark and that of the late

10th/early 11th-century church at Sherborne, and suggests that masonry of this date was encased by later rebuilding. However the lack of archaeological evidence would seem to argue against a substantial masonry building being erected during the late Saxon period and it is possible that the chalk wall foundations unearthed during excavations within the present Cathedral building (Hammerson 1978) represent the only remains of earlier church buildings. Evidence from the stone types used at triforium level would also argue against the survival of a building dating from the late 10th /early 11th century. Excavations at parish church sites in the City of London suggest that late Saxon ecclesiastical buildings were constructed using ragstone and re-used Roman ceramic building materials (Cohen 1994). Thus, the layout of the Minster remains elusive.

It seems likely that the important location of the *monasterium* at Southwark adjacent to the crossing point of the Thames, and the fact that royal and noble interests in the nearby tideway are recorded, meant that there was some development of the church during the mid to late 11th century, and the archaeological evidence certainly indicates increased levels of activity on the site; however, the plan of this *monasterium* is also unclear.

It is likely that large-scale construction work took place on the site during the post-Conquest period, as evidenced by the use of Caen and Reigate stone (in both Phases 1 and 2, i.e. the *c.* 1106 and later 12th-century construction phases). After the loss of territory in Normandy in the early 13th century there was a decrease in the amount of Caen stone imported (Tatton-Brown 1990, 76). Reigate stone was used in large quantities in London from the 11th century onwards, initially on royal projects, for example at Westminster Abbey and in large public works such as London Bridge in 1176 (Clifton-Taylor 1972, 117). The use of Reigate stone at Southwark could be indicative of 12th-century links with Surrey quarries, a possibility that is further supported by the documentary evidence concerning grants to the priory in the Reigate area. For example, during the early 12th century the Earl of Surrey, William de Warenne, endowed the priory with Kirkesfield, or Crechesfield, the church at Reigate where his Surrey castle stood (Higham 1955, 31). Thus the foundation of the Augustinian priory of secular canons in 1106 (Phase 1) meant the rebuilding of parts of the *monasterium* church to create a cruciform church with a central tower, probably without aisles to both the nave and choir, but with apsidal chapels to the north and south transepts. The form of the choir's east end is suggested to have been a short apse and this relatively unimpressive foundation reflects the early status of the founders.

It is worth noting that of the 197 Austin canon houses identified (Binns 1989, 118–159), in 1981 the number subjected to some form of archaeological investigation was only in the region of a 20% sample; evidence of early architectural form is even rarer (Hall 2000, 43). This means that any suggestions of a 'standardised' plan form relating to the houses of the order are based on only a small sample, within which are demonstrable differences relating to location, patronage and so on. Comparison

with other English and continental examples (Hall 2000) suggests an apsidal form for the east end of the priory church in its original construction, while the indirect but compelling evidence investigated during the standing building recording programme lends further weight to this hypothesis.

The examination of the masonry in the northeast transept chapel and the triforium provides evidence for an intermediate phase of building between the original early 12th-century foundation and the rebuilding of the 13th century after a destructive fire, and it seems likely that building works were on-going throughout the 12th century across the priory buildings. It is possible that the involvement of William Giffard, perhaps in association with Pont de l'Arche, brought a series of changes to the priory and may have instigated a change in rule (i.e. regularisation), and therefore a change in priory layout, including that of the church itself, to accommodate communal structures essential to regular, monastic life. These changes could have been influenced by the reforming ideals of the Cistercian order, who favoured square ended terminal walls for their monastic churches, such as those found at Tintern (Gwent). Giffard himself was influential in the foundation of Waverly (Surrey), the country's first Cistercian house, in 1128. However, while the extension of the east end at this time is clearly demonstrated by the nature of the construction surviving at triforium level, the form of the choir can be reconstructed in two ways. The first scenario (see Roffey 1998a; 1998b; 1999) conjectures a change from apsidal to square end in both the choir and transept chapels as early as the 1120s–1130s. Archaeological evidence in support of this is found in the northeast transept chapel, if the re-use of the decorative string course stone in the eastern wall is accepted as dating evidence (see Roffey 1998b), and the possibility that the blank west wall of the retro-choir was once an external wall. This supposition that the terminal walls were square ended presupposes Giffard's involvement and Cistercian influence. It is also worth noting the possibility that these changes in the northeast transept chapel did take place at this time but that they represent the extent of Giffard's involvement; it has been suggested that this development 'does not impinge on the apsidal east end (of the choir), so it is not rebuilt at this time, although it is likely Giffard planned to do so had it not been for his death in 1129' (Hall 2000, 55).

A second scenario, that the transept chapels remained apsidal in form and that the choir was extended together with an apsidal ambulatory, during the mid-late 12th century is also proposed here as the more likely sequence of development. The archaeological evidence for a development of this nature is found at both ground and triforium level, as outlined above. Documentary evidence and comparative examples also support this hypothesis. It is known that the priory was well-patronised during the mid–late 12th century and it may be that materials for the reconstruction were provided through the influence of the priory's benefactors. William Giffard was succeeded as Bishop of Winchester by Henry of Blois (1129–73), an extremely influential churchman and the brother of

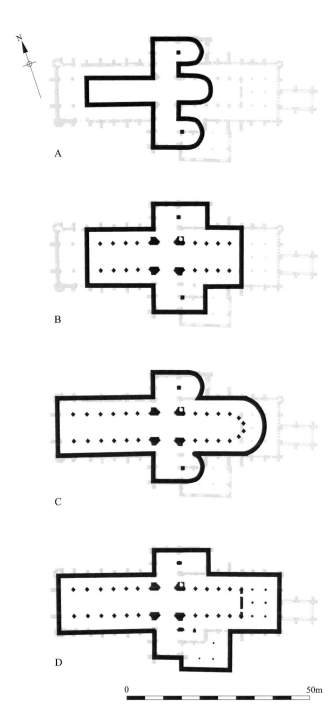

Fig. 74   Proposed phases of development of
Southwark Cathedral (scale 1:1,000)

A)   suggested reconstruction of the priory church c. 1106
(Phase 1)

B)   suggested reconstruction of the priory church c. 1130
(after Roffey, 1998b)

C)   alternative reconstruction of the priory church 1120s–
1190s (Phase 2)

D)   suggested reconstruction of the priory church 13th
century (Phase 3)

King Stephen. There are two facts about Henry of Blois
that are relevant to a discussion of the development of the
priory at Southwark: the first is that two children of King
Stephen were buried at Holy Trinity Priory, where the
construction of the presbytery (of a similar plan form to
that proposed at Southwark) is dated to c. 1150 (Schofield
and Lea 2005, 144). This, together with the documentary
evidence concerning the foundation of Augustinian houses
during the reign of Henry I, demonstrates an interest in
and patronage of the order by members of the royal family
and officials of their court. Secondly, Henry of Blois was
educated at Cluny and a close friend of the abbot, Peter the
Venerable, who visited England in 1130 (Clanchy 1989,
104–105). The Cluniac order favoured apsidal rather than
square east ends, thus it is likely that the east end extension
at Southwark, if influenced by Henry of Blois, was of
apsidal form.

The evidence from other Augustinian houses in London
also suggests that an apsidal end was at this time the more
common form. The surviving east end of St Bartholomew
the Great, founded in 1123 is apsidal with an ambulatory,
while at Holy Trinity Priory (founded 1108), the suggested
reconstruction of the east end c. 1150 shows that the choir
terminated in three single storey chapels, the central one
being an octagonal apse (Schofield and Lea 2005, 140).
Interestingly with regard to the transept chapels, those
at Holy Trinity Priory were apsidal internally but with a
square external plan. Other monastic churches in London
do show a development from apsidal to square end,
however this is generally dated later. For example, at the
Cluniac abbey at Bermondsey, the squaring off of the east
end occurred in the late 12th or 13th centuries (Grimes
1968, 214), while the rebuilding at St Paul's incorporating a
square east end is also dated to the 13th century (Hall 2000,
42). Outside London, the Abbey of St Augustine in Bristol
shows a square ended plan form of 'early English' date,
while at Winchester itself, the apsidal end was replaced
by a square east end during the 13th century. Finally, it is
intriguing to note that the apsidal end to chancels and side
chapels is almost unknown in Surrey (VCH 1914, 436),
demonstrating the priory's links with London and the
wider world rather than the rural hinterland to the south.

Such changes, it can be argued, brought the priory
more in line with religious reform as well as providing
more room for a larger, and more regularised order of
monks who, no longer confined to a small choir in direct
spatial relationship with the public nave, were now in the
more exclusive confines of the extended choir. Evidence
for former sockets in the easternmost crossing piers also
suggest this part of the church was further screened from
the body of the crossing and the nave at this period.
Increased provision of devotional space may also have been
a reason for the extension eastwards of many of the greater
churches, including St Mary Overie. More space was
required for altars to patron saints, for shrines, feretories
and processions and for the cult of the Virgin (shown in the
proliferation of Lady Chapels), which grew in popularity
during the late 12th century (Hall 2000, 25).

The building work in the choir heralded other developments within the priory during the latter part of the 12th century. Evidence from the examination of moulded stone fragments suggests that the cloister was rebuilt at this time. Surviving medieval fabric in the nave also indicates construction during this period; for example the Prior's doorway on the north aisle is dated to *c.* 1160, while Dollman's records of the nave capitals suggest a late 12th-century date. At the west end of the south wall of the nave is a battered stretch of wall arcading with capitals, which suggest a late 12th-century date. The designs of the westernmost bays of the nave differ from the rest and there are exceptionally large piers second from the west (illustrated in Moss and Nightingale 1818, these are not shown on either the RCHM 1930 or Dollman's 1881 plans; see Fig. 33), which may suggest earlier masonry has been encased (Cherry and Pevsner 1983, 566). The rebuilding was apparently carried out after the style of the French influenced 'Canterbury' (early Gothic) school of architecture (Lethaby 1914, 155–160). The dating of the roof bosses of the choir may suggest that alterations had begun to be made to the choir itself from 1180 onwards (as they were at Lichfield).

The masonry remains found in excavations in Trench 4 attest to the westerly extension of the church in the 12th century following the regularisation of the priory and the generous benefaction of, for example, King Stephen, who issued it a grant of a stone house in London once owned by William Pont de l'Arche (Carlin 1996, 68).

It is during this period that the priory of St Mary was at its zenith, with its church extended and decorated in the latest continental style, wealthy and influential patrons, the building of the hospital dedicated to St Thomas à Becket and its prime location next to the reconstructed London Bridge, at the start of the pilgrims' route to Canterbury.

The eastern arm of Lichfield Cathedral is the best comparison for the development in form (Hall 2000, 44), although the construction of the square end is dated to a slightly earlier period (however, as noted above, it is possible that transformation of the east end had begun in the period before the fire). At Lichfield, the complex rebuilding of the choir and presbytery, (defined as 'Norman Transitional I') transformed the apsidal choir, with its narrow ambulatory into a square end of seven bays with four eastern chapels began in *c.* 1170 – 1180. It appears that while the external walls of the ambulatory and the choir were removed the apsidal arcade remained for some time. The rebuilding was inspired by the fact that apsidal sanctuaries encircled by ambulatories were falling out of fashion by the late 12th century, that more choir space was required for the canons and a feretory was needed for the relics of the local saint (Rodwell 1993, 23–24). It is interesting to note that the retro-choir has also been known as the Lady Chapel, which could suggest the presence of a devotional altar in this area. The form of the retro-choir built at Southwark is uncommon, with Lichfield noted as the only other surviving English example. In Scotland, this construction type is found at Glasgow Cathedral (Rodwell 1993, 24). Decorative alterations made to the capitals at

Lichfield (during the 'Norman Transitional II' period) are comparable to those found at Christchurch, Oxford and at Canterbury dating to *c.* 1180–90. This further suggests that the building work at Southwark was inspired by contemporary late 12th-century style, although the majority of the construction took place during the early 13th century after the fire. Despite the undoubted damage caused by the fire, it appears that much of the structure of the 12th-century church survived and provided the framework for the rebuilding of the 13th century.

Natural disasters meant a prolonged period of stagnation during its subsequent rebuilding in the 13th century and into the early 14th century. However, the continuing importance of the priory within the local area is demonstrated by the construction of the parochial chapel of St Mary Magdalene and the establishment of major ecclesiastical residences such as the sumptuous palace of the Bishop of Winchester encouraged further residential development. A distinctive feature of 14th-century Southwark was the acquisition of houses by lay magnates and gentry (Hines *et al* 2004, 32). By the late 14th and early 15th centuries, the population of the area was gradually recovering from the devastating effects of the Black Death, and alterations and repairs were made to the priory church, including the reconstruction of the south transept by Cardinal Beaufort, the building of the west front and alterations to the chapel of St Mary Magdalene during the 15th century (Cherry and Pevsner 1983, 564). The priory was the setting for many major social as well as religious events, such as the marriage of Edmund Earl of Kent to the daughter of the Duke of Milan in 1406, and the establishment of chantry chapels such as that of the poet John Gower, indicate continuing lay patronage of the priory (see Hines *et al* 2004). Thus during this period the priory was at the heart of a growing and affluent Southwark, formally under the control of the Bishop of Winchester.

Evidence for possible 13th-century repair work was revealed in and around the southwest door to the Cathedral and the retro-choir. In the following century the Lady Chapel was added at the eastern end of the retro-choir and the south transept was rebuilt, although the archaeological evidence for this may also suggest another rebuild in the first quarter of the 15th century. Following that, a porch was added to the southern wall of this structure. Also, contemporary with either reworking of the south transept, was a possible rebuild of the St Mary Magdalene Chapel. The frequency and scale of these rebuilds and expansions is testament not only to the misfortune of the priory, but also to its importance. Upon each disaster the expense and often protracted timescale of repair was felt to be justified not only by those who used or inhabited the priory, but more notably by those who financed it whether for reasons of *kudos* or, more likely, status.

With regards to those inhabitants, skeletal remains excavated within the Chapter House were undoubtedly those of priors, two buried within stone sarcophagi. Assessment of the skeletons has revealed that the individuals lived a wealthy lifestyle and enjoyed a rich diet, as would have befitted their positions in what was one of the most imposing institutions in medieval Southwark. Although alterations continued to be made in the period leading up to the Dissolution, these can largely be seen to be either reactive (for example the necessary rebuilding of the nave roof after the collapse of 1469), or relating to the internal layout of the building in the case of the early 16th-century reredos. That only twelve canons survived to be pensioned off after the Dissolution suggests that the priory had declined in importance by this time, and that some of the buildings may already have been falling into a state of disrepair. This is confirmed to some extent by the major rebuilding required during the 17th century.

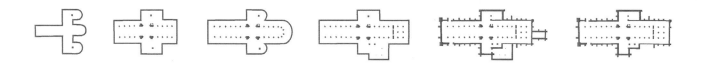

Chapter 4 The Post-Medieval Church of St Saviour

Chris Mayo and Nathalie Cohen

with Philip Armitage, Sarah Carter, Natasha Dodwell, Märit Gaimster, Chris Jarrett,

Ken Sabel, Duncan Sayer, Kathelen Sayer and John Shepherd

On the 27th of October 1539 the last prior, Bartholomew Linsted, surrendered the Priory of St Mary Overie and lost control of the church and priory buildings (Carlin 1996, 75). By comparison with some priories, St Mary Overie largely escaped destruction and defacement; at the nearby Greyfriars Monastery in Newgate Street grave monuments were destroyed in 1547 (Weinreb and Hibbert 1995, 348–349), at St Mary Spital roof lead and building stone was stripped and sold (Thomas *et al* 1997, 130–133) and at Bermondsey Abbey extensive demolition took place (Heard 1997, 14). At Southwark Cathedral there is no historical record of any systematic demolition of the priory's buildings; this is mirrored by a lack of such evidence in the archaeological record. The ease with which the priory church passed through the Dissolution may be a result of the willingness of the prior to yield it, which led to him being paid a large annual pension of £100 and given a house 'within the close' (Page 1974, 484). As the priory was dissolved and the buildings to the north relinquished, the church was renamed as the Parish Church of St Saviour.

Even though the priory church did not suffer any deliberate damage, the Dissolution resulted in the building falling into disrepair, the same fate that befell the majority of religious houses in the country. At St Saviour's the disrepair lasted until the early 17th century when the parishioners bought the church from the crown and then repaired it, an example of which could be areas of brickwork internal to the retro-choir (Hines *et al* 2004).

After the events of 1539, the former priory's conventual buildings passed into the control of Sir Anthony Browne. Either he or his son and namesake, who held the title of Viscount Montague and from which the name Montague Close may have originated (Taylor 1833, 132), lived in the prior's house (Raymond 1999), while the other buildings were used as stables.

Following Linsted's surrendering of the church building to King Henry VIII, he and the remaining twelve canons were pensioned off. The priory church then became the Parish Church of St Saviour and the parishes of St Margaret and St Mary Magdalene were amalgamated with it. An Act of Parliament confirmed the arrangement noting that St Mary Overie's was a 'very great church and very costly to be maintained in due repair' (Higham 1955, 102–103). The Chapel of St John the Evangelist (northeast transept chapel) was used as a vestry and as a place where rates and taxes were assessed and paid (Stevens 1931, 50), while the retro-choir was used in 1555 for the examination of some of the Marian martyrs (Stevens 1931, 61). During the later part of the 16th century, the retro-choir was leased out as a bakehouse, and ovens and kneading troughs were installed within the building. Livestock was also housed in the retro-choir during this period (Concanen and Morgan 1795, 78).

In the early 17th century, 'the rectory and church, the burying ground and all glebe land, tithes etc' were bought by the vestry for the parish (Higham 1955, 158) and the church was repaired in many places. The retro-choir was also restored to the church in 1624 and the 'ruines and blasted estate…were repaired, renewed, well and very worthily beautified' (Stevens 1931, 61). A fire in 1676 damaged the eastern end of the church, and alterations and repairs continued to be made by the parishioners (both structurally and to the fixtures and fittings of the church) during the 18th century (Dollman 1881, 16).

It was not until the 19th century that the church was thoroughly restored by George Gwilt. Renovations were undertaken to the east and south of the former priory church between 1818 and 1824, and both the chapel of St Mary Magdalene and the Bishop's Chapel (formerly part of the Lady Chapel at the east end of the church) were demolished at this time (RCHM 1930, 59). A letter from Gwilt dated 15 May 1821 highlights the dilapidated state of the building at the time, he found 'the East End of the church to be so exceedingly ruinous and its present state so highly precarious, that I consider it prudent to advise you that a single day ought not to be lost in taking it down' (LMA ref: P/92/SAV/1971). In 1838 the now roofless nave (Fig. 75) was pulled down and rebuilt by Henry Rose (Cherry and Pevsner 1983, 564). The floor of this new church was many feet higher than that of the present nave and was 'only remarkable for its excessive ugliness' (Daniell 1897, 211). This was subsequently replaced by a new nave in the Victorian Gothic style designed by Sir Arthur Blomfield and built by Thomas Rider (1890–7). In 1905, diocesan reorganization saw the parish church

Fig. 75   View of the nave during restoration (Hawkins 1934)
Reproduced by kind permission of the Guildhall Library

become a Cathedral and regain its earlier dedication as the Cathedral and Collegiate Church of St Saviour and St Mary Overie.

A number of programmes of clearance, rebuilding and renovation were undertaken throughout the 19th century, which were to leave the fabric and landscape of the church in the form that it took at the time of the Millennium Project. One of the main reasons for work around the church was the construction of John Rennie's London Bridge between 1823–31 (Weinreb and Hibbert 1995, 483), a process that also markedly affected the north and south banks of the Thames as new approaches were built. With the position of the new bridge upstream from the old, the northern end of Borough High Street was realigned, taking it closer to the church than before and necessitating massive alterations in the immediate

vicinity. The demolition of the Bishop's Chapel and Chain Gate buildings in 1830 for example were a direct result of this project (C. L.R.O. ref. P.D.151.3 1823; Dollman 1881, 18). Misplaced aesthetics were also used to justify the destruction of the Bishop's Chapel, as it was deemed that the dilapidated condition of the structure 'impeded the supposed 'grand vista' of the approach to the new bridge' (Dollman 1881, 18); the same fate befell the vestry of the church of St Olave on Tooley Street in 1831 (Malden 1967, 152). More fortunate though was the retro-choir of St Saviour's Church, which itself was intended for demolition. A poll within the parish of St Saviour's Church in 1832, which 'for two days presented all the appearance of a contested parliamentary election' (Dollman 1881, 19) saw the preservationists win by a majority of 240 votes (The Gentleman's Magazine 1832, 101).

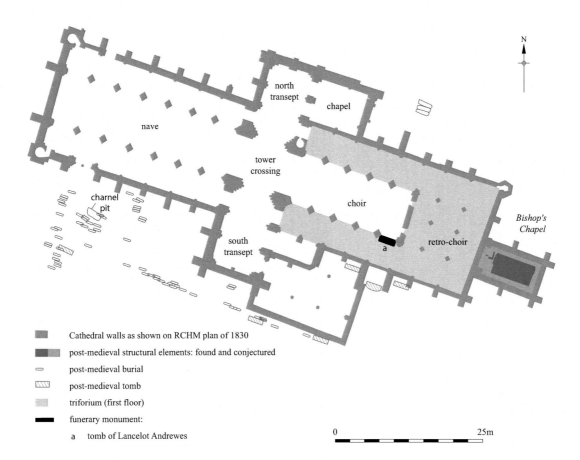

Fig. 76   Elements of the post-Reformation church as revealed through archaeological excavation
(scale 1:625)

The nave

Remodelling of the southwest doorway

Evidence for the redevelopment of the southwest door of
the priory church was found in Trench 18. The medieval
foundations discussed above, interpreted as being of the
Norman church or a 13th-century repair, had been altered
with the addition of a mortar deposit. It was seen across the
entire doorway and scars at the top suggested that it once
seated a threshold that survived only as very fragmentary
stonework at 3.95m OD. Within the threshold mortar-
rubble appeared to have been used to in-fill the space. No
datable elements were associated with these remains and
therefore documentary sources represent the only basis for
assigning them to any particular period. An illustration
of the church from 1647 shows an imposing two-storey
gabled porch structure (Fig. 77); the implication of this is
that it post-dates the nave because the roof of the porch
blocks part of one of the windows. The latest pre-1661

Evidence for both the constructive and destructive
processes of 19th-century regeneration was seen during the
groundworks around the Cathedral (see Fig. 94).

rebuild of the nave that can be traced from historical
sources was in the 15th century (Carlin 1996, 70). Another
illustration of *c.* 1750 shows that the porch had been rebuilt
in a simplified style, which remained until its makeover in
the 1830s as part of the beautification of the church (Fig.
78). Comparison of this simplified porch with the earlier
more grandiose one suggests that their components and
dimensions are the same. As such the foundations may
have been identical between the 15th century and the
1830s, and the remains in Trench 18 may therefore date
from between the 15th century and 1661.

A clear construction trench for the 19th-century façade
was visible as a narrow linear cut in only one place, in
Trench 18 exterior to the south aisle. Of note was that it was
filled with approximately 60% disarticulated human bone;
a similarly high proportion was seen around the steps in
the south graveyard leading up to Cathedral Street. This
demonstrates a typical tendency during this period to re-
inter disturbed skeletal remains as backfill rather than in
distinct charnel pits, as seen for example during the course
of recent work at Spitalfields and Bermondsey Square (E.
Sayer, *pers comm*). That said, one small and shallow charnel
pit was excavated in the south graveyard of the Cathedral.
Such features confirm the density of burials and the high
frequency of disturbance in the graveyard.

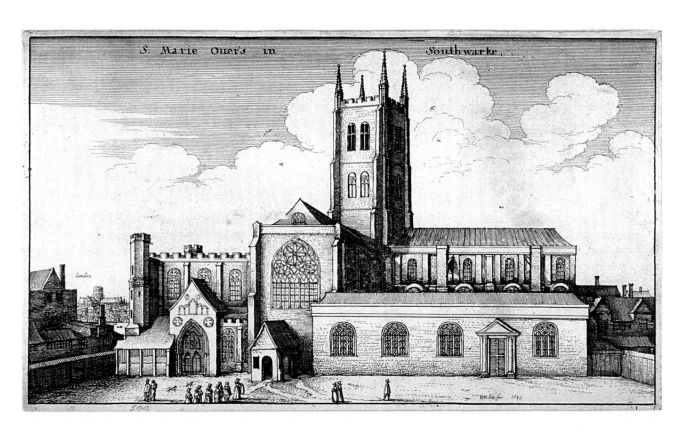

Fig. 77   Hollar's 1647 view of St Saviour from the south

Reproduced by kind permission of the Guildhall Library

Fig. 78   View of St Saviour from the south (Cole c. 1750)

Reproduced by kind permission of the Guildhall Library

The choir and triforium

As noted above (see Chapter 3) two post-medieval phases (Phases 5 and 6) were identified in the study of the triforium masonry (see Fig. 39, Fig. 40, Fig. 41).

Phase 5, 17th–18th centuries

It is suggested here the ashlar Reigate stone masonry of the east end with its distinctive horizontal and vertical tool-marks, and including contexts 48, 53, 64, 80, 82, 85 and 88, represents 17th- or early 18th-century rebuilding undertaken by the parishioners of St Saviour's Church, either after the acquisition of the church building during the early part of the century, or after the fire of 1676. The original rubble core of the choir walls is visible in places on the south side (65, 72, 83), demonstrating that where possible the original materials were retained beneath the

new cladding. On both the north and south sides of the choir, masonry of the 12th and 13th centuries is also visible at the base of the elevations (66, 67, 69, 75, 76, 77, 78, and 131). Finally, at the east end, there is evidence for a post-medieval roof-line of two gables, in the form of roof scars (63) running across the 17th-century stonework and a central roof support (61) built of brick.

Phase 6, 1822 restoration

Evidence for Gwilt's restoration of 1822 is clearly visible in the triforium, firstly in the rebuild of the roof. The uppermost courses of the choir walls have been reconstructed in places (for example 19, 40, 95 and probably 27 and 104) and the choir, retro-choir and aisle walls on the north and south sides of the building all show evidence for the insertion of pad stones and support blocks for the iron roof struts (including contexts 29, 46, 68, 71,

ST. SAVIOUR'S CHURCH.

ST MARY MAGDALEN'S CHAPEL.

Fig. 79   View of the interior of the St Mary Magdalene Chapel (Moss and Nightingale 1818)

Reproduced by kind permission of Southwark Local Studies Library

and 86). As well as introducing new yellow sandstone blocks, earlier Reigate stone masonry was also re-used. Gwilt also built the stair turrets to the clerestory at the north and south of the east elevation in sandstone (49, 51, 57 and 134) at this time, where Dollman's illustrations suggest that none existed before.

The south transept and chapel of St Mary Magdalene

Images of the St Mary Magdalene Chapel produced in 1647 and 1818 are contradictory and therefore provide useful evidence for the post-medieval development of the chapel. They both show a classical façade; that Inigo Jones only introduced the classical system of architecture into Britain in the early 17th century indicates that there is likely to have been major rebuilding in the mid 17th century. The earlier illustration (Fig. 77) shows five openings with the door (with a triangular pedimented door case) forming the

second opening from the east, while later engravings (such as that of Cole *c.* 1750, Fig. 78 and Moss and Nightingale 1818, Fig. 55) show the door in the third bay from the west with a segmental pediment. Dollman's plans and elevations (1881) all concur with the 1818 engraving that there were only two windows to the west of the door and that there was likely to be a single window to the east of the door. This is likely to have always been the case, as even the earlier illustration shows the chapel the same length relative to the chancel behind. Differences in the configuration of the roof are likely to be part of the reconfiguration of the chapel, for example in 1578 and the 17th century (Malden 1967, 155).

Archaeological evidence of alterations to the chapel was found in an internal north–south wall foundation in Trench 18. It was two bricks wide and is thought to have been a sleeper wall beneath the chapel floor, which would have been above *c.* 4.0m OD. The bricks used in the build date from the second half of the 15th century to *c.* 1700, and indicate that the chapel was re-floored.

Fig. 80   View of Southwark Cathedral from the southeast showing the area of the Mary Magdalene Chapel immediately after demolition (Yates 1825)

Reproduced by kind permission of the Guildhall Library

The chapel was described by Nightingale thus in 1818:

'The chapel itself is a very plain erection. It is entered on the south, through a large pair of folding doors leading down a small flight of steps. The ceiling has nothing peculiar in its character; nor are the four pillars supporting the roof, and the unequal arches leading into the south aisle, in the least calculated to convey any idea of grandeur or feeling of veneration. These arches have been cut through in a very clumsy manner, so that scarcely any vestige of the ancient church of St Mary Magdalene now remains. A small doorway and windows, however, are still visible at the east end of this chapel; the west end formerly opened into the south transept; but that also is now walled up, except a part, which leads to the gallery there. There are in different parts niches which once held the holy water, by which the pious devotees of former ages sprinkled their foreheads on their entrance before the altar. I am not aware that any other remains of the old church are now visible in this chapel. Passing through the eastern end of the south aisle, a pair of gates leads into the Virgin Mary's Chapel.' (Walford 1878)

The demolition of the St Mary Magdalene Chapel in 1822 reduced the superstructure of the building to foundation level, elements of which were excavated in Trench 19. The area was then landscaped with paving stones incorporating ledger slabs. Substantial deposits of demolition rubble were found as make-up for the paving across the area to the south of the choir and retro-choir, chiefly comprising pieces of worked Kentish ragstone and Reigate stone masonry likely to have come from the chapel. The substantial levelling of the area of the St Mary Magdalene Chapel, combined with the small areas of investigation, limited the available evidence of its demolition.

The foundations of the 19th-century façade designed by George Gwilt were seen in Trenches 4, 18 and 20, mostly in the form of stepped brick footings but also reusing earlier masonry ones. At the southwest corner of the south transept, the medieval foundations in combination with a new footing, probably a rubble core with a Roman Cement render, had been used as the base for the new cladding. With this the 19th-century buttress foundation had a north–south length of 2.4m, 0.8m longer than the medieval one.

The retro-choir

As will be discussed further below, a reduction in the status of the church following the Dissolution, combined perhaps with increasing pressure on space in north Southwark, led to buildings encroaching on the area immediately around the church and in the 1550s the retro-choir was leased out as a bakery and pigsty (Malden 1967, 155). Brickwork was recorded in the elevations of the north and south walls of the retro-choir at triforium level, fragmentary sections of

which could relate to secular use of the building during the immediate post-Dissolution period. However, it is likely that that the majority of brick use in this area relates to later post-medieval and modern renovations and repairs. A combination of old masonry and new brick footings could be seen beneath the 19th-century re-facing of the retro-choir and evidence of Gwilt's 1822 restoration was visible in the insertion of pad stones and support blocks for iron roof struts in the retro-choir walls.

The Lady Chapel

Evidence was seen for the remodelling of the interior of the Lady Chapel from a brick repair on the internal face of the southern chapel wall. The bricks are likely to date to between the 15th and 17th centuries, although because brick was a high status material in the 15th and early 16th century and the example here was used in a relatively hidden location, a 16th- to early 17th-century date is more likely. The brickwork, and indeed the internal faces of both chapel walls had been covered with a render. The date range for these bricks corresponds well with the Dissolution and the neglect that followed it in the 16th century. The chapel at this time, and until 1624 (Malden 1967, 155), was used for secular activities and the repair may have come about as a result of that use.

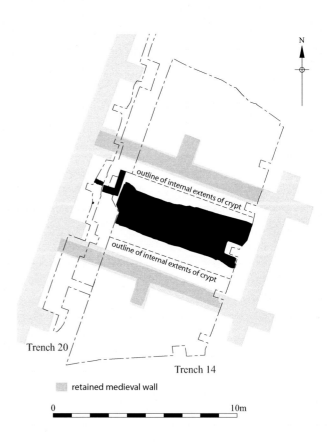

Fig. 81 The conversion of the Lady Chapel to Bishop's Chapel (scale 1:200)

Conversion of the Lady Chapel to Bishop's Chapel

In the 17th century the Lady Chapel at the east end of the church was converted to incorporate a brick-vaulted crypt for the burial of Bishop Lancelot Andrewes, who died in September 1626 (Welsby 1958, 259). Thereafter the building was known as the Bishop's Chapel. The effigy of Bishop Andrewes now stands in the south choir aisle.

Lancelot Andrewes

Lancelot Andrewes was born in the parish of All Hallows, Barking, in 1555. He was educated at Merchant Taylors' School and then at Pembroke Hall, Cambridge, where he proved an exceptional scholar and, by adulthood, the master of 15 languages.

In 1589 he became the vicar of St Giles at Cripplegate and the master of his former college. He was offered two bishoprics by Elizabeth I at Salisbury and Ely but declined them both. However, he took the latter see in 1609 when offered it by James I, following positions as the Dean of Westminster in 1601 and the Bishop of Chichester in 1605. He became the Bishop of Winchester in 1619.

Bishop Andrewes was noted in life for his abilities as a preacher, and in death for the leading role he had played as a translator at the Hampton Court Conference in 1604 that led to the production of the Authorized Version of the Bible in 1611 (Cross and Livingstone 1977, 52).

He died at Winchester Palace in 1626. The date of his death is variously given as 21st September (Moss 1818, 85), 25th September (Welsby 1958, 259) and 26th September (Cross and Livingstone 1977, 52).

The conversion of the chapel had a minimal impact on the superstructure of the building, but its interior was completely overhauled. The barrel-vaulted crypt had an internal length of 7.4m and a calculated width of *c.* 3.5m. The crypt's western wall was positioned at a distance of 1.5m from the east end of the retro-choir. In this gap was a set of steps central to the crypt with an approximate internal width of 0.75m that allowed subterranean access from the chapel's entrance. The structure had vertical brick walls on the north and south sides to a height of 0.75m, from which the vault was sprung. At its highest point

Fig. 83   The effigy of Bishop Andrewes in the south choir aisle

the crypt measured 2.27m internally. The western wall of the structure was built in an approximation of English bond, and incorporated a niche with a triangular arch, presumably to hold a lantern. The sill of the lowest step was exposed, at a height of 0.3m from the floor. The upper courses of the western wall, and to a corresponding height around the interior of the crypt, were coated with render. The crypt was floored at 2.1m OD with unglazed tiles imported from the Low Countries, which are known to have been used in London from *c.* 1600.

The material used to backfill the space around the crypt extended internally right up to the walls of the chapel; this process had removed any traces of the previous internal arrangement of the Lady Chapel. It was also a process that would have presumably required specialist, or just plain fearless, building skills because the chapel was essentially being undermined internally while the crypt was dug.

Any floor surface within the Bishop's Chapel had been completely robbed, presumably when the chapel was demolished in 1830. A mortar layer above the backfill around the crypt, at an upper height of 4.93m OD, may have been the bedding for a tiled floor. The steps from the retro-choir into the chapel (The Mirror of Literature, Amusement, and Instruction 1832) were probably retained from the medieval structure, and would have been removed during George Gwilt's renovation work in the 1820s (Hines *et al* 2004). The change in level between the retro-choir and the Bishop's Chapel can be seen in Dollman's long section through the Cathedral (1881). The drawing shows that the floor levels had probably changed little since the 14th century, as the column bases shown in both building elements were both in proportion to the columns. The new chapel's floor was at least slightly higher than the old floor level in the Lady Chapel, as demonstrated by the fact that the material backfilling around the crypt covered the fragments of painted plaster surviving on the chapel walls as discussed above.

The Bishop's Chapel remained structurally unaltered through the post-medieval period, but was repaired on at least one occasion. This is shown by the discovery of a piece of lead window came, from the crypt, which bears the

Fig. 82   The vault of the Bishop's Chapel after excavation, looking west (2m scales)

Fig. 84   The Chapel in the Church of St Saviour Southwark, as published (1825) by Robert Wilkinson, 125 Fenchurch Street

inscription '[EDW]ARD [PI]NDER 1676'. In that year, a fire damaged the eastern end of the priory church including the Bishop's Chapel, and the piece of came is undoubtedly from its repair.

During excavations within the crypt, graffiti was seen on the internal render. One inscription on the south side was merely the painted word 'James'. However, on the north side the name 'Edwa[r]ds' was carved into the render with a date that possibly read '26 February 1757'. The presence of this particular graffiti indicates that the crypt was being accessed for at least 131 years after the burial of Bishop Andrewes. Moss (1818, 83–84) names individuals who he says were buried in the 'Bishop's vault', indicating the crypt itself. One such individual was a Chief Cashier and Governor of the Bank of England, Abraham Newland, who before his death in 1807 oversaw the first issue of the one-pound note. The contents of the crypt were removed prior to the chapel's demolition in the 19th century, and Bishop Andrewes' monument was sited in its current position to the south of the choir.

The process of demolition at the east end of the Cathedral, carried out as part of the 1822 restoration, was clearly visible because of the higher finished ground level and because it was left as a 'soft' garden, aside from a narrow pavement around the retro-choir. The barrel-vaulted crypt was found to have been backfilled with layers of material including masonry, and therefore it seems that following the removal of the body of Bishop Andrewes to the south aisle, his crypt was used as a convenient disposal place for the demolition material from the chapel above. A substantial quantity of disarticulated human bone was also found in the backfill (over 28% of all the bone recovered), showing that the material originated from elsewhere in the graveyard as well. It is certain that some of the masonry from the chapel would have been robbed and re-used; for example, no finished floor surface was present within the building even though a surface-bedding layer was. Above this level several layers of demolition material were found across Trench 14, made up primarily of crushed mortar and distinctly lacking in suitable quantities of stone or brick, indicating the robbing or re-use of building material. It is possible that some of the material was re-used in the remodelling of the church; examples of the 19th century re-use of earlier stone can be seen in the roof of the nave at the triforium level, where medieval corbels are supported by iron struts.

Post-medieval funerary monuments

In total, 159 ledger slabs and 84 wall monuments and chest tombs were recorded at the east end of the Cathedral, ranging in date from the 13th century to the present day. Ledger slabs were recorded in the tower crossing, north transept, south transept, retro-choir, north and south choir aisles, chancel and high altar. Memorials located in the main body of the church were not examined, with the exception of the tomb of John Gower, which formed part of a separate study (see Hines *et al* 2004). For the purposes of this volume, a plan of the ledger slabs in the retro-choir (Fig. 86) has been reproduced. The ledger slabs and wall monuments were described in sequence using a numbered series for each location. Several of the monuments recorded are discussed in detail, numbers in square brackets (eg [L708]) refer to full catalogue, which can be found in the site archive.

The church itself has always been regarded as both a prestigious and spiritually rewarding final resting place, having the prayers of the faithful resounding around one's mortal remains for centuries to come. The growth in popularity of the chantry chapel (and associated endowments), particularly during the 14th and 15th centuries, demonstrates the desire of the secular community for commemoration within ecclesiastical institutions, be they parish churches or monastic establishments. Thus, funerary monuments became part of the architecture of the church. The type and location of chantry constructed depended on the wealth and status of its benefactor and although the construction of these memorials was made illegal in 1547, post-Reformation commemorative art seems to have taken up this principle (Llewellyn 1991, 106). By the late 17th century the vogue for grand burials spread from primarily royal and aristocratic circles to the growing number of middle class enriched by trade and later, industrialisation (Jalland 1996, 195).

English Canonical Law, from the time of King James I states that 'Every parishioner, and everyone dying in the parish is entitled by law to burial in the parish churchyard or burial ground whether or not he was a member of the church of England or, indeed, even a Christian ...there is no right (however) except under faculty, to burial in the church itself' (Moore 1967, 92–95). A 'faculty' would have to be obtained before one could be buried within the church, presumably only those parishioners with enough money and status were able to ensure this. 'Monuments, as markers of the place of burial, were permanent manifestations of this investment in space. Their very location was a sign of power' (Llewellyn 1991, 105). Further to this, the construction of a vault as a dynastic burial chamber, which was popular between the first quarter of the 17th century and the second quarter of the 18th century, was also the preserve of the wealthy (Litten 1991, 197).

The funerary monuments at Southwark Cathedral provide an interesting sample of post-medieval burial commemoration. The most common memorials are the ledger stones set into the floors of the transepts, crossing, choir, choir aisles and retro-choir. Examples also survive in the churchyard, representing the floor of the former parochial chapel of St Mary Magdalene. The majority of the slabs date from the 18th and early 19th centuries; they consist mainly of rectangular black marble and Yorkstone slabs, with a basic inscription, detailing the name of the deceased and their position held in life. Most have been laid in commemoration of more than one individual and some are decorated with heraldic roundels. Over twenty-five different occupations have been recorded, and an interesting variety of social classes are represented. Of the earlier slabs (of the late 17th /early 18th century) two demonstrate clearly the points mentioned above regarding the status of individuals and the location of their monument; at the high altar is a memorial to John Appleby Esquire, who died in 1680 and his wife Dorothy (died 1682) [L802]. They are described as good benefactors to the parish. Also located near the high altar is a black ledger slab with an inscribed coat arms [L808] in memory of Sir Richard Oldner (died 1719). Other examples of 18th-century occupations include: in the south choir aisle [L707] Mr George Farmer (died 1796), 'Hop Factor' and [L719] Mr John Corner (died 1733), citizen and dyer, in the north choir aisle [L514] Henry Kendall, Warehouseman (died 1778), [L510] Mary Davis, wife of John Davis, Coal Merchant (died 1749) and [L507] John Wright, Distiller (died 1702).

The burial vaults at St Saviour's Church are largely unexcavated, with the exception of that beneath the choir

Fig. 85   Recording the floor plan and ledger slabs in the south transept

©SCARP

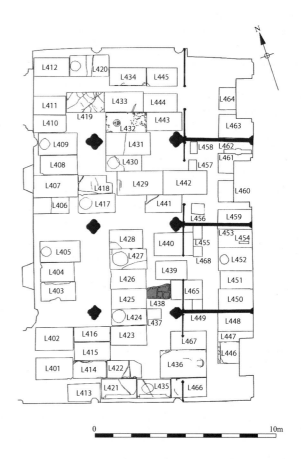

Fig. 86   Floor plan of ledger slabs in the retro-choir (scale 1:200)

©SCARP

and at the east end, as discussed above. Many of the ledger slabs refer to the existence of family vaults and the stones themselves show signs of their removal to accommodate interments at different times in the form of chipped edges. However, it is clear from examination of antiquarian drawings, and from the evidence presented on the slabs themselves (in the form of truncated stones and cracked or broken areas) that many of the ledgers (in particular those of the retro-choir) are not *in situ*. It may be that some of the slabs were removed from the nave during the 19th-century rebuilding and references to family vaults may refer to structures there.

Antiquarian records also record the movement of chest tombs and wall monuments around different parts of the building. It is known that the tomb of John Gower was temporarily relocated from the north nave aisle to the south transept (Hines *et al* 2004, 35) and also the medieval effigies of the north choir aisle are not *in situ*. The post-medieval monuments relating to the use of the building as a parish church have also moved around the structure. A rare (in Southwark Cathedral) surviving example of a brass monument, the memorial to ten-year old Susanna Barford who died in 1652 is known to have been moved from the floor of the retro-choir to the wall of the south transept (Taylor 1833, 116). Many of the monuments were originally located in the Bishop's Chapel and St Mary Magdalene's Chapel and were moved into the main body of the church after the chapels' demolition during the early 19th century.

Conclusions

The recording project established that while the wall monuments and chest tombs are in good condition, many of the ledger slabs are cracked and worn, and consequently the descriptions are indecipherable. If preservative measures are not taken (that is, that they are either removed, covered or visitors to the Cathedral diverted around them), they will deteriorate further. If these precautions cannot be followed then they should be preserved by record, transcribed and individually photographed and entered into a database where they could be related to other parish records. The preservation, either directly, or indirectly through accurate recording of the monuments is extremely important as they not only form part of the archaeological record but are primary historical documents within themselves.

We can learn much from such monuments. Developments in costume, armour and weaponry, for example, can be studied from memorial effigies, while social and demographic information regarding wealth and status, occupation and infant mortality can be gleaned from inscriptions. A study of the location of the memorials informs our understanding of both the original positions of the monument, and of the areas of the church that have undergone repair or alteration. It can therefore be seen that the funerary monuments from Southwark Cathedral can tell us much about the social, economic and religious development of the church, and parish.

The former claustral buildings

The west range

Archaeological evidence was found for the remodelling of parts of the priory buildings in the early post-medieval period. Structural alterations were made to the eastern side of the wall in Trench 5 that may have previously formed part of the cellarer's block. It was modified with brick (dating from 1450 / 1480 to *c.* 1700), chalk and Reigate stone only surviving on the wall's eastern side. The presence of Reigate stone in the eastern face implies that that side was internal. A layer of mortar excavated from a position abutting the earlier phase of this wall is interpreted as a bedding surface, possibly for a tiled floor, and associated with the later build. Such a floor would have been at *c.* 2.7m OD. A make-up layer that was excavated underneath the mortar contained pottery dating from the late 17th to 18th centuries. This floor is significantly higher than three layers of compacted silt and sand in Trench 4 at 2.08m OD that were also surfaces, and therefore they may have been within a sub-basement. A make-up layer below these contained clay tobacco pipe bowls dating from 1690 to 1710, and also a gold earring of 17th-century date. Jewellery of this period is extremely rare from archaeological excavations and this example is particularly striking. It takes the form of a fragment of twisted gold wire finished with a small blue glass bead (Fig. 87). The only known parallels for items of this type come from 17th-century coral and pearl earrings

Fig. 87 17th-century gold earring

from Italy (Concetta di Natale and Abbale 1995), although any speculation on whether this is an actual Italian example or representative of the spread of technology and techniques needs to be tempered by the very rarity of such finds on archaeological sites. The dates of these features suggest that at least some of the priory buildings were remodelled and maintained, for it seems that many of the structures fell into disrepair not long after the death of Browne in 1548 (Taylor 1833, 132), who, as established above, had adapted the prior's house in the precinct as his residence at the Reformation. An example of this was found in Trench 5 where a cesspit was lined with bricks dating from 1340/1480 to the 16th century, yet the pit had been backfilled in the 19th century, indicating that the bricks were re-used perhaps from the priory buildings themselves.

The east range

Nothing was revealed archaeologically of the east range north of the chapter house, which was demolished in the 19th century. Contemporary images show the eastern claustral range modified for later occupation and in various states of repair; by 1835 the buildings appear ruinous (Fig. 88).

The chapter house

In the early 17th century the chapter house was used as a pot house to house a Delftware kiln. Dawson, excavating in the 1970s revealed part of this kiln, the earliest remains of which probably date to *c.* 1613 (Dawson 1976). Although part of a brick wall and stone floor to the stoke hole from a later phase of this kiln were found preserved below modern service pipes (see Fig. 109), during the Millennium excavations most of this kiln was located to the west of Trench 1 and was not revisited. A later kiln built against the eastern wall of the chapter house was, however, uncovered and is discussed in detail below (see Chapter 5).

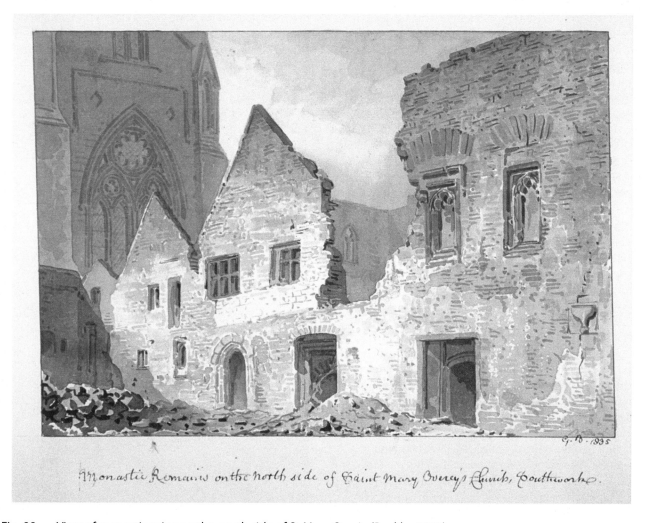

Fig. 88   View of monastic ruins on the north side of St Mary Overie (Buckler 1835)

Reproduced by kind permission of the Guildhall Library

The cemeteries

Burials in the southern graveyard

The Millennium excavations included a substantial process of landscaping in the southern graveyard of Southwark Cathedral to replace retaining walls, re-lay paths and pavements, and install floodlighting around the building's façade. This allowed the keyhole investigation of human burials within the graveyard in places where ground-penetrating works were necessary (see Fig. 76). As such, the investigations were not comprehensive and therefore the skeletal material recovered is of very limited value archaeologically. Because excavation was only confined to the areas defined by the new construction, complete grave cuts, and therefore firm stratigraphic relationships, were often not fully exposed. However, the work has revealed large assemblages of material associated with post-medieval burial activity around the Cathedral, for example tombs, coffins and coffin furniture.

Human remains and associated accoutrements were found in Trenches 16, 17, 18, 21, 22 and 24. Within these layers, a number of cemetery soil horizons could be seen, generally comprising a greyish-brown sand clay silt. Artefactual evidence from these layers did not necessarily reflect their stratigraphic position, indicating the high level of disturbance to the ground from burial activity. Yet, the fact that the layers were discernible could be evidence for ground raising; not merely landscaping but perhaps with a more functional purpose, to increase the depth within which bodies could be interred. This is implied in an engraving (Moss and Nightingale 1818, see Fig. 55) depicting men working within the graveyard by the entrance to the St Mary Magdalene Chapel, which is shown at a considerably lower level. The graveyard is also shown in the engraving to contain numerous headstones, which had been removed during 19th- or 20th-century landscaping.

The base of the cemetery soil horizons was not observed in any trench, for the work only went to the required formation level for the new installations: at the lowest point this was approximately 3.5m OD in Trench 17. All observed burials within the graveyard were extended supine inhumations and aligned east–west. Of the 77 burials that were found in the southern graveyard, 58 were present as skeletal remains (75%), seven were present as coffins (9%) and twelve were brick-built tombs (16%). Of the coffins, three were timber, three were lead and one was iron. The latter would have been a very expensive funerary item, indicating the wealth of its owner and, accordingly, it was found near the main southwest doorway of the church. Likewise for the lead coffins, which were also near the 'prime' location by the main door.

Amongst the cemetery soils were pieces of coffin furniture, ranging from numerous coffin pins and tacks, to 106 individual grips and six breastplates. Indeed the high number found during the Millennium excavations is further evidence for a wealthier cemetery population than might be expected. This could be an indication of preferential treatment being given to wealthy individuals

in a burial ground of very limited size, only 0.25 acres (Reeve 1998, 235), perhaps leading to the prime plots being reserved for benefactors while the poorer population were left with lower status plots away from the church, for example at the Cross Bones Burial Ground on Redcross Way (Brickley *et al* 1999). Some of the coffin grips were ornately decorated with cherub heads, while the coffin plates were elaborately decorated; one bore the inscription 'Mrs Anna ...., Died ....1806, Aged .... years' within a decorative frame of flowers and shells (Fig. 89). Assemblages of coffin furniture of this kind are uncommon and as such, their typology is still developing. However five of the six types of coffin grips from Southwark Cathedral are comparable to those from an assemblage from excavations in the crypt at Christ Church Spitalfields (Reeve and Adams 1993), the burials from which dated between 1729 and 1847. Therefore the Millennium excavations assemblage can be tentatively assigned a similar date range. Furthermore, that human burial in the graveyard at St Saviour's Church was forbidden in 1853 (Malden 1967, 154) provides a *terminus ante quem* for the burials and funerary material found.

The 77 burials found during the investigations in the south graveyard are undoubtedly only a tiny proportion of the actual cemetery population. The quantity of disarticulated human bone gives a clue to the far higher figure: post-medieval pits around the Bishop's Chapel (see below) contained over 20.6% human bone out of all bone

Fig. 89   Early 19th-century lead coffin plate, with decorative frame of flowers and shells

recovered, occurring as a higher percentage than all types of animal bone represented: for example sheep (20.1%), cattle (18.8%) and pig (6.8%).

Coffin furniture

The most frequently occurring and best preserved category of funerary material from Southwark comprises 106 individual coffin grips of six types (a complete catalogue of these is available with the archive), five of which are of types identified at Spitalfields (Reeve and Adams 1993) and one is not. This unfamiliar grip was of a simple square handle with thick or heavy grip; its simplicity may suggest that it is of a type more commonly found on wardrobes and cabinets of the period than coffins. The material identifiable had similarities with the Spitalfields find group which, was in use between 1729 and 1847, although this may not be the complete date range over which this material was in use, as no complete typology of coffin material exists at present. Unfortunately, with the exception of the one elaborate but corroded lead name plate described above (3934), so decayed it required x-ray examination to see the date of 1806, none of the surviving fragments of coffin plates recovered were able to provide a more exact date for the assemblage. However, comparison with similar collections of grips from other sites suggests that the assemblage recovered from the burial ground at Southwark Cathedral was in use up to around 1850. This burial ground and the associated Cross Bones burial ground at Redcross Way, Southwark, were under pressure as a result of public health reforms, and the latter cemetery went out of use in 1853, probably as a direct result of the Burial Act of the previous year and it seems that, as stated above, burials ceased in the small and overcrowded Southwark Cathedral burial ground at the same time. As a direct result of this pressure on small burial grounds much material from earlier burials would have been replaced by later interments and, unlike the crypt burials of Spitalfields, the majority of surviving burials within this churchyard are likely to be from the latter half of the date range. Pressure on urban burial grounds was so great that grave diggers were often cutting through even recent graves to fit in the newly deceased (Chadwick 1843) reputedly frequently resorting to drink to cope with the stench (Morley 1971), and this is supported by the large quantities of disarticulated remains found in cemetery excavations (cf Sayer 2001)

The limited range of style of grips recovered during this excavation may not be a true reflection of the variation within the cemetery. The presence of an iron coffin (3717), so rare and expensive that it was probably commissioned specifically for that interment, suggests that if the cemetery were divided up into prestige-related areas, the trenches excavated covered generally wealthy areas. Indeed, five lead coffins and the numerous lead coffin plates (see Fig. 89) indicate expensive decorative embellishment, arguably less common within burial grounds than vaults. The volume of coffin material, pins, plates and grips within the cemetery is very high, and although much is the result of a mass production industry, it was still expensive. The five lead coffins, iron coffin and the hand made lead coffin plate all required various degrees of skilled labour and time invested in them. It is of interest that all of this material was located within the southern side of the cemetery, avoiding the 'darker' northern side, a superstition in decline during the 19th century (Daniell 1897) and very much in conflict with the need for space. While this practice is still evident elsewhere, for Southwark, with its particularly small burial ground, it very much suggests a conservative or traditional cemetery structure still in place among the wealthiest right up to when the ground ceased to be used for burials.

A conservative estimate of the minimum percentage of decorated coffins with either grips, name plates, or material-securing studs is 42%, an extremely high figure when compared to 31.4% from excavations at St Bride's lower churchyard and 23.4% from Cross Bones burial ground (Brickley et al 1999, 26). Assuming that St Bride's cemetery holds a good cross-section of a community, it could be inferred that the two Southwark cemeteries served two different strata of the population; Cross Bones is likely to have been the burial place of temporarily housed people in Southwark who were not members of the parish and also non-Anglicans, as there is no evidence that the ground was consecrated. This suggests that the remains still interred and those excavated from Southwark Cathedral are those of the emerging middle class Anglicans and some reasonably wealthy individuals (such as the individual within the iron coffin).

Other finds associated with the burials include coffin nails; simple square nails were the most common type of construction material used. A single copper-alloy pin fragment is probably a shroud pin. Three graves contained clay tobacco pipe fragments; these may be residual or the smoking material used by gravediggers.

Burials to the north of the church

To the east of the northeast transept chapel, excavation in a small area for a new lightwell for Montague Chambers revealed three deep shaft graves containing a total of 24 burials (see Fig. 76). The earliest grave cut was at the south end, with the other two dug later in a northerly direction. These were all substantial cuts in the region of 3.0m deep, down to the natural gravel, the bases at an average level of 0.14m OD. The burials had been stacked on top of each other within the graves, and showed brown staining and timber remains indicating that all had been contained within coffins (Fig. 90. Fig. 91).

From the early 17th century, the pot houses of the Montague Close pottery industry occupied the position to the north of the north choir aisle. Despite a quantity of artefactual material recovered from the fills of all three graves dating to the second half of the 18th century, they must post-date 1830 when the eastern pot house, which stood over the position of the lightwell, was demolished (Dawson 1976, 57). In addition, a single bone button found in one of the graves is of 19th-century date. They

Fig. 90   Burials to the north of the church

must also pre-date 1853, for in that year further burials were forbidden in the churchyard of St Saviour's Church and in the Cross Bones Burial Ground to the southwest (Malden 1967, 154). Further refinement of this date range came from a skeleton that had undergone a post-mortem examination indicated by certain cut marks on the skull. Given that such a process was illegal until the Anatomy Act of 1832 (Chamberlain 1999), it is more likely that this skeleton is an example of a legal dissection, and the three graves may therefore be dated between 1832 and 1853. This suggestion in further confirmed by evidence from the vestry minutes of St Saviour's Church which record negotiations with the trustees of Borough Market in 1832 to obtain their assistance in purchasing land on the north side of the church for additional burial ground. In 1849 the wardens stated that they had enclosed a small piece of ground on the north side of the church for burial (Brickley et al 1999, 9, 13). Dawson suggests the most reasonable place for this is in the angle between the north transept and the choir (G. Dawson, pers comm). The 1st edition Ordnance Survey shows a wall running east–west from the northeast corner of the northeast transept chapel to the almshouses to the east (see Fig. 3), which presumably formed the northern extent of this burial ground into which the three shaft graves were dug.

From the fill of the earliest, most southerly, of the graves [351] a small, copper-alloy medal was retrieved. This small copper-alloy medal (Fig. 92) represents one of the most successful Catholic items produced in the 19th century. Known as the Miraculous Medal, it originated with visions of the Virgin Mary by Sister (now Saint) Catherine Labouré, a novice at the Sisters of Charity at Chatillon-sur-Seine. The obverse of the medal depicts Mary standing on a globe, with the inscription 'O Mary, conceived without sin, pray for us who have recourse to thee'. The reverse shows a cross over a large 'M', and below are two hearts; one encircled in thorns, symbolising Christ, and the other pierced by a sword, symbolising Mary.

Production started in 1832 and already by 1836 the Miraculous Medal was produced in a number of languages,

including English, Polish, German and even Chinese. The popularity of the Miraculous Medal soon led to production outside France, and it was estimated that over 20 million medals were produced between 1832 and 1837. The medal became associated with the movement towards acceptance of the Immaculate Conception by the Catholic Church, something that was acceded to in 1854 when the dogma of the Immaculate Conception was defined by Pope Pius IX (Ajmar and Sheffield 1994).

The presence of a Catholic item within the graveyard of an Anglican church is not necessarily unusual when it is considered that the Church of St Mary Overie was a parish

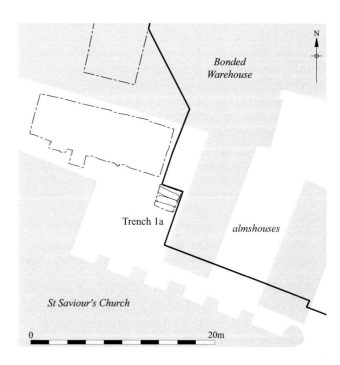

Fig. 91   Post-medieval burials to the north of the church in relation to buildings shown on the 1st edition Ordnance Survey map of 1872 (scale 1:400)

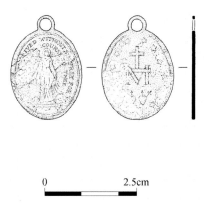

0   2.5cm

Fig. 92   The 'Miraculous Medal' (scale 1:1)

church, and therefore a Catholic parishioner would have been entitled to burial there.

The high concentration of burials excavated from the lightwell, 24 stacked burials in three graves over a 21-year period, indicates the scarcity of space within the churchyard by the mid-19th century. This is a common scenario in the first half of the 19th century, when the population of London more than doubled resulting in overcrowding in the available graveyards. The problem was first addressed in 1832 when a new burial ground was licensed off the Harrow Road, following the lobbying of Parliament by George Frederick Carden. His petition to Parliament in 1830 stated that 'in many churchyards the number of interments is so great, that time is not afforded for the decomposition of bodies; and that, in consequence, many shocking spectacles present themselves to the public eye' (Reeve 1998, 214). An effective resolution to the problem, however, was not reached until the passing of the Burial Act in 1852.

The wider area to the north of the church had changed dramatically following the Dissolution. After the acquisition of the cloisters by Sir Anthony Browne the family suffered a downturn so that by the late 17th century all records of them have disappeared. By 1740 the property was owned by the Overman family who oversaw a period of structural expansion. Dollman cites an Act of Parliament, which states that by 1775 the area contained 'about sixty houses and four wharfs' (1881, 29). It was also under the auspices of Mrs Alice Shaw Overman that the almshouses were built in 1771 (Roberts and Godfrey 1950, 44). These were short lived, for Roberts and Godfrey record their demolition in 1830 to make way for the new bridge (1950, 44). Following its construction new almshouses were built, then demolished in October 1879 (Dollman 1881, 29). When considered with the evidence for burials to the north of the church in the lightwell excavation, a scenario is revealed of competition for space, with the burials being 'inserted' into available soft ground, in this case immediately to the east of the post-1830 almshouses (see Fig. 91). Analysis of the skeletal remains from the lightwell graves has revealed that the assemblage comprised twenty-one adults, one sub-adult and two infants. An assessment of age was based on the stages of dental

eruption and epithyseal union, on the degree of dental attrition (Brothwell 1981) and where possible on changes to the pubic symphysis (Brooks and Suchey 1990). Male and female adults were recovered in almost equal numbers, and the majority of these had lived past the age of 45, consistent with a 'normal' cemetery population. The low number of infants and lack of neonates is untypical given the date of the bodies, in a period of high child mortality. One of the skeletons had marks on the left femur, which may be the result of a practised amputation (Dodwell 2001, 144). The remains demonstrated a high-incidence of *ante-mortem* tooth loss, dental caries and calculus, indicating that the individuals represented in the shaft graves suffered from a lack of dental hygiene, and a sugary diet.

A particular feature of the fills and surrounding material of the shaft graves was the high quantity of disturbed and disarticulated human bone. Although this material could not be dated, and may well have originated from similar post-medieval graves, it is possible that they represent earlier burials. Medieval priories nearly always included land set aside within the precinct for the burial of monks. Such graveyards are typically found 'between the transept and the chapter-house' (Crossley 1943, 43). In the case of St Mary Overie this accords well with the area to the north side of the church, near to the lightwell. As discussed above graves, interpreted by Dawson as those of priors, were found during the 1970s within the chapter house, and in the cloisters to the west (Dawson 1976, 48). There seems no reason why similar graves may not have been inserted to the east of the chapter house in the lightwell area.

Domestic land-use around the church

The remains of a hovel

An upstanding wall was recorded by the southwest entrance to the Cathedral that would have formed the backing to a fireplace; the constituent tiles showing signs of scorching (Fig. 93). Aligned north–south, and standing to a height of *c.* 0.75m, it was built of roof tiles arranged in herringbone coursing with vertical dividers. It had been

Fig. 93   Recording the remains of the hovel by the southwest doorway

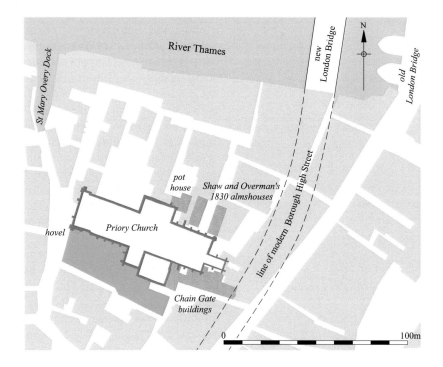

Fig. 94   19th-century landuse around the church (based on Dollman 1881) (scale 1:2,000)

Fig. 95   Copper-alloy buckle (2cm scale)

Fig. 96   Copper-alloy mount or strap-end
(for scale see Fig. 97)

repaired and conserved, probably in the 20th century, but the tiles of the original build date to after 1480. The base of the wall, currently at 4.83m OD, indicates that the floor of the structure would have been below that level. The wall is in the same position as a structure shown on an impression of the church in 1661 (Malden 1967, opp. 154); the same structure is shown on a later plan where it is marked as a 'hovel' (Dollman 1881, plate 3). It is historically depicted as a small lean-to building constructed against the south aisle, to the west of the main door (see Fig. 77).

Land-use exterior to the Bishop's Chapel

The conversion of the Lady Chapel to the Bishop's Chapel coincided with developments external to that structure. These began with ground-raising layers deposited prior to the construction of dwellings. Archaeological and historical evidence has shown that, following the Dissolution in the second half of the 16th century and into the 17th century, the priory church fell into disrepair, as described above. It was a reduction in the status of the priory church after 1539, perhaps combined with an increasing need of land for development, which led to a number of buildings, industrial and domestic, being built in very close proximity to the church. As discussed above the retro-choir was leased out as a bakery and a pigsty in the 1550s (Malden 1967, 155), and the Montague Close pottery industry commenced operating to the north of the church in the early 17th century (as discussed in Chapter 5). Such degradation in the status and sanctity of the church, both internally and externally, was typical of the period; for example, part of Greyfriars Monastery was used for the storage of herrings and wine at this time (Weinreb and Hibbert 1995, 234). The land-use exterior to the Bishop's Chapel provides further evidence of this encroachment of secular activities on the church.

On the southern side of the Bishop's Chapel, a number of ground-raising layers were excavated down to the formation level for the Millennium project. These deposits were unremarkable, mostly comprising sandy silt. The lowest layer in the sequence, which was not fully excavated, contained a large quantity of pottery ranging in date from the medieval period to the 17th century, whilst the uppermost contained pottery ranging from the 15th to 17th

centuries. A copper-alloy belt or sword-belt buckle and a decorated copper-alloy mount or strap-end were recovered from these layers, which had a combined thickness of 0.65m, to an upper level of 4.85m OD, and may have been deposited to compensate for the raised floor level within the chapel following the construction of the barrel-vaulted crypt

The copper-alloy annular buckle (Fig. 95) is complete, 47mm wide and 45mm long, with a central bar, set back and simple decoration of incised transverse lines. Its size suggests a belt or sword-belt buckle. Such annular buckles represent a form with a long period of use, stretching from c. 1350–1650; buckles of comparable size, with a similar decoration of incised oblique lines have been dated to the 15th and 16th centuries (Cunningham and Drury 1985, fig. 26 no. 10; Whitehead 2003, 52 no. 287). The beautifully decorated copper-alloy mount or strap-end of early post-medieval date found within one of the layers may have originated from a book clasp (Fig. 96). Both sides bear incised decoration, with a pattern of squares and nicks with radiating lines on one, and a six-petalled rose on the other.

Two pits, excavated within these layers, served for waste disposal. The stratigraphically lower pit contained 17th-century material including pottery and animal bone, and the upper pit contained similarly dated pottery and two ivory handles.

A similar sequence was seen on the north side of the Bishop's Chapel. The excavated sequence here began (at formation level for the new works) with two layers of sandy silt that contained 17th-century pottery ([3363], [3364], not illustrated). Above one of these layers, in the area to the west of the buttress of the northern chapel wall, was a very crude, and therefore possibly temporary, cobbled surface at 4.27m OD. This area yielded a notable assemblage of delftware wasters dating from 1660–80, indicating the use of the land to the north of the chapel as a convenient dump for material from the pottery kilns just around the church. One waster came from a charger with a Wanli style panel, possibly direct evidence of the output of the adjacent kilns. Delftwares in general formed over 60% of the pottery found immediately to the north of the Bishop's Chapel.

Following the ground-raising to the south of the chapel, the area was developed structurally. The sequence began with two walls of a building at a distance of c. 2.4m from the southern chapel wall. Both had east–west elements, offset by a later rebuild, that then returned south, forming the northern extent of the ground plan, giving an internal east–west dimension of 3.25m (see Fig. 100). These walls were built with bricks that date from the 17th or very early 18th centuries, and 17th-century pottery was found in the construction backfill of one. Material that was excavated from the area within the walls was probably a make-up layer for a floor surface, which would have sat above 4.35m OD.

A rebuild was observed in the east–west section of the building's wall, which was cut into the make-up layer. The masonry in this new section of wall comprised a brick skin on the northern face, with the southern face made of a crude lime mortar, possibly a method of cheap

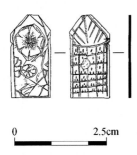

0   2.5cm

Fig. 97   Copper-alloy mount or strap end (scale 1:1)

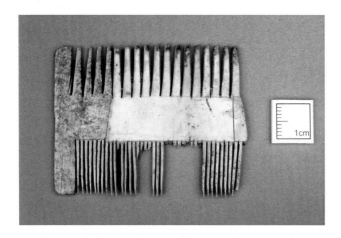

Fig. 98   The ivory comb (1cm scale)

construction, and with its east–west alignment offset from the earlier two walls. The bricks in this modification have been dated to the 18th or early 19th century.

With the construction of these walls, an enclosed yard area was created between this building and the southern wall of the Bishop's Chapel, with a north–south dimension of *c.* 2.4m. A number of features and surfaces were excavated in this area. The earliest in this sequence included an ovoid pit, which contained 17th-century pottery and an ivory comb (Fig. 98), and a small linear cut, possibly a gully or the remains of a robbed yard wall, the backfill of which was also 17th century in date. The comb from the pit is a characteristic find from 16th- to 17th-century contexts. The fine teeth on the comb were designed, as with similar examples today, for the removal of head lice.

The area was developed using the chapel wall as much as possible, and the chapel buttress which the yard enclosed was used on its east and west sides as the convenient corners for two brick-lined pits (see Fig. 100). On the west side a rectangular pit measuring 1.5m north–south by 1.09m east–west was cut, with 17th-century brick, chalk and re-used Reigate stone lining to its southern and eastern edges. The opposite two sides were formed by the masonry of the buttress, which on its western face had been rendered, presumably in an attempt at waterproofing. The faces of the walls of the pit were covered, in places, with a layer of encrusted cess; however, the fills of the pit were more typical of rubbish disposal, implying that the cesspit had been regularly emptied before being deliberately backfilled; the two fills in the pit contained 17th-century pottery. An alteration to the masonry of the west face of the buttress, where two small cuts into the level above the chamfer course had been lined with bricks dating from the 15th to 17th century, may have been designed to support a cover over the cesspit.

A similar pit on the east side of the buttress was brick-lined on its eastern and southern sides, giving total dimensions of 1.72m north–south by 1.3m east–west. The south face of the chapel wall within the pit was lined with roofing tiles to allow for easier emptying of the pit. Three fills were excavated containing 17th-century pottery

with a notable quantity of animal bone in one; like the neighbouring pit to the west, it is likely that this feature was a deliberately backfilled cesspit. That both of these cesspits were backfilled shortly after their construction is perhaps because of the unhygienic conditions created by two such features enclosed within a narrow yard.

The ground at the top of the western pit was paved with a brick surface, which is likely to have originally extended to the eastern pit as well. A roughly north–south aligned row of bricks were laid with further bricks at right angles to this, all on their bed. The surface, at 4.92m OD, sat on a mortar bedding above a make-up layer that contained 17th-century pottery. The yard surface had been repaired at least twice with areas of broken brick, Reigate stone, flint and chalk.

A small and heavily truncated section of brick wall of late 17th-century date was found to the east of the yard area and represents all that was found of the neighbouring building.

The buildings represented by the walls to the south of the Bishop's Chapel are shown on a number of plans as 'Chain Gate Houses', the name referring to the thoroughfares which were 'common open boundaries with chains and posts' (Dollman 1881, 30). Documents relating to the compulsory purchase of the properties for demolition in the 1820s list the occupier of Chain Gate House No 6, the better surviving of the two, as George Stringer (C.L.R.O. ref. P.D.151.3 1823). The heavily truncated wall to the east of No 6 was the remains of No 7 Chain Gate, which belonged to James Macfarlin (C.L.R.O. ref. P.D.151.3 1823). The properties are shown on Fig. 100; this plan reveals a convincing correlation between the archaeological remains and Dollman's work in terms of position and includes the altered rear wall of No 6 Chain Gate as was found in Trench 14.

Both cesspits were in the rear yard of No 6 Chain Gate and served that building, although it is possible that the eastern pit was shared with No 7. They were part of a terrace of houses of fairly low status shown on Dollman's plan (1881) as having been demolished in 1822. They were of an urban form, one room wide and their floor plan consisted of one or two rooms extending back from the street. A winding staircase was located at the back of the front or between the front and rear rooms and the chimney stack also situated between the two rooms. The rebuild noted at the back of No 6 Chain Gate conforms to a bay window shown by Dollman (1881, pl. 3a) and indicates a structural alteration to the building. The absence of entrance halls leading from the front doors to the staircases in many of the buildings shown on the plan, and the fact that the front walls are shown as being of lightweight construction, suggests that most (including No 6) were shops; they are described as such by Dollman: 'Within and without the Chain Gate barriers were houses and shops' (1881, 30). The rear wall of No 6 facing onto the yard was found to have brick foundations and is shown by Dollman (1881) as a lightweight structure. The rear wall is therefore likely to have been timber-framed by the early 19th century, with the brickwork representing a plinth. The configuration

Fig. 99   Excavated remains of No. 6 Chain Gate, looking east (1m and 2m scales)

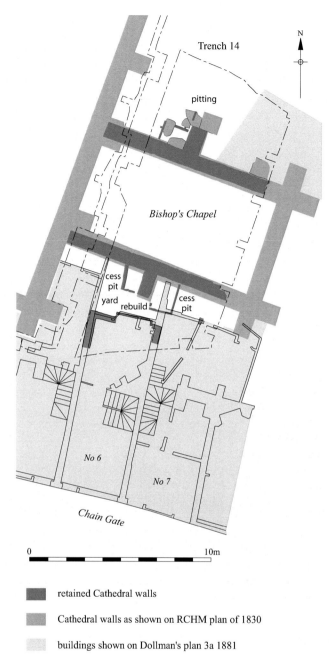

Fig. 100   Detail of excavated Chain Gate buildings and pitting to the north of the Bishop's Chapel (scale 1:200)

(nb the outline of the Bishop's Chapel and east end of the church is taken from RCHM 1830, whilst other building evidence is taken from Dollman 1881 and the two do not correlate perfectly)

of the foundations suggest that the back wall may have been brick at one time and that it represents the line of an earlier brick foundation in line with those either side that was cut through to build the lightweight rear extension, indicated on the historic plan. The upper floors may have had brick fronts and rear walls supported on bressumers. The party walls to the sides of No 6 have brick foundations that were one and a half bricks thick. The floor plan suggests that this may have widened to two bricks thickness in the front room in the party wall between Nos 5 and 6 Chain Gate (Dollman 1881). The rear room was heated with a corner fireplace with an adjacent stove. The shop appears to have been unheated. With foundations of one and a half to two bricks thick, the building may have been two storeys high and are depicted on Hollar's 1647 view of Southwark Cathedral (see Fig. 77).

The Chain Gate Houses produced quantities of glass fragments, mainly deriving from common late 17th- or 18th-century 'English' wine bottles in naturally coloured, thick, olive green glass. Amongst the remainder were identifiable fragments of drinking glasses and beakers, including two examples illustrated here, one (Fig. 101.1) is a fragment from the base of a pedestal beaker in natural, weathered pale green glass with a folded foot and a visible pontil scar, of late 16th- to mid 17th-century date. The other (Fig. 101.2) comprises three adjoining fragments of colourless glass with a grey tint from the base and sides of a cylindrical beaker, with a pushed-in base and a visible pontil scar. It has an applied base ring in the same metal

with rigaree decoration and an additional applied band of rigaree decoration, also in the same metal, on the body of the beaker and is of late 16th- to late 17th-century date.

The structural sequence seen to the south of the chapel was not mirrored to the north; rather the area immediately adjacent to the chapel's wall contained eleven pits, which were irregularly spaced and often intercut (see Fig. 100;

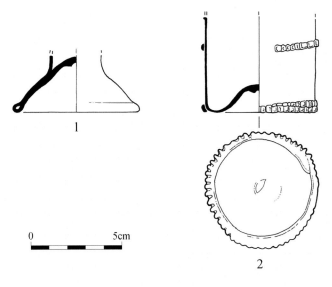

Fig. 101   Examples of post-medieval glass recovered from the Chain Gate buildings (scale 1:2)

Fig. 102   Chain Gate buildings during excavation with cesspits adjacent to Bishop's Chapel (visible in background), looking northeast

due to the intercutting nature of the pits not all of them are visible). It is likely that they were used for rubbish disposal over a period dated between the 17th century and the 19th century, from artefacts in the fills. One pit contained a blacking bottle with the stamp of J. Bourne, Denby, and the excise duty stamp 'EX 11', dated from 1817–34. The uppermost pit was cut from 4.18m OD.

The remains of two poorly-surviving walls were found to the west of the buttress on the north chapel wall, and it is possible that they originally enclosed a brick-lined pit like those seen to the south (Fig. 102). The backfill of one of the construction cuts of these walls contained 17th-century pottery. Another very poorly-built wall extending north from the buttress may have been a garden wall.

The excavation of the areas to the north and south of the Bishop's Chapel produced an assemblage of clay tobacco pipe bowls and stems that can be traced to manufacturers both locally and further afield. The parishes around, and including, Southwark were a major centre for clay tobacco pipe production in the post-medieval period, and kilns have been excavated at the Arcadia Buildings on Great Dover Street (Dean 1980, 372), at 15–23 Southwark Street (Cowan 1992, 61) and at Tabard Square on Long Lane (Killock forthcoming). The identifiable stamps on tobacco pipes from the excavation are listed below, together with their names, location and dates of production.

I B   James Brooks, St Olave's (1704)
H S   Henry Stenard, St Olave's (1724)
W W   William Wilder, Whitecross St (1717–63)
I T   James (Joseph) Tester (1805–28)
W W   William Williams, Kent St, Borough (1823–64)
           or William Watson, Silver St, Lemans Pond, (1809–11)
J B   James Brixley, Horsleydown (1828–40)
G G   George Greenland, Bermondsey (1828–32)
J W   John Williams, Kent St, Borough (1828–42)
T W   Thomas Wooten, Borough (1820–46)
I C   James Critchfield, London (1828–94)
J S   James Swinyard, Hooper St, Westminster Road (1828–56)
I F   James Frost, Borough (1836)
C CROP   Charles Crop, Hoxton and Kingsland (1856–1924)

Analysis of the faunal remains recovered from layers and pits around the Bishop's Chapel reveals a typical post-medieval dietary assemblage, with an emphasis on sheep (33.7%) and cattle (28.0%). Pig, wildfowl, domestic fowl and rabbit are also represented.

The arrangement of the land to the north and south of the Bishop's Chapel raises some small discrepancies between historical records and the archaeology. To the south Dollman's plan (1881, pl. 3A) shows a yard area with a wall that should extend to abut the chapel wall. The survival of the brick-lined pit on the east side of the buttress in the marked position of this wall, together with Dollman's accurate portrayal of the inserted bay window, implies that the rear of No 6 Chain Gate was never constructed as planned. Given the date of Dollman's publication (1881) and the date of the demolition of the buildings (before 1830) it is likely that his source material included older plans that pre-dated a re-working of the yard area of No 6 Chain Gate resulting in the 17th-century pitting. However, given the detailed nature of the plans and the unlikelihood of 17th-century plans bearing such a level of accuracy, it is also possible that he was using blueprints for the Chain Gate Houses which were altered upon construction to present the structural and yard arrangement observed archaeologically.

The configuration of the land to the north of the chapel as shown on the same plan shows a large structure, positioned to the east of the buttress and abutting the chapel. A drawing made from the northeast of the chapel (Dollman 1881, plate 42; Fig. 103) implies that this structure was timber clad and two-storey, and is may have had some type of foundations that would be expected to manifest themselves archaeologically. That no structural evidence was found in this position in Trench 14 suggests either that Dollman is inaccurate or that the post-demolition landscaping in this area after 1830 thoroughly removed any traces of the building, which appears, from Dollman's view, to be much less substantial than the Chain Gate buildings.

19th-century and later structures

Elements of other 19th-century or later structures around the Cathedral were seen. These include: the current boundary wall of the graveyard (which post-dates 1830); the Organ House (late 19th century); the steps leading from the south graveyard up to Borough High Street, built between 1910 (The Daily Graphic 1910, 4) and 1912 (The Builder 1912, 265–266). Also seen was the construction cut for the subterranean boiler room. This 20th-century structure was a massive undertaking, involving the excavation of a trench over 10.5m by 9.5m, and at least 2.0m deep. Such works would have no doubt disturbed a great many burials, yet no correspondingly large sized assemblages of charnel were recovered in the areas of the south graveyard that were investigated, suggesting that the disturbed bone was re-interred elsewhere.

From amongst layers of topsoil and cemetery soil that were excavated around the Cathedral were found fragments of window glass. They are all post-medieval in date, and their stratigraphic origin limits their intrinsic usefulness,

Fig. 103 View from the northeast of the Bishop's Chapel (from Dollman 1881)

Reproduced by kind permission of Southwark Local Studies Library

but they provide an insight into the way in which the priory church and early Cathedral of the 20th century may have been glazed. The fragments are all decorated, good quality, natural green and cylinder blown. The homogeneous quality of the pieces has led to the suggestion that they originated from the same window, yet they were found over a wide area in the south graveyard and around Trench 14, and therefore it seems more likely that they are evidence of a period of glazing rather than one window.

Fig. 104 Old London Bridge, July 1830, previous to its removal for the new line of approach

Fig. 105   View of a building at the northwest corner of Southwark Cathedral
(Yates *c.* 1825)

Reproduced by kind permission of the Guildhall Library

The fragments bear painted decorations that allow a tentative identification of the scenes; images of crenellations, fluted columns, architectural fragments and foliage are considered to depict buildings. Whilst the dates of these fragments are stratigraphically unknown, they have parallels in 16th-century donor windows. An example of carved architectural foliage can be seen below a surbased arch above Bedygfeld Shelton and his wife, donors to St Mary's Church in Shelton, Norfolk. Other fragments of window glass reveal a scene of an individual showing a brow and hairline, a scene of a wing and the lower limbs of a possible saint. Another small fragment depicting a geometric design was made using a technique that was introduced in the 15th century.

Post-medieval Discussion

The post-medieval church

The upheaval of the Dissolution in 1539 left the Priory of St Mary Overie in a state of disrepair caused by neglect rather than deliberate damage, including the use of parts of the church as a bakehouse and pigsty. The church reverted to its purely religious function in the early 17th century when the parishioners bought it and embarked upon a programme of repair that was to continue until the 18th century; an example of this work may include the remodelling of the southwest doorway. The claustral buildings passed into the private ownership of Sir Anthony Browne, who oversaw their remodelling rather than rebuilding. They were further

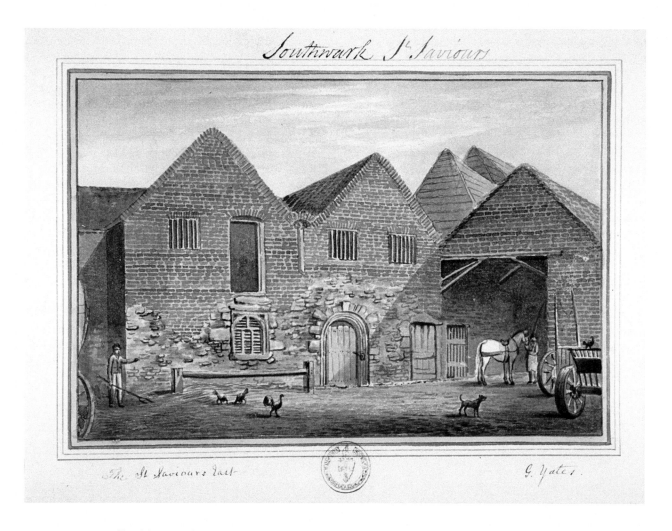

Southwark S.t Saviours

The St Saviours East   *G. Yates.*

Fig. 106   View of buildings in disrepair to the northwest of Southwark Cathedral (Yates 1825)

Reproduced by kind permission of the Guildhall Library

reworked to incorporate the Montague Close pot industry (see Chapter 5), before being cleared in the 18th and 19th centuries to make way for warehousing.

Following the death of Bishop Andrewes in 1626, the Lady Chapel was remodelled with the construction of an internal barrel-vaulted crypt to house his body. Renamed the Bishop's Chapel, it was given a new lease of life that was to be shortened by the encroachment of Southwark upon its walls, and eventually left it in a condition described as 'unsightly and dilapidated' (Dollman 1881, 18). It was demolished in 1830, eight years after the removal of the St Mary Magdalene Chapel, to allow for the construction of the new approach to London Bridge (Fig. 104). At about the same time, a programme of renewal works around the Cathedral by George Gwilt led to new façades for the retro-choir and much of the southern elevation of the building. The demolition material from the 19th-century works has revealed the re-use of building rubble in make-up deposits around the south graveyard, and has provided an idea of the nature of the building's fenestration.

The human remains excavated from the southern graveyard and to the north of the north aisle demonstrate the intensive use of the site for burial and also provide evidence for either zoning of interment or the increased

pressures on the church caused by 19th-century death-rates. Burials in the southern graveyard were largely seen to be typical of a wealthy cemetery population, buried in expensive iron and lead coffins, or with coffin furniture. Parallels for this Southwark Cathedral assemblage can be seen at Christ Church Spitalfields (Reeve and Adams 1993), and suggest an 18th- to 19th-century date range. In contrast, however, were three shaft graves containing 24 individuals excavated on the north side of the Cathedral. Analysis of artefactual evidence and historical sources has shown that the burials dated between 1832 and 1853; they represent a population with bad dental health and include an individual who had undergone a practised amputation and a post-mortem examination. Such factors suggest that these people were poorer than their counterparts in the south graveyard, and that the north side of the Cathedral was being used for lower status burials; especially considering the less tranquil nature of this particular area. Such zoning may have been the intended motives of the generous benefactors who contributed to the post-medieval repairs and beautification of the church. Yet given the date of the shaft graves, it is also possible that they represent a response to the 19th-century problem of burial, caused by the overcrowding of existing graveyards and a growing death-rate resulting from increased population and unhygienic conditions, resulting in the cholera outbreaks of the 1840s (Raymond 1999, 26).

Domestic land-use around the church

Excavation in Trench 14 revealed intensive land-use external to the Bishop's Chapel that can be seen as evidence for both the reduced status of the 16th- and 17th-century church following the Dissolution and the increased pressure of urbanisation in Southwark in the 18th and 19th centuries. The sequence began with ground raising deposits contemporary with the conversion of the Lady Chapel which then, in the 17th century, formed the bedding for a terrace of buildings less than five metres away from the chapel's south wall. These were low status structures that combined functions as both shops and dwellings. The archaeological remains revealed an alteration to one of the buildings with the insertion of a bay window at the rear; this, and the rest of the structure, reflects Dollman's plan of the arrangement (1881) with the exception that the rear extent of the building is smaller than he shows,

possibly as a result of his use of inaccurate source material. The rear of the properties included yard areas that initially incorporated cesspits, but these went out of use by the end of the 17th century, perhaps as a result of the confined nature of the yard. The buildings themselves were used until their demolition, with the Bishop's Chapel, in 1830. Their occupants in 1822 have been traced from historical records as George Stringer and James Macfarlin.

The encroachment of waste pits to the north of the chapel and terraces to the south shows the fervent nature of land-use in Southwark in the post-medieval period, with an increasing population resulting in the maximum use of space. Early 19th-century images of the church environs depict this clearly (see Fig. 105, Fig. 106). This overcrowding, combined with unsanitary conditions, may well have led to ill-health of the local population that resulted in the need for shaft grave burials such as those found on the north side of the church. By the 19th century the environs of the Millennium excavations contained an ecclesiastical institution, light industry, a main thoroughfare in London Bridge, retail and residential activity all within 100m of each other.

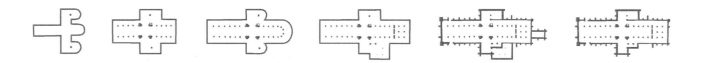

Chapter 5   Delftware Production at Southwark Cathedral

David Divers and Chris Jarrett

Tin-glazed earthenware or delftware is defined as a twice-fired ceramic; firstly the vessel was formed and fired (the biscuit ware stage) and then the vessel was decorated with a lead glaze containing oxides of tin and fired a second time to produce a finished product. Contemporary terms for this ceramic were gallyware and whiteware, the term delftware being adopted in the early 18th century after the Dutch production centre of Delft. During the late 16th–18th centuries there were three main types of pottery made in London, a coarse red earthenware, stoneware and tin-glazed earthenware. It is the latter, largely because of its artistic and collectable nature, that has received the most attention, archaeologically, in museum catalogues, or for the enjoyment of the collector and connoisseur.

Archaeologically, there have been many excavations of delftware pot houses, and their products have been recorded in dumps. For example, wasters of late 16th- to early 17th-century date have been found associated with the first London tin-glaze pot house at Aldgate (Edwards 1999; Edwards and Stephenson 2002; Blackmore 2005). One other tin-glaze pottery existed on the north bank of the Thames: this was the Hermitage Pot house, Wapping (Tyler 1999), while on the south bank of the Thames, excavation work by the Museum of London on kiln sites at the Pickleherring Rotherhithe pot houses and others in Lambeth are reported in a monograph (Tyler et al 2008). Additional publications for production sites in the Lambeth area include that of Vauxhall (Edwards 1981; 1982; 1984), Norfolk House (Bloice 1971) and further to the west, late 18th- to early 19th-century wares at the Mortlake kiln (Stephenson 2003, Tyler et al 2008).

Some waster dumps are associated with the Thames foreshore (Egan 1978, 156–159) and these have been studied in depth at Mark Browns Wharf (Orton 1988) and Adlard's Wharf, Bermondsey (Jarrett 2002). Dumps of wasters dating to the third quarter of the 18th century and probably originating from the Lambeth High Street kiln, were used to infill cesspits at the site of Lambeth Bridge House (Jarrett 2003). Important studies for the typologies of delftware vessels occur in Bloice (1971), Noël Hume (1977), Orton (1988) and Edwards (in prep), while the most recent review of the industry is Stephenson (1999).

Therefore a fairly comprehensive understanding of the London delftware industries and its production centres is emerging and results of excavation at the Montague Close kiln add to the corpus of knowledge. To date the delftware wasters recovered from the 1969–74 excavations of the two Montague Close kilns have not yet been reported on fully, but summaries have appeared (Dawson 1971b; 2006). Tin-glazed pottery finds from dumps in the vicinity of this kiln have been published (Dawson and Edwards 1974, Bird et al 1978) while waster dumps excavated at Hibernia Wharf and attributed to the Montague Close kiln contain fragments of elaborate salts in the shape of figures with Afro-Caribbean features (Stephenson 1999, 265). The pit also produced bowls, possible bottles, chargers, dishes, jars, a probable puzzle jug, plates and porringers dating to the last quarter of the 17th century. Decoration on these wares is largely geometrical with interlinking arcs, rosettes, swags and pyriform motifs. A blue and white charger has a central design of a bird sitting on a plinth surrounded by a Wanli border, but different to the typical c. 1625–50 versions (Tyler et al 2008, 24–25). The current excavations found, in common with previous investigations, evidence for production solely of delftware, and considering its long period of operation, only large, meaningful deposits dating from the late 17th century up to the kiln's closure in c. 1755 are discussed here. In contrast to Montague Close, other pot houses in Southwark, such as those at Bear Garden and Gravel Lane also produced stoneware (Britton 1987, 46).

The pottery waster deposits studied here consist of a large c. 1660–80 dated dump recovered from the area of the Bishop's Chapel and deposits associated with the substantial remains of a kiln built against the northern wall of the Priory's northeast transept chapel. The wasters come from various phases of building, reconstruction and backfilling of the kiln. Evidence for the pottery production of the early 17th-century pot house is unfortunately absent and no production waste was found with the largely demolished second, western kiln.

History of the Montague Close pot house

The documentation for the delftware pot house at Montague Close has previously received detailed publication (Garner 1946; Dawson and Edwards 1974; Edwards 1974; Britton 1987) and a précis is presented here. This pot house was in operation for some 142 years and was established in 1612 with delftware production beginning in

1613. It is notable for being the second delftware pot house in London and the first one in Southwark and on the south bank of the Thames; the Dutch potter Jasper Andres having established the first London delftware pot house in 1571 at Aldgate. These potteries were both located within buildings of former religious establishments; the Aldgate kiln was within the precinct of the Holy Trinity Priory, subsequently called Dukes Place after the reformation, and the Montague Close pottery was located in buildings of the former Priory of St Mary Overie.

In November 1612 Edmund Bradshawe took a lease on part of the frater belonging to Montague Close and with Hugh Cressey a patent/monopoly was granted to them on the 5th August 1613 to make 'earthenware in the manner of Fiansa', a reference to Italian tin-glazed ware. An initial record for a shipment of 40 tons of clay from Norwich to the pot house is recorded for the 13th January 1613/14 and indicates a start for pottery production around this time, with subsequent deliveries of 30 tons of clay in both July and October (Public Record Office Port Book E190/484/7). Bradshawe and Cressey's patent indicates the types of products they produced: all sizes of paving tiles, dishes and other pots, the range of pots made in Fiansa, as well as enigmatic garden 'posts'. The patent also tells of foreign workmen brought and employed purposely for making pots. Bradshawe left the partnership in 1614, and Cressey, the manager of the pot house, became partners with the knight Sir Thomas Smith and the merchant Rowland Hellin. Cressey had litigation over his Fiansa patent with Christian Wilhelm shortly before c. 1613 and in 1620 against Samuel Sotherne, the latter making the point of the duplicity of Fiansa ware, as it was no different to the gallyware patented by Jacob Jansen or Johnson in 1571 and made by him thereafter. However, by 1624 the Fiansa patent was probably redundant, despite the Statute of Monopolies for that year not mentioning it and Cressy probably surrendered the lease of the pottery in 1625.

The next tenant to occupy the Montague Close pot house between 1627–1633/4 was a potter previously employed at Aldgate, by the name of Jacob Prynn. After him, a period of ownership ensued by London businessmen until c. 1670 (Dawson and Edwards 1974, 59–60). However, in 1634/5 a brick pot house or workhouse, built upon old foundations was leased to John Humphreyes (a member of the Haberdashers' Company). Thomas Irons was a potter dwelling in a small tenement of the pot house and he appears to have been the main leaseholder in 1642 and was in active partnership with John Townsend and Thomas Ball. From 1646 the water-powered Armoury Mill on the River Ravensbourne, Greenwich, was leased for 21 years to Thomas Irons and other members of the Haberdashers' Company, for the grinding and milling of colours and other materials for glazes.

With the death of Thomas Irons the partnership was transferred to Thomas Harper who ran the pottery between 1668–1702 with his colleague Daniel Parker. Under Harper's tenure there was an increase in the number of apprentices who include two well-known potters, Mathew Garner and Moses Johnson, who were prosecuted as master

potters by John Dwight in 1695 for infringement of his stoneware patent. Harper was also an important voice against the import of foreign pottery between 1672 and 1694 and on the Excise duty imposed on earthenware and glass between 1695–98. This duty apparently had an unfair economic effect on potters. Thomas Harper died in 1702, but one of his main workmen, Richard Crew, was probably running the pot house from around 1695 until his death in 1707/08. The succeeding owner was Samuel Wilkinson who had been apprenticed to Thomas Harper in 1695. The Montague Close pottery was particularly prosperous during the 1720s, so that by 1727 a lease was taken out for 61 years on the Clink Prison, probably for the use of warehouses, and a pottery was operating there by 1746. Around 1735 the Montague Close pottery appears to have been run by Thomas Bodle and then managed by him from 1735 for Richard Davis and Son, whose names are listed in Kent's Directory of 1752 as 'Potters, Montague Close, Bankside', but they may have been merchants rather than potters themselves. The last time the pottery is referred to in Kent's directory is 1755, the date given for its closure, as the next time Richard Davis and Son are mentioned is 1759 when they were located next to Joiner's Hall, Upper Thames Street and described only as Merchants. The Clink pot house was managed by James Taylor, but also owned by Richard Day and Son from 1752 until its closure in 1762/3 and the Montague Close pottery therefore probably transferred its operations to the Clink.

Documentary evidence shows that during its long history the personnel at the Montague factory moved to other delftware pot houses, not just in London eg Gravel Lane, Norfolk House, Pickelherring, Rotherhithe and Hermitage, but also John Bissick established a pot house at Brislington, Bristol, in the 1640s or 1650s and Matthew Garner managed a pot house in Dublin by 1718 (Tyler *et al* 2008, 117–118). So the skills learnt by personnel at the Montague Close establishment were transferred throughout London and to other parts of the British Isles.

THE KILNS

The earliest kiln remains revealed during the 1970s excavations at Montague Close probably date to c. 1613 (Dawson 1976). This first kiln (western pot house) had been built in the remains of the former chapter house, one of the old monastic buildings, the eastern wall of which was found during the excavations. Although part of a brick wall and stone floor to the stoke hole from a later phase of the kiln were found preserved below modern service pipes (see below and Fig. 109), most of this kiln was located to the west of Trench 1 and was not revisited.

A second kiln found during the previous excavations was attributed to a 'new pot house' first mentioned in a lease of 1681 (Dawson 1976, 55); it was these remains that were investigated during the Millennium excavations and part of this kiln has now been preserved in a permanent display area in the Cathedral's Millennium building. The kiln itself had been built in the corner between the

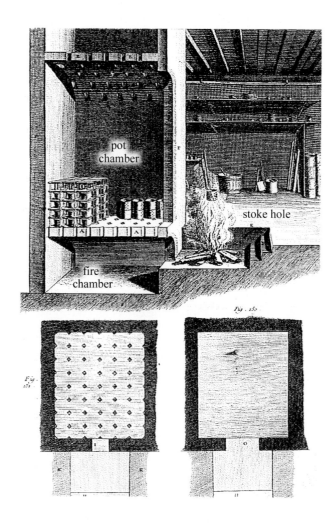

Fig. 107   Plan and cross section of a kiln as illustrated by Diderot

northern wall of the northeast transept chapel and the eastern wall of the chapter house, which had housed the original Montague Close kiln.

Tin-glazed earthenware was produced in rectangular kilns, and these have been described and illustrated in contemporary literature (Bloice 1971, 149: eg Diderot 1725–65; Piccolpasso 1548; Bolswards 1794; Paape 1794). The kilns at Montague Close are probably most similar to that illustrated by Diderot (Fig. 107; Archer 1997, 16). The kiln consisted of three main component parts. Heat was provided by a fire in the stoke hole, which was drawn through the flue into the fire chamber, then into the pot chamber above and out through the chimney. This simple up-draught system was controlled primarily by a series of vents in the pot chamber floor, but also by altering the size of the flue to control air flow from the stoke hole into the firing chamber. The lower parts of the kiln which can be seen in Diderot's illustration (Fig. 107) correspond to those found during excavation, which have survived because they were constructed in a basement, below ground level; the pottery would have been fired at contemporary ground level.

The architecture of the kiln buildings

The architecture of the building that housed the kiln is of interest. It is shown on two historic engravings. An engraving of 1813 shows that the two storey building that stood on the site of the kiln, to the northeast of the chapter house, dated back to before the mid 17th century (Fig. 108). A window on its east wall is large, rectangular and mullioned and the roof is steeply pitched. An engraving of 1817 by W G Moss (Moss and Nightingale 1818) shows the building (to the northeast of the chapter house) as

Fig. 108   View from the northeast of the chapter house in 1813 (engraved by T. Higham from a drawing made by W. Deeble for the Antiquarian Itinerary)

having the same gabled and steeply pitched roof. The pitch indicates a roof that probably dates to before the early 18th century. The fact that it sags is also indicative that it was of some age in 1817, as the roof timbers must have warped. This dating evidence shows that the building that housed the kiln still stood at the beginning of the 19th century. The front (north) elevation of the facing building in both engravings is late 18th to 19th century in date and is three-bayed with a central door. The fenestration is characteristically industrial and the window openings are wide with segmental arches, suggesting that the building that housed the kiln continued in industrial use into the 19th century and the addition of a fashionable façade indicates that its use was profitable.

The western pot house

To the west of the chapter house wall were found the remains of an east–west aligned brick wall and stone floor, surviving below a service trench. These represent a small surviving fragment of the kiln identified in earlier excavations (Dawson 1976) and little more can be said of this kiln.

The eastern pot house

Kiln 1

A north–south orientated linear cut containing unbonded flint nodules [538] was interpreted as part of a wall or foundation perhaps for a timber framed building, or a partition wall within a building, constructed against the eastern side of the chapter house housing the kiln.

The earliest kiln remains found, which date to the late 17th century, comprised two brick walls [66] (and [897], not illustrated), which formed part of the stoke hole, and associated burnt layers between these walls representing internal surfaces set within the structure formed by the wall foundation above (Kiln 1, Phase 1). The walls apparently defined the eastern and southern sides of the stoke hole, with a 1.25m wide flue leading south, presumably into the firing chamber. The whole structure was built in a deep construction trench. A floor surface of broken peg tiles survived to the east of the kiln, presumably forming an internal surface within the pot house. Nothing survived of the firing chamber for Kiln 1 which was destroyed during the construction of Kiln 2 although the base of what may have been a construction cut for Kiln 1 indicated the fire chamber's floor may have been as low as 1.3m OD. It has been assumed that the Kiln 1 firing chamber occupied a roughly similar location to that of its successor (Fig. 109).

There was evidence of modifications to Kiln 1 in the form of two north–south orientated brick walls [116], [109] built onto the remnants of the original walls (Kiln 1, Phase 2). These indicated that the stoke hole was about 1.6m wide and at least 1.5m long, although the northern end was truncated. The stoke hole had a floor of bricks laid on edge

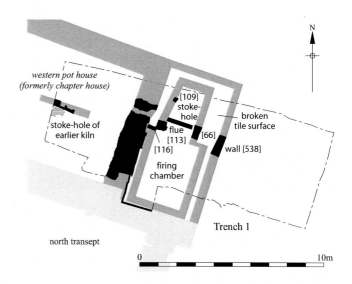

Fig. 109   Kiln 1, in relation to the earlier kiln recognised by Dawson in the chapter house (scale 1:200)

at 1.80m OD while the flue had a compacted earthen floor at a similar level. A thin wall of brick stretchers [113] one brick high was built across the entrance of the flue and was presumably added to regulate the flow of hot air into the kiln.

Later a floor of stone blocks was added to the flue raising its base by about 0.3m making the brick feature across the flue redundant (Kiln 1, Phase 3, not illustrated). A similar stone block, resting on layers containing quantities of pottery wasters, was all that remained of this floor which had once extended throughout the stoke hole and possibly into the fire chamber.

The pottery associated with this phase of Kiln 1 suggests a late 17th- to early 18th-century date, the tin-glaze decoration indicating a date after 1680. That so many modifications were carried out to the structure during its use indicates a desire to continually refine and improve the working of the kiln. However, ultimately it seems these modifications were not enough and dumps of kiln waste dated to *c.* 1730 found within the structure signified the end of Kiln 1's use prior to its reconstruction on an east–west orientation.

Kiln 2

Kiln 2 was rebuilt about 1730 in the same location but on an east–west alignment, rather than the north–south arrangement of the original. It appears that the north–south-aligned flint foundation [538] remained and a brick floor surface was built adjacent to it to the east, some 0.5m lower than the peg tile surface to the west at 2.66m OD. The bricks which made up this floor suggest that it was not laid until the 18th century and thus whilst it may represent a modification to the structure surrounding Kiln 1 in its later phases, it is likely to be a new floor associated with Kiln 2. However, this floor only survived where it lay directly below part of a wall, interpreted as being associated with

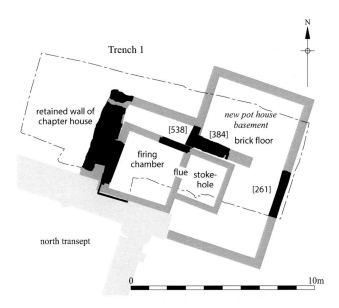

Fig. 110   Kiln 2 showing suggested extent of the basement for the new pot house (scale 1:200)

Kiln 2. Dawson indicates that the floor was once more extensive and that it was associated with Kiln 2 (Dawson 1976, 55). Interestingly, whilst the pot house now occupied a new building, the kiln structure still utilised the external walls of the north transept of the church and the chapter house as its western and southern boundaries.

The earliest surviving masonry associated with the realigned kiln took the form of walls built around the edges of a deep construction trench (Kiln 2, Phase1). Only the northern and western sides of this were identified, the latter built directly against the external face of the chapter house wall. However, the full dimensions of the chamber represented by these walls could be determined as the southern wall was presumably built along the northern side of the northeast transept chapel but was obscured by later brickwork, whilst the eastern wall survived only as a scar at the east end. The walls were about 0.5m wide and survived up to 1.39m high, built of brick with occasional courses of sandstone ashlar blocks bonded with a sandy clay which

Fig. 111   Excavating the kiln, looking southwest

had become fired during the use of the kiln. The sandstone blocks would have been included in the structure for their refractory properties, allowing the structure to withstand the stresses caused by the intense heat generated. Similar stone blocks have been found in this role elsewhere, such as at Dwight's Fulham stoneware kilns (Green 1999, 46). The sandy fabric of some of the bricks would also have had refractory properties. These walls would have created a space measuring 3.4m by 3.2m, housing the kiln's firing chamber, with a chimney above venting the kiln.

A scorched compacted internal kiln floor surface in the fire chamber area, recorded at 1.66m OD was associated with this phase of Kiln 2. The fire chamber area was later resurfaced, demonstrating its repeated use. Another area of scorched floor to the east, and 0.2m higher than the fire chamber floor, was presumably associated with the stoke hole although no remains of the walls of this were found.

External to the kiln an east–west orientated stone and brick wall [384] was built on top of the brick floor, to the north of the stoke hole area. This was presumably internal to the pot house and may have given added stability to the stoke hole structure. A James 1 farthing (1619–25) was recovered from the fabric of the wall. To the east a north–south aligned brick wall [261] may represent the eastern wall of the basement that housed the kiln.

A barrel-vaulted fire chamber was built within the masonry shell of the fire chamber described above, extending to the east. This appeared to be a later addition or rebuild of Kiln 2 (Kiln 2, Phase 2). New walls were built against the brick and stone walls of the shell, along with a barrel vaulted roof, part of which survived as the western arch of the fire chamber (Fig. 111). The foundation of the northern wall was stepped out to the south, from where the barrel vaulting arches were sprung. The base of a second arch was seen to the east of the first and a third arch was documented by Dawson (1976), but subsequently destroyed. The internal dimensions of the fire chamber thus constructed were approximately 3.5m east–west by 3m north–south, though the chamber was subsequently extended to the east (see below).

All the bricks in this structure were of a sandy fabric and slightly thicker than typical bricks of the period. They were known as 'Windsor' or 'Hedgerley' bricks and are often mentioned in 18th- to 19th-century writings as being ideal for use in kilns (eg Langley 1748, 14). The structure also incorporated a course of floor tiles also in a sandy fabric, again ideally suited for use in this type of structure.

Internally all the brickwork was vitrified due to the intense heat generated during firing. Long vents between the arches and the end walls allowed heat to rise through the kiln (see Fig. 113). Bricks connecting the tops of the arches and the end walls, or scars on the vitrification indicating the position of such bricks, divided the long vents into eight short lengths. These bricks would have provided additional support for the arches and would also allow better control of the kiln temperature. Above the firing chamber the pot chamber, or oven, had a brick floor at 3.72m OD perhaps indicating contemporary ground level; there was also some evidence that ceramic floor tiles overlying this brickwork were used to control the vents and therefore the temperature.

Modifications to Kiln 2

The addition of an east–west-orientated brick wall [389] may represent a later expansion of the kiln to the east (Fig. 112). The wall was more substantial than the earlier ones and was bonded with mortar rather than the sandy clay used in most of the other kiln walls. If this element were associated with an expansion of the fire chamber, the increased size (c. 4.4m long) would have allowed for the addition of one extra arch. A small element of north–south wall [370] defined the western end of the fire chamber and flue. This may have been built to control the airflow from the stoke hole into the firing chamber.

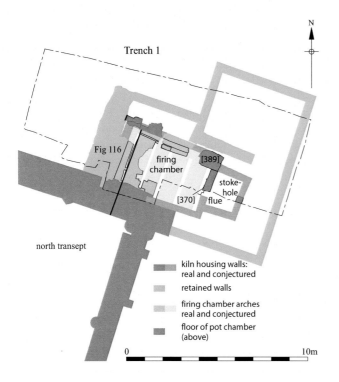

Fig. 113   Kiln 2, looking west (1m scale)

Fig. 112   Modifications to Kiln 2 (scale 1:200)

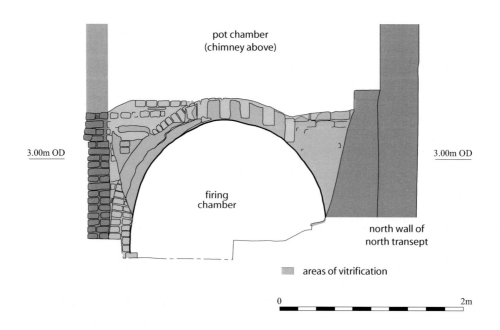

Fig. 114   West-facing elevation through Kiln 2 (scale 1:40)

A sequence of floor surfaces and other features in the flue and firing chamber indicated the repeated use of the kiln and continuing efforts to maintain and modify it. At the entrance into the firing chamber and flue area, was the eastern end of a shallow cut, which may have removed evidence of earlier surfaces. It respected the wall, and contained a compacted burnt surface at 1.80m OD that gradually sloped down into the fire chamber. This floor was succeeded by a stone and brick floor of which very little survived. A second brick floor survived better but like its predecessor, its remains were restricted to the flue area and did not extend into the main part of the firing chamber. The third floor extended throughout the fire chamber.

At the eastern end of the kiln was the stoke hole room which appeared to be a later addition to the original kiln, possibly associated with its expansion to the east. Its earliest components were a north–south brick wall with occasional stone courses; it survived to a height of 1.2m. Previous excavations had shown that this wall had returned west at its northern end abutting the new brick wall.

The earliest surviving stoke hole floor, at 2.08m OD was made of sandstone blocks bedded on a sandy layer. This was superseded by a brick floor on mortar and a further brick floor on sand. This last surface brought the floor up to the same level as the top of the wall at the entrance from the stoke hole into the flue (2.30m OD).

Disuse of the last fire chamber floor of Phase 2 was followed by internal modifications to the flue and fire chamber, although the evidence for this lay on the very limits of the excavation area (Phase 3). Dumped deposits of burnt material overlay the disused brick floor. A type E ointment pot recovered from these deposits indicates a date no earlier than 1750 for the alterations. In the flue area, the northern face of a brick wall was revealed in the southern edge of excavation along with a brick floor, which extended into the fire chamber. The wall was in the same location as the original eastern extent of the Kiln 2 fire chamber shell, possibly indicating a reduction of the chamber's size, or another attempt to control the heat flow through the flue. A clay tobacco pipe bowl dating to 1730–60 came from the construction cut for this wall.

The original fire chamber floor was covered by a 0.3m depth of dumps, which appeared to be truncated at their western end. It is possible that this vertical edge is the impression of a robbed out wall, against which the layers had been dumped. If this is the case, then the upper internal scorched floor layer is associated with these modifications and indicates the reduced size of the firing chamber, perhaps to just over 2.0m long (Phase 4).

A series of dumps of pottery production waste inside the kiln signified its final disuse. Analysis of these wasters suggested the upper dumps contained slightly later wares (consequently these deposits have been sub-divided into Kiln 2, Phase 5.1 for the lower fills and Kiln 2, Phase 5.2 for those above). Despite the slight temporal difference in these two groups of material they were generally contemporary and confirm that this kiln continued in use up until the documented end of production at Montague Close in 1755.

THE POTTERY

Chris Jarrett

The waster deposits excavated here and associated with the Montague Close pot house contained biscuit ware and the final glazed ware, delftware, also called tin-glazed earthenware. These dumps also contained kiln furniture, a fluted dish mould and other moulded items, such as the lugs for porringers, which are individual to the pot house.

Manufacturing technology

The clays and their preparation

The biscuit ware was made of a mixture of three clays; first, a 'fat' clay, almost certainly the coarse sandy clays used by the local redware potters, renowned for shrinking. The second, a 'lean' clay, which is high in calcium carbonate to prevent shrinkage. The third clay was required to lighten the fabric in order for the tin-glaze to remain opaque rather than discoloured by a red body; such whitening clays might include pipe clays (Archer 1997, 13). Calcium carbonate-rich clays also made it easier for the tin-glaze to fix to the body (Britton 1987, 12). It is known that from the initial production period at Montague Close the lean clay was shipped from Norwich. This clay was probably from the same geological source as that obtained by Jasper Andres and Jacob Jansen, the first Dutch potters to make delftware in this country, at Cringleford, close to their Norwich pottery established in 1571. The latest known transport of clay from Yarmouth to London is 1680 and later sources of 'lean' clay used by the London delftware potters were obtained from Boyton in Suffolk until 1725. A new source of clay was found at Aylesford in Kent in 1681, documented as a supplier to Thomas Harper at Montague Close (Britton 1987, 12; Archer 1997, 13).

Chemical analysis of the fabrics from a number of the London delftware pot houses has importantly shown that although the 'fat' clay used was very similar, there are subtle differences and each pot house can be distinguished. Therefore the pothouses used different clay pits, probably extracted locally (Hughes 2008). As the Montague Close pothouse was located in a built up area, some distance from open land in the 17th and 18th centuries, obtaining very local sources of clay would have been difficult. It would therefore have been interesting to chemically test the Montague Close fabrics to see how different or similar the fabrics are to the nearest pothouses: Pickleherring to the east and the Lambeth kilns to the southwest.

In 1697–8 John Dwight gave an account of delftware making at Lambeth. The mixing of the clay indicates it was in a ratio of three barrels of red, five of blue (lean) and seven or eight of white clay. These were mixed in a cistern or settling tank with water until a thick colloid was formed, a process called 'washing' or levigation. The clay was then sieved and the water allowed to evaporate in another tank until the consistency of the clay was acceptable for wedging and then working into the desired shapes (after Weatherill and Edwards 1971, 164). Archer (1997, 14) points out that some 17th-century chargers show that the different types of clay were also wedged together, rather than mixing the clays in the washing process. Examples of this technique were found on this site in one of the dump layers excavated to the north of the Bishop's Chapel [3364] with saggars in a marbled fabric.

The fabrics

A change can be seen over time in the different types of fabrics used at the pot house; as they become increasingly better mixed and finer textured. The three constituent clays, and or their inclusions, can be more readily seen in the earlier, mid 17th-century fabrics.

Kiln furniture from the 1660–80-dated dump deposit shows great variety in the degree of marbling:

Colour: Red (7.5R 5/8) with occasional, moderate and heavy marbling with a white (?pipe clay) (2.5 Y 8/1) streaks. Fabrics are hard with a rough feel and fine texture. Inclusions consist of abundant, ill sorted, grey and iron-stained quartz, 0.2–0.5mm, sparse, ill-sorted, sub-rounded red and/or black iron ore compounds, 0.02–1.5mm, sparse, ill-sorted, sub-rounded marl up to 3mm, very sparse fresh water shell. Very sparse angular flint up to 3mm.

The biscuit ware 'domestic' forms are in fairly uniform fabrics, and finer than the kiln furniture:

Colour: light red (10R 7/6) to pink (5YR 8/3) and are hard, a smooth to rough feel and a texture described as smooth: fine under the lens. Inclusions consist of moderate to abundant, irregular sub-rounded white and iron-stained quartz up to 0.2mm. Sparse red iron ore compounds, up to 0.5mm, sparse, elongated ?ferro-magnesium, up to 0.3mm. Sparse, irregular, sub-rounded white ?marl up to 0.3mm. Often vessels have a pinkish-white slip (10R 8/2).

The fabrics associated with Kiln 1, Phase 2 and the Kiln 2, Phase 5 dumps are generally finer than the 1660–80 dated group and some of the kiln furniture, such as the type 1 saggars, are near-identical to the domestic wares.

The kiln furniture, such as the shelves, is mostly made of a light colour firing fabric and the marbling is visible only under the microscope.

Pale yellow 2.5Y 8/3 with pink 5YR 8/3 streaks. Hard, smooth feel, fine to irregular texture. Moderate to abundant, ill-sorted sub-rounded white and pink quartz up to 0.3mm. Sparse, rounded, red iron ore compounds.

Domestic wares are variable in their colour range, varying from white (2.5Y 8/1) or pale yellow (2.5 8/2–8/3) or oxidised colours ranging between light red (10R 7/6), reddish yellow (5YR 7/6) to pink (5YR 7/4, 8/4), but can be variegated with lighter colours, often observed on the rims of plates. The coarseness of the fabrics can vary between fine and moderately fine but inclusions are always present. They are best described as:

Hard, fine to smooth feel and a fine texture. Inclusions consist of moderate to abundant, ill-sorted, sub-rounded clear/grey quartz up to 0.3mm. Sparse flecks of black iron ore, occasional, ill-sorted, rounded, white marl up to 0.7mm.

Vessel forming

Handforming (largely for kiln furniture) and wheel-throwing methods were both used to make the Montague Close pot house products.

Handforming

Kiln furniture items such as pegs, shelves, trivets and the type 2 saggars (open-ended cylinders with pairs of triangular piercings) as well as domestic wall tiles were made by rolling out slabs of clay which were either cut to shape or forced into moulds, probably made of wood. These items usually have one surface with moulding sand, either placed on the work surface the clay was rolled on or used to line the moulds for the easy removal of the article. The type 2 saggars were slab-built by joining the narrow ends of the rolled out length of clay together. On the domestic tiles there are pinpricked holes found in some corners, which are part of the forming process. More-complete examples were found at Norfolk House with the holes found in two diagonally opposed corners (Bloice 1971, 121, 141–142).

The wall tiles were formed from lengths of rolled clay placed between two laths fixed to a board and then rolled with a heavy lead cylinder coated with copper to give the tile a smooth surface. After a period of drying the tiles were shaped using a handled, wooden square pattern with metal edges, the underside of which had two to four pins (making the holes in the corner) which held the tile secure while trimming. This process was developed sometime before 1700 and previous to this squares were cut from rolled pieces of clay and placed into wooden or metal frames and then rolled (Archer 1997, 16).

Moulds

There is evidence for the use of moulds on the site, which were almost certainly used to form the lug handles of porringers. A mould (Fig. 115.1) recovered from the site indicates that fluted dishes or cracknels were also made, despite their scarcity in the waster deposits.

Wheel throwing

The majority of vessels were wheel thrown on a simple kick-wheel, with documentary evidence indicating initially only the use of a square piece of iron and in the 18th century a jolly (a vertical lathe) for the trimming and final smoothing of the vessels. Trimming was very visible on bases, particularly the roughly made type 1 and 2 saggars. Paring or knife-trimming on plate bases, particularly the recessed examples, could also be seen where drag marks caused by a tool resulted in quartz and other inclusions leaving drag lines or scratch marks.

Handles were simply luted on to the vessel and there was no attempt at mortising composite parts, for example on the pharmaceutical spouted jar (Fig. 118.4) where a circular hole was cut into the shoulder, the spout was simply luted over the opening and not inserted into it.

Many of the biscuit wares, particularly in a layer dated to 1660–80 have a white slipped surface, a practice found decreasingly in the 18th-century kiln groups. Where the biscuit ware was likely to fire a red colour a white-slip would have aided the glazes to maintain their desired colours.

Initial Firing

Once the vessels were thrown, required handles etc applied and the vessel finished, they were put to dry on 'stillions' or 'stillings'; trestles or wall brackets in a drying room. This was probably located in the pot house building on the east side of the courtyard. Once dry, the vessels would have been taken to the kiln and stacked within. At this initial stage the vessels were probably not placed in saggars, but on the shelves (see kiln furniture below), which were probably stacked several layers high to make a framework supported by the kiln bars or girders as suggested by Bloice (1971, 142). Once the kiln was filled the firing process could start, using wood for fuel as coal produced gasses that could be detrimental to the tin-glazes. Firing took several hours to reach the required temperature of 950/980°C to 1000/1050°C, which then would be maintained for twenty-four to forty-eight hours and needed constant attendance (Britton 1987, 11; Archer 1997, 16). The kiln was allowed to cool for approximately two days and then the biscuit ware was unpacked and made ready for the next stage; glazing. Delftware could not be fired in one go as the differential shrinkage of the vessel body during its first firing would cause the glaze to crawl and so distort any patterns and leave bare patches.

Glazing

In England, lead-based tin-glazes were used; made from 10 parts of fine white sand, 4 parts soda, 3 parts pot ash, 10 parts lead and 3.3 parts tin, with the addition of copper filings and a small amount of cobalt (Ray 1968, 86). Roasting these ingredients in the kiln then made a frit, which was ground; the Montague Close kiln using the water-powered Armoury Mill on the River Ravensbourne, for this process. However, other kilns in London used windmills or mills on site to do the grinding (Britton 1987). The glaze was then made into a liquid solution with water. Other metals were added to produce different colours, cobalt for blue, manganese for purple hues, iron to give red, antimony for yellow and copper to give green. A c. 1700 development of mixing cobalt and antimony together gave a better, more reliable green colour (Black 2001, 13). However, a limited range of colours appears to have been used at the Montague Close kiln, namely blue, white and perhaps some purple. Dawson also found limited evidence for polychrome wares from his excavations (Britton 1987, 43). Tin was an expensive metal to buy and therefore, in

the 17th century, chargers more often than not only had a tin-glaze on the interior of the vessel and a plain lead-glaze on the exterior. However, most vessels would have been initially dipped entirely into liquid glaze, although the underside of many closed vessels, such as albarellos, mugs and jugs were not glazed. Subsequent decoration with a brush, etc, would have taken place after the initial background glaze had dried. Repetitive designs could be achieved by using a stencil where the pattern was pricked out on to paper (called a pounce paper) and patting the surface with a muslin bag filled with ground charcoal, which revealed the design on the vessel. The motifs could then have their outline and shading painted using coloured glazes (Archer 1997, 18). However, painting a design onto unfired tin-glaze is difficult as the surface is absorbent and does not allow for any corrections (Black 2001, 14). Therefore, a degree of mental determination on the part of the decorator was necessary to execute the design as any dithering could cause a botched result.

The final firing

Once the biscuit wares had been decorated and allowed to dry, they would be ready for firing. Many kiln furniture forms were utilised, as they were important in stacking the vessels or protecting them from the gasses and flames produced during firing and to maintain the vessel in an even temperature. Unfortunately, very few scars were recorded on the vessel wasters or the saggars from the excavations making it difficult to determine how the vessels were stacked within the kiln; and the accepted practices known from documentary and other excavation work have been applied here. For the 17th and early 18th century trivets were used to keep chargers and other open vessels separate from each other as they were stacked horizontally and inverted, on top of each other inside the type 1 saggars. If bases were scraped free or wiped clean of glaze (as were the rims of ointment pots) then vessels could be stacked base to base inside saggars and would not stick together.

Type 2 saggars are present on the site from the 1660–1680s and these were used to fire plates and dishes, the underside of the rims being placed upon the pegs inserted through the triangular holes of the saggar. A layer of plates or dishes was therefore built up inside this saggar. Both types of saggars could then be stacked either on the shelves or on top of each other (depending upon their rim and base diameters) and sometimes secured with pads of clay. A lid may then have been placed on the rim of the top saggar.

Only one glazed rim of a plate or dish was found on the inside of a type 2 saggar, while the overlapping outline of two glazed vessels was found on a shelf recovered from a dump layer [3364] to the north of the Bishop's Chapel, which may imply that some glazed vessels were not protected by a saggar, unless an upended one was placed over it.

There is evidence that biscuit and glazed wares were fired together and at Norfolk House it was suggested that the delftware may have been fired at a higher level in the kiln than the biscuit wares, some of the latter being found with glaze drips on them (Bloice 1971, 144). There are a few items from the Montague Close kiln groups that suggest this was also happening there, including a biscuit ware plate with white-glaze drips. The second firing lightens the body of the vessel and makes it softer, perhaps because of the glaze coverage (Bloice 1971, 141).

Once the firing was complete and the pottery was unloaded from the kiln, successfully fired vessels were ready for retailing.

Waster evidence

At the Montague Close pottery the main quality control was at the biscuit ware stage where many vessels were discarded perhaps, but not necessarily, due to their oxidised colour. Vessel warping may have been an important reason for wastage as in the case of Britton's types I and K shaped plates found in the final infilling of the kiln (Britton 1987, 194). Another minor problem in this period was the shrinkage of bases, resulting in holes on two ointment pots of type D shape. There were a number of incidences of vessels with unfired or under-fired glazes; examples include a plain whiteware vessel of *c.* 1730 Britton's type E, in the form of a bowl or dish dated *c.* 1660–80 and a *c.* 1755 chamber pot. Many of the plain blue ware Britton type I plates deposited *c.* 1755 have uneven glazed surfaces with raised, thickened bands of glaze runs. A hemispherical bowl dated *c.* 1730 with a hooked rim had a 'burst bubble' glaze, while another dish was soot damaged and two sherds discarded *c.* 1730–50 had blackened glazes.

Vessel forms

The classification codes for vessel shapes are those used by the Museum of London Specialist Services (MoLSS), who use Britton's dishes and plate vessel shape categories (Britton 1987, 194). The form dates are derived from the archaeological sequence associated with pottery production, namely a dump and kilns.

Table Wares

Bowls

Bowls are defined as open shapes with a rim diameter equal to or greater than the base and a height of one third or more of the rim diameter (MPRG 1998).

Hemispherical bowls have a hemispherical body profile and footring and come in a wide range of sizes. They have been divided into two sub-categories according to their rims. Type 1 (Fig. 115.2) has a simple rim with little or no embellishments and rim diameters ranging between 100–270mm, the most common rim sizes being 140–160mm and 220mm. Larger examples may represent punch bowls. One decorated example is present in a blue on white floral design (Fig. 119.3) and is dated *c.* 1730–40. The second

type has down-turned or hooked rims (eg Fig. 115.3) with diameters ranging between 180–300mm, the majority having a diameter of 240mm. Only one decorated example was present with a plain blue tin-glaze. The hooked rim bowl is known from excavations with Wanli and bird on rock style decoration, which dates from the second quarter of the 17th century (Archer 1997, 100), but first occurs here in wasters dated 1660–80. The simple rimmed examples are only apparent with the abandonment of the kiln (*c.* 1755) and therefore seem to be a later development here, but punch bowls are known *c.* 1660 (Archer 1997, F.3, 285). One other decorated sherd came from a rimless *c.* 1755 example and has a pendulous flower design (Fig. 119.16).

The earliest rounded bowl shape was found as a single example dated *c.* 1680–1700. It has a slightly everted, rounded rim (Fig. 115.4). Other vessels with this general shape occur as a body sherd with suggestion of an everted rim dated *c.* 1700–30, but also in the form of base sherds of a *c.* 1755 date, one flat (Fig. 115.5), the other with a foot ring, possibly representing a porringer.

The simple rim of a straight-sided bowl was also recovered and is dated *c.* 1700–30 (Fig. 115.6).

Dishes

Dishes are defined as open shapes with a rim diameter equal to, or greater than that of the base and have a height of between one third and one seventh their rim diameter (MPRG 1998).

Chargers are dishes, in large open forms, with footrings (Britton 1987, 184). Most of the recovered sherds are difficult to classify to a specific type. Examples of footrings recovered have diameters ranging between 80–100mm, very occasionally with suspension holes. One sherd has polychrome decoration in style D (TGW D) with a yellow and blue geometrical/floral design on white and an external blue lead glaze, but it is almost certainly residual. Britton's type C dishes (Fig. 115.7 – Fig. 115.13) have a rounded profile with rim diameters ranging between 200–300mm, most frequently 230mm, and base diameters ranging between 80–120mm, and here were recovered from a deposit dated *c.* 1660–80. The rims are variable, and they can be hooked (Fig. 115.7), but are more often simply thickened and rounded (Fig. 115.8 – Fig. 115.10), although they also can be internally stepped or lid-seated. The latest type-C charger comes from a deposit dated *c.* 1680–1700.

The latest type of charger present is of Britton's type E, with a broad everted rim (240–340mm in diameter), short wall and rounded base with a footring (not illustrated). Traditionally this charger type was in production for a long period of time. The 1602-dated charger depicting probably the Tower of London and a legend including Queen Elizabeth is of this type (Britton 1987, 105 no 25). However, this shape is first present from *c.* 1730. Generally, charger production on the site is dated to the 17th century. Chargers were a redundant form by *c.* 1740, but shape E is generally accepted as a late 17th-century development imitating Chinese porcelain imports (Archer 1997, 70).

A number of different types of flared dishes were recorded (Fig. 115.14), first with simple slightly thickened

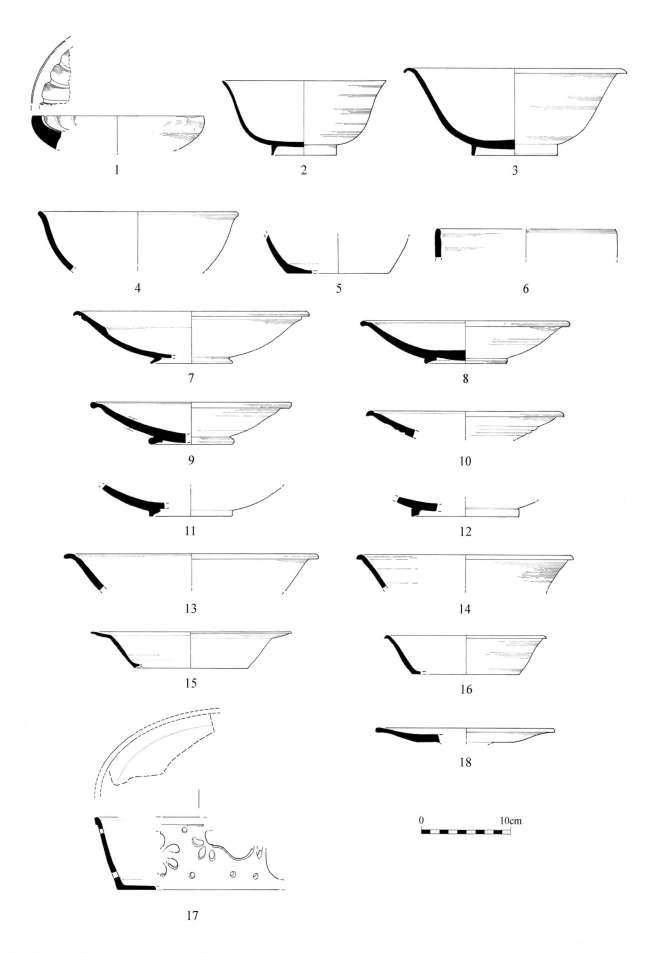

Fig. 115   Delftware bowls (scale 1:4)

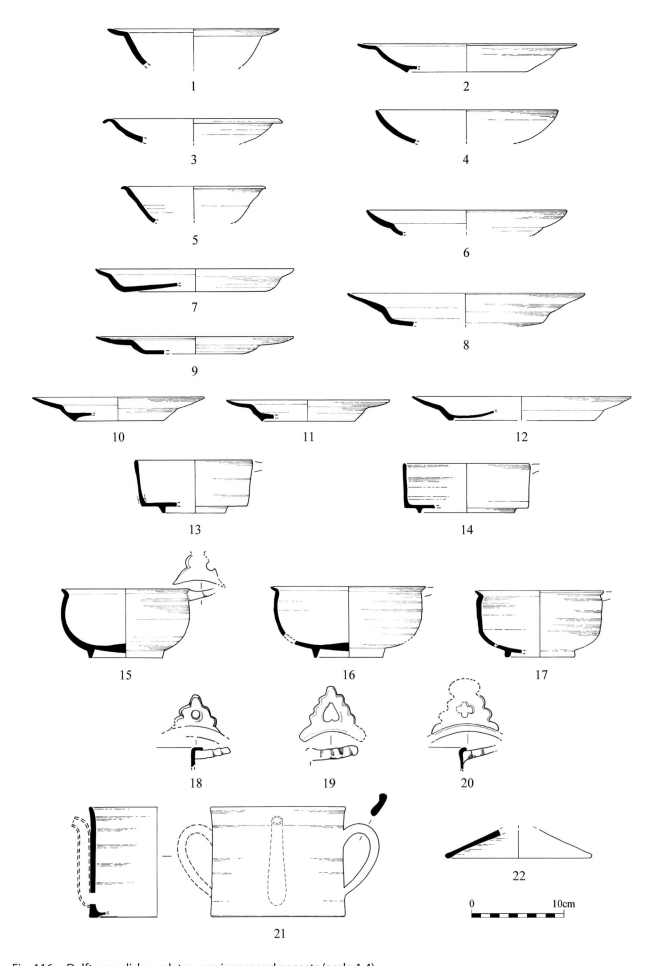

Fig. 116   Delftware dishes, plates, porringers and possets (scale 1:4)

everted rims, or thickened and bevelled rims, and second with a narrow everted rim type (Fig. 115.15). There was also a single small flared dish with a thickened rim (Fig. 115.16). Bases are generally flat, but one example has a recessed base (Fig. 115.15). All flared dishes occur in the *c.* 1755 kiln abandonment dumps.

Despite a fragment of a mould for fluted dishes (Fig. 115.1) being recorded from a *c.* 1755-dated context, only two sherds of a fluted dish were recovered, a biscuit ware rim dated *c.* 1700–30 and a glazed body sherd (see Fig. 119.5), decorated in dark blue on light blue, probably in the style of Chinamen in grasses (TGW F), dated 1670–90.

Two examples of oval dishes were found dated to *c.* 1755, both with squared rims. The most complete example has flared walls and is decorated with circular piercings around the base and the wall has cut-outs in a floral pattern (Fig. 115.17).

Two rims from small dishes or saucers are present with rim diameters of 138–140mm and may be of a type with pedestal bases (Fig. 115.18). Such forms usually date to between *c.* 1680–1720 (Orton and Pearce 1984, 56–57, fig. 26.115) and here are present only between *c.* 1700–30.

The majority of rounded dishes have a broad everted rim (Fig. 116.1 – Fig. 116.2) with diameters between 180–230mm, most being 210mm, while those with surviving bases are recessed (Fig. 116.2). This form may equate to soup plates and are deeper examples of Britton's type K plates (Britton 1987, 194). Other rare rounded dish variants have hooked or slightly hooked rims (Fig. 116.3) and all these types are dated *c.* 1755 as is simple rimmed rounded dish (Fig. 116.4). Rare amongst the wasters are small rounded dishes with rim diameters ranging between 110–160mm with rounded or slightly thickened rims (Fig. 116.5). and dated between *c.* 1730–55.

Plates

There is a limited range of plate types. Britton's type H plates have a rounded exterior, flat base and an internal thickening at the rim wall angle (Fig. 116.6 illustrates a variant). Such plates are usually dated to the late 17th and start of the 18th century, but they are rare amongst the wasters. Plates with a simple or primitive shape, where the internal and external vessel profile are the same (Britton's type I), are the most common type (Fig. 116.7 – Fig. 116.9). There are a number of versions distinguished by the size of the rim, most have a narrow everted version (Fig. 116.7) but others have a broader rim (Fig. 116.8 – Fig. 116.9); diameters range between 180–280mm, but most are 220mm in size. Glazed examples are largely present in plain blue, but a plain white example was recorded and a number are present in style H (see decoration below, Fig. 119.13–Fig. 119.18). During the excavation these simple plates were restricted to the *c.* 1755 backfilling of the kiln dumps, though they are known to date from *c.* 1690 (Garner and Archer 1972, 81). Another late 17th- to early 18th-century type of plate is Britton's type J plate with a flared exterior and internal thickened, angular profile. It

is rare amongst the waster deposits from this pot house as three examples only were present and these were probably residual, this being an antiquated shape by the middle of the 18th century.

The final type of plate is Britton's type K with mostly broad, everted rims, the walls externally rounded or flared and internally short and angled. The recessed base starts close to the change in wall to base angle (Fig. 116.10 – Fig. 116.12). These plates are dated from *c.* 1730 (Garner and Archer 1972, 81) and are restricted to the *c.* 1755 kiln backfilling.

Porringers

Porringers are categorised as small bowl-shaped vessels with a horizontal, often lobed, lug and shallow footring on the base. The lug was usually made in a mould and they are therefore usually specific to a pot house, unless they were sold on to another kiln with the closure of a pot house. The form had two main functions, firstly as a tableware for the consumption of semi-liquid foods and secondly for a pharmaceutical function as a bleeding bowl (Archer 1997). Three types of porringers can be distinguished and have temporal significance.

Type A porringers have a straight-sided walls and are dated to between *c.* 1660– 1730 (Fig. 116.13 – Fig. 116.14). Type B porringers have a rounded profile and simple, upright rim. A single example was recovered, with style D glazing, decorated internally with four blue horizontal bands and an external lead glaze. It is dated to *c.* 1660–80 but may represent a domestic item rather than a product of the kiln. Type C porringers have a rounded body profile, an everted rim and first date from *c.* 1700 but, from the excavation, were much more common in the *c.* 1755 dumps (Fig. 116.15 – Fig. 116.17). Three porringer lugs were recovered from the same dumps: one with a circular central hole (Fig. 116.18), another with a heart-shaped hole (Fig. 116.19) and a third with a cross-shaped piercing (Fig. 116.20).

Possets

Posset pots were used for drinking wassail (a mixture of apple pulp and spiced wine) or posset (milk curdled with wine or some other alcohol) and were popular in the 17th century and at the beginning of the 18th century. Three posset pots of a cylindrical type (Fig. 116.21) with simple rims (140–160mm in diameter), two opposed vertical loop, strap handles and a slightly recessed base were present and date to between *c.* 1660–80. The spouts start at the base and are fixed to the vessel wall except for at the top where they are angled outwards. Contemporary flanged lids for the posset pots also occur (Fig. 118.19 – Fig. 118.20). Fragments of posset pots, including a cylindrical type, were also found with phases of the kiln dated to between *c.* 1700–30, but the form is redundant thereafter.

Salt

A pedestal base was recovered that could possibly belong to a salt, but several other forms also have such bases (see wet drug jars). A plain white tin-glaze example is illustrated (Fig. 116.22).

Drinking forms

The drinking forms were generally fragmentary and difficult to distinguish, particularly cups from mugs, and mugs from jugs. Cups are distinguished as having a rim diameter greater than the base diameter and height, and by having a vertical loop handle, while mugs are classified as having a greater height than rim and base diameter and have one or more vertical loop handles (MPRG 1998). Cup rims were distinguished here by having thinner walls than the mug rims. The distinction of these forms has also been a problem with other biscuit ware waster dumps, where bases survived but other parts were missing, but here there are more rims than bases (Orton 1988; Jarrett 2002).

No complete profiles of jugs could be reconstructed and fragments were assigned to jugs on the basis of size and other shape criteria, though some sherds assigned to jug types may well be those of mugs and vice versa. Most jug fragments would appear to be from a rounded shape with simple rims and a variety of bases; flat, concave and slightly splayed. There is some evidence of typological changes, but these probably do not reflect the changes in jugs as a whole. The flat base of a small rounded jug with wire marks is dated 1660–80, while jug bases dated *c.* 1700–30 can be flat or a pedestal with a concave underside. Splayed jug bases first appear *c.* 1730 and are also found in *c.* 1755 along with concave examples. One other jug type was found dated *c.* 1755 as the body sherd of a barrel shaped vessel.

Cups

A number of thin-walled sherds with simple rims and body sherds have been assigned to a general cup category. There are also a number of small handles with oval or D-shaped profiles that seem appropriate for cups. The form occurs between *c.* 1700–1755. A possible *c.* 1700–30 cup rim is tin-glazed with an external design of purple bands and a floral motif on white (Fig. 119.4). The handle terminals in all groups have at the base the end turned up and pushed back on to the handle, and there are some with coiled or spiralled ends of a *c.* 1755 date.

A single rim sherd from a capuchine with a deep neck is dated *c.* 1755 (Fig. 117.1)

Rim sherds from flared-shaped cups are dated *c.* 1700–30 (Fig. 5.11.2) and *c.* 1755 with rim diameters ranging between 70–110mm.

Rounded-shape cups are more common, present in most groups associated with the kiln but always fragmentary. They have rim diameters ranging between 70–100mm but show no increase in size over time. The base sherds are mostly of a short pedestal type with a concave underside (Fig. 117.3) but examples with footrings are dated *c.* 1755.

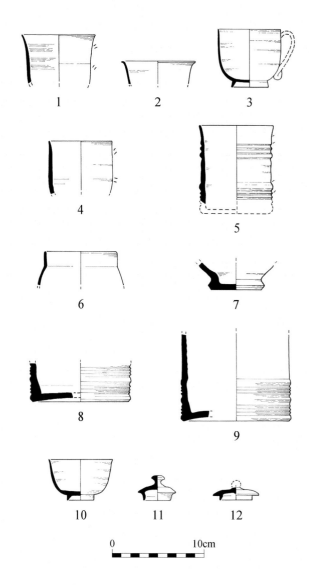

Fig. 117   Delftware cups, mugs, tankards and teawares (scale 1:4)

As straight-sided cups were only noted by their rims (Fig. 117.4), this form may be interchangeable with straight-sided mugs and tankards. These cups are dated *c.* 1700–30 and *c.* 1755 and have rim diameters ranging between 70–120mm.

Mugs

A single cylindrical mug rim is dated *c.* 1755 with a diameter of 100mm (Fig. 117.5). It is decorated with ribs at the top and bottom of the vessel and is a squatter version of the tankards (see below).

A small number of rounded mugs are recorded with those dated *c.* 1700–30 having simple upright rims, both with diameters of 90mm. One vessel has a shoulder (Fig. 117.6). Some examples dated *c.* 1755 have simple everted rims and a body sherd has a rod handle terminal formed into a spiral.

Small rounded mugs were largely dated 1660–80 and recorded as having globular bodies and splayed bases (Fig.

117.7), one showing evidence for knife trimming. The rim of a small rounded mug was also present and dated *c.* 1755 with a rim diameter of 80mm.

Tankards

Bases of tankards with concave undersides were recognised from the *c.* 1755 dumps and are decorated with horizontal ribs of different sizes (Fig. 117.8 – Fig. 117.9). The innovation for this lathing probably came from the local and other English stoneware tankards.

Teawares

Saucers

Saucers were dated to *c.* 1755 and have simple rims ranging in diameter between 120–140mm, while the bases have a shallow footring. The form was scarce amongst the wasters recovered, but one decorated example in style H was found (Fig. 119.19).

Tea bowls

Tea bowls are defined as cups without handles and have a footring (Fig. 117.10). They are present from *c.* 1700 but are particularly notable around 1755. The rim diameters range between 60–80mm but the low frequency of these vessels do not show a temporal increase in size. The decrease in the price of tea during the 18th century resulted in tea wares slowly increasing in size. There are two sherds decorated in style H both with external floral designs.

Teapot lid

Two small, flanged lids were recovered with diameters of 40 and 50mm, and dated to *c.* 1755. One is complete and one has a missing knob (Fig. 117.11 – Fig. 117.12). These lids have been recorded as possible teapot covers, as they are comparable in size to other contemporary examples in other pottery types, for example Staffordshire-type white salt-glazed stoneware dating to the 1740s and 1750s. However, no evidence for teapots was recorded and these lids may equally have been a cover for another vessel type.

Hygiene Wares

Pharmaceutical

Albarellos or gallipots are defined as cylindrical jars, waisted at the top and bottom of the body and, although functionally they are viewed as containers for medical ingredients and preparations, the form was used for the storage of a wide range of items such as cosmetics, groceries and paints (Archer 1997, 379–380). Albarellos from the site are present from *c.* 1660 and from *c.* 1700–30 in the kiln, but all are fragmentary and few complete profiles could be reconstructed. The rims range in diameter between 96–200mm, but are most commonly 100–120mm in size. The rim profiles are mostly thickened and bevelled (Fig. 118.1), and occasionally collared (Fig. 118.2) between 1700–30, but the *c.* 1755 examples are simply rounded in profile and

everted to some extent. Bases are splayed (Fig. 118.3) and show no real typological changes except for horizontal grooves on two examples dated *c.* 1700–30.

A biscuit ware spouted jar of a cylindrical, shouldered type was recorded and dated *c.* 1755 (Fig. 118.4). Its rim is everted and a circular piercing made on the shoulder with the collared, tubular spout luted on the exterior and not socketed into the hole. Although the function of this vessel is not certain, it does seem more likely that it had the same function as a pharmaceutical wet drug jar and was used by the apothecary to store liquid preparations such as syrups and oils.

The evidence for the manufacture of wet drug jars (for syrups and oils used by the apothecary) on the site is slim and restricted to hollow pedestal bases (see Fig. 116.22). However, no tubular spouts were recovered (except for the spouted jar above) and these hollow pedestals could equally belong to candlesticks, salts, nozzled vases or could indeed be lids.

The site produced a wide range of ointment pots reflecting some chronological changes in the form. Type A has a narrower splayed pedestal base than the globular body (Fig. 118.5) and the one example recovered is dated *c.* 1700–30. Type B has a splayed base wider than the cylindrical body (Fig. 118.6) and two examples are dated *c.* 1700–30, one being plain blue glazed with a rim diameter of 80mm. This type probably dates to the late 17th and early 18th century (Archer 1997, J.14, 385).

Type C has a cylindrical shape, waisted at the neck and base with the rim, body and base having similar diameters (Fig. 118.7). It is the main type of ointment pot between *c.* 1700–30 with a decline in the number of examples by *c.* 1755. Rim diameters range between 40–80mm reflecting the range in sizes, in addition to taller examples, but those with a diameter of 60mm are more common. One example is white-glazed. This shape is dated *c.* 1700–1770 (Archer 1997, J.16, 386).

Type D is categorised as having a narrower pedestal base and is less globular in shape than type A (Fig. 118.8). It first appears in a *c.* 1730 context as a single base example; it is one of the main types in *c.* 1755 but is almost absent in the latest kiln backfill dumps. Rim diameters range between 50 and 70mm with 60mm being the most frequent. When glazed, plain blue examples are more common, but three examples dated *c.* 1755 are decorated in style H with darker blue vertical straight and or curvilinear lines (Fig. 119.6 – Fig. 119.8) and one additionally with a scroll. This type of decoration is more common on mid 18th-century ointment pots. Type E has a pedestal base narrower than the body, most frequently with a vertical, slightly rounded wall with rims everted to a greater or lesser degree (Fig. 118.9 – Fig. 118.11). A variant was found with a more closed shape. It was made in a range of sizes with diameters of 32–90mm, but more ointment pots of this type occur with a diameter of around 70mm and only plain blue glazed examples were encountered. This shape first appears on the site in contexts dated between *c.* 1730–50 as minimal numbers but is the main *c.* 1755 type. Typologically it is dated to the late 18th century by its narrower base compared to its rim (Archer 1997, 387)

Type F is a hemispherical bowl shape with a narrow pedestal base (Fig. 118.12). It is rare on the site with two examples found of which only one had a measurable rim diameter at 62mm. Types F and G ointment pots occur within deposits dated to the abandonment of the kiln and therefore here seem to date to the 1750s. Type G has a globular, closed shape with a narrow pedestal base (Fig. 118.13) and only four examples were recovered, with rim diameters ranging between 38–60mm.

Storage or dispensing jars are defined as cylindrical or shouldered-shaped often with a concave base, while the rims show some chronological change. A bevelled type was recovered dated *c.* 1700–30, but the *c.* 1755 examples have mostly simple, thickened rims (Fig. 119.11), simply everted (Fig. 119.9) and a triangular profile with a flat top (Fig. 119.10). Rim diameters range between 70–220mm but the majority fall between 100–120mm. Decorated forms are only dated to *c.* 1755 as multiple blue horizontal bands either on a white or paler blue background (TGW H) tin-glaze.

Sanitary wares

The wide flat rim of a deep dish shaped vessel has been identified as a probable barber's bowl by the presence of a pair of piercings (Fig. 118.14). Complete barber's bowls have a circular cut-out (for the customer to hold under his chin) in a wide rim and a depression to hold a soap ball (Archer 1997, 316–317). Piercings are not necessarily a prerequisite for barber's bowls, but a *c.* 1740–50 example in the Warren Collection has them (Ray 2000, 48). The earliest known example of this form has a date of 1681, while the example here is dated *c.* 1755 (Ray 2000, 48).

The chamber pots recovered from the excavations are fairly uniform in shape, often with everted rims, but hooked or down turned rims also occur, sometimes undercut (Fig. 118.15 – Fig. 118.18), many have a neck, globular bodies and shallow footrings on a flat or slightly concave base. Rim diameters range between 140–240mm but the most common range is 180–200mm. The handles are of a vertical strap type, attached in the London area post-medieval potting tradition to the rim (but here on the rim underside) and below the middle of the body, the end of the terminal always folded, often pinched and pushed back on to the handle. Many of the chamber pots either have a shallow horizontal incised line or light cordon or sometimes both at the base of the neck. Glazed examples are either plain white or plain blue. There is a development within chamber pot types in the southeast England area with a continuous production of narrow rim shapes, as exclusively found at Montague Close, but chamber pots with broad rims are known (see Britton 1987, No. 47, 116), they are an innovation of the late 17th century, lasting until the early 18th century. Fig. 118.18 is a possible exception having a narrow flat rim and so does not quite fit into either category. Chamber pots are present in the kiln deposits between *c.* 1700–55, but only in the final backfilling of the kiln are they an important manufactured form.

Lids

There are two flanged lids that were almost certainly covers for the posset pots found with them and dated *c.* 1660–80. They have rim diameters of 160 and 180mm with a domed profile and rounded knob (Fig. 118 .19– Fig. 118.20). Both are in a red fabric and are white slipped and one example has a stacking scar on the underside. These lids have been dated by Noël Hume (1977, 93) to 1650–75, while Archer (1997, D10, 262) suggests a 1650–55 date for paralleled examples, which have bosses. Other flanged rims are dated *c.* 1755 including an example with a domed top with a diameter of 140mm, but is unlikely to have been a cover for a posset pot.

Jars

Jars are difficult to define but generally have a rim and base smaller than the vessel's maximum diameter.

A number of jars with rounded body shapes are present and are difficult to place in the conventional repertoire of delftware forms. The rims are mostly simply everted (Fig. 118.21) with diameters between 100–180mm and are mainly dated *c.* 1755 except for an example with a burnt, blackened tin-glaze dated *c.* 1730–50. These rims could be from wet drug jars, 'ginger jars' or possibly nozzled flower vases, but without the associated diagnostic spouts and nozzles it is difficult to be certain of the exact forms. One other rounded jar also has a simple everted rim and a splayed, concave base sherd.

Other forms

A single basal sherd of a strainer with three circular piercings is dated *c.* 1755.

Candlesticks

Two upright candlesticks were recovered and dated 1660–80 (Fig. 118.22 – Fig. 118.23). Both are incomplete and consist of a hollow, conical pedestal base constricted into a cylinder with a single drip tray. These are dated to 1640–1700 by Noël Hume (1977, VI. 16, 70) and Archer (1997, G4. 327) dates similar examples to *c.* 1680. A third hollow, conical base also dated 1660–80 may also be from a candlestick, but could alternatively be from a salt or nozzled vase.

Patty pans (squat straight-sided jars)

Four examples of squat straight-sided jars (containers) are dated *c.* 1700–30 with rim diameters ranging between 120–140mm, all with everted, bevelled rims and a circular groove below the rim (Fig. 118.24). One later example (Fig. 118.25) of this form is dated *c.* 1755 and it has a rounded everted rim and a rounded wall, the base being slightly concave. They were used for chopped, cooked meats (i.e. pâté).

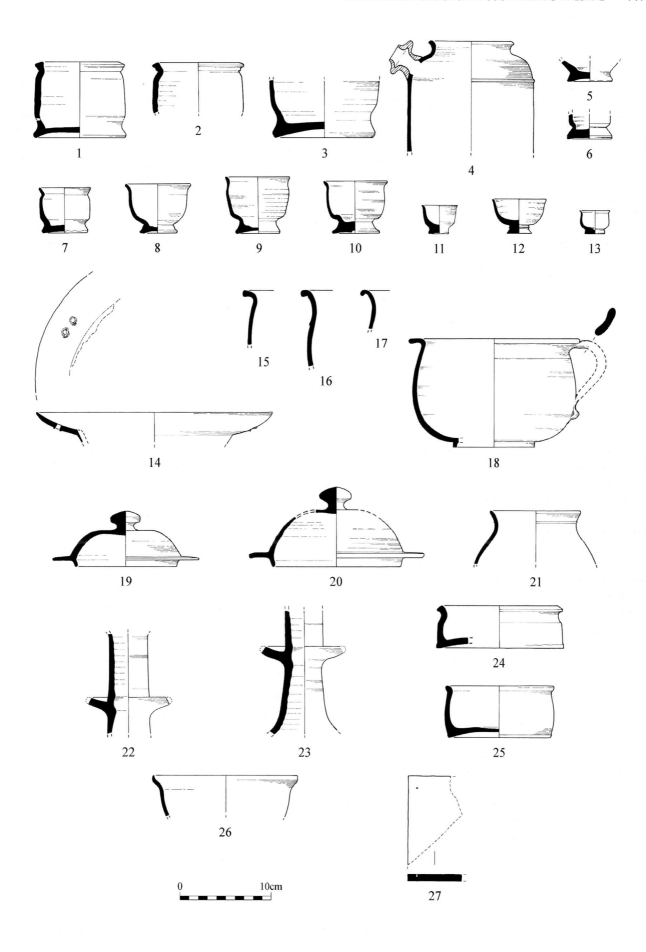

Fig. 118   Delftware sanitary wares and other forms (scale 1:4)

Urn

A single rim sherd was recovered from an urn, dated *c.* 1755 (Fig. 118.26). The rim is upright with a diameter of 160mm and the body profile is curved. Larger delftware urns were often used as decorative containers for flowerpots, but smaller examples were used ornamentally at each end of a mantelpiece, perhaps to hold flowers or feathers. Similar biscuit ware examples dating to the third quarter of the 18th century were found at Lambeth Bridge House, and were probably made at the Lambeth High Street kiln (Jarrett 2003, fig. 5.21, 36–37), but larger examples for holding flowerpots are known from at least the late 17th and early 18th century (Jarrett 2000, fig. 9.6, 130).

Vase

A rim of a possible vase dated *c.* 1755 was recovered. Decorated in style H, it is everted and decorated externally with a diamond diaper border above a floral design (Fig. 119.12).

Wall Tiles

Fragments of blanks for wall tiles were recovered and dated to between *c.* 1730–55 (Fig. 118.27). The tiles were formed on a layer of fine moulding sand and have bevelled edges while some examples dating from *c.* 1755 have a small pointed stab mark in at least one corner of the tile. No complete tiles or sizable fragments were recovered and therefore the whole dimensions are not known, but they are in excess of 95mm, while the thickness of tiles ranged between 6–8mm. One (*c.* 1755) biscuit ware tile was found with a reddish brown surface deposit, probably an unfired glaze or slip. This sort of waster was also found at Norfolk House where it was believed that the coating was applied before the biscuit firing, but the authors found it difficult to explain (Bloice 1971, 142). Only one glazed tile fragment was found, plain blue in colour.

Decoration

The glazed wares have been classified according to Orton (1988, 321–327) and expanded by reference to the Museum of London Specialist Services classification.

Generic designs not covered by the classification system (TGW): these are mostly blue and white wares dating to the late 17th and 18th centuries and at their simplest comprise blue horizontal bands on such forms as the dispensing/storage jar. Other sherds with blue on white designs include a Britton's type H plate with blue 'dots' and an external lead glaze (Fig. 119.1), dating to the late 17th century. Another sherd has four dots in a diamond pattern. A more complex design with horizontal blue bands and simple floral motifs, dated *c.* 1740–50 was found on a fragment of a hemispherical bowl with a simple rim and another with a possible Chinese scroll design (Fig. 119.2 – Fig. 119.3). Purple on white decoration was restricted to a possible jug with purple bands and a floral design (Fig. 119.4).

Style C

Plain white (TGW C), plain whitewares are dated from *c.* 1630 and throughout the 18th century, but are most common in 17th-century deposits. Two sherds are present in a layer dated *c.* 1660–80 and examples came from all phases of the kiln. Forms decorated in plain white ware are bowls and dishes, chamber pots, ointment pots, plates of Britton's type I, porringers of type C and hollow pedestal bases belonging either to salts or wet drug jars or another form.

Plain blue

Plain blue glazed wares (TGW BLUE) date from *c.* 1630 into the early 19th century, although domestic deposits show that they are rare in the 17th century but common thereafter. The colour can vary from a mid to duck-egg blue. This is the most common glazed ware in material from Kiln 1. Plain blue forms are represented by hemispherical type 2 bowls (hooked rims), a medium rounded bowl, chamber pots, a rounded cup, ointment pot types B, D and E, plates of Britton's type I, a porringer and a wall tile.

Style D

Mid 17th-century geometrical or polychrome designs (TGW D) are rare from the excavations. There are three vessels dated 1660–80, firstly as a charger with blue bands and a possible star motif and secondly as a porringer of shape B with four internal horizontal blue bands, both with external lead-glaze. A residual charger sherd occurred in the latest *c.* 1755-dated dump with a yellow and blue geometrical-floral design and an external blue lead based glaze.

Style F

The 'Chinamen in grasses' (TGW F) style was current between *c.* 1670–90 and a sherd of a fluted dish (Fig. 119.5) present in Kiln 2, Phase 1, is decorated with landscape elements executed in this style, but in dark blue on a light blue background. This sherd is possibly residual.

Style H

Although 17th-century Ligurian *berettino* wares share this dark blue designs on a paler blue background (TGW H) colour scheme, an inspiration for this style may well have been the inferior blue and white Chinese porcelains being imported at this time. Stylistically this decoration dates to *c.* 1680–1800. The simplest designs are found on the ointment pots, particularly of shapes D and E, decorated with alternating vertical blue lines of either different lengths, or

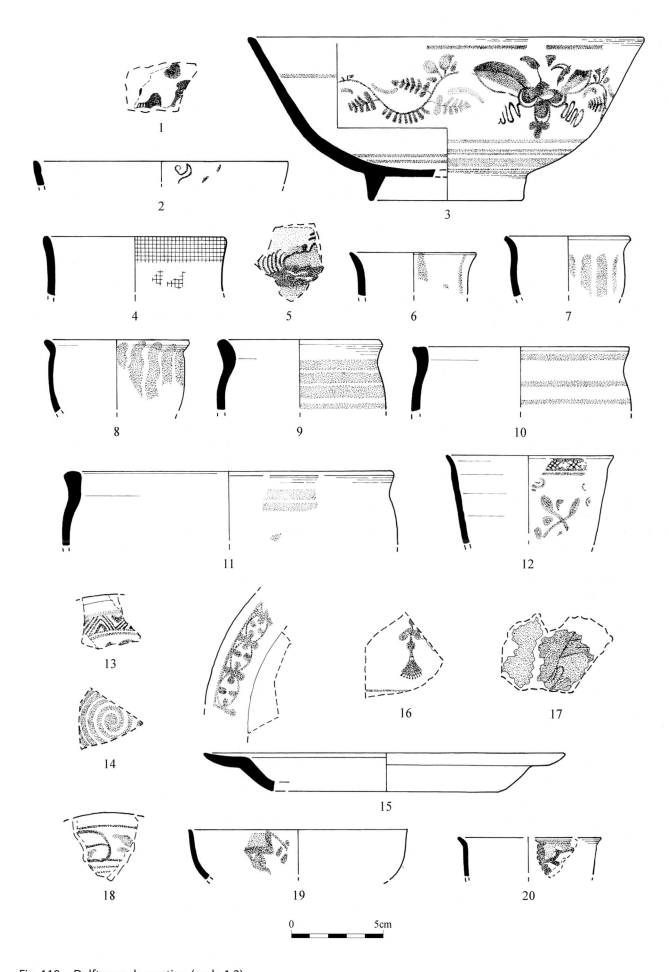

Fig. 119   Delftware decoration (scale 1:2)

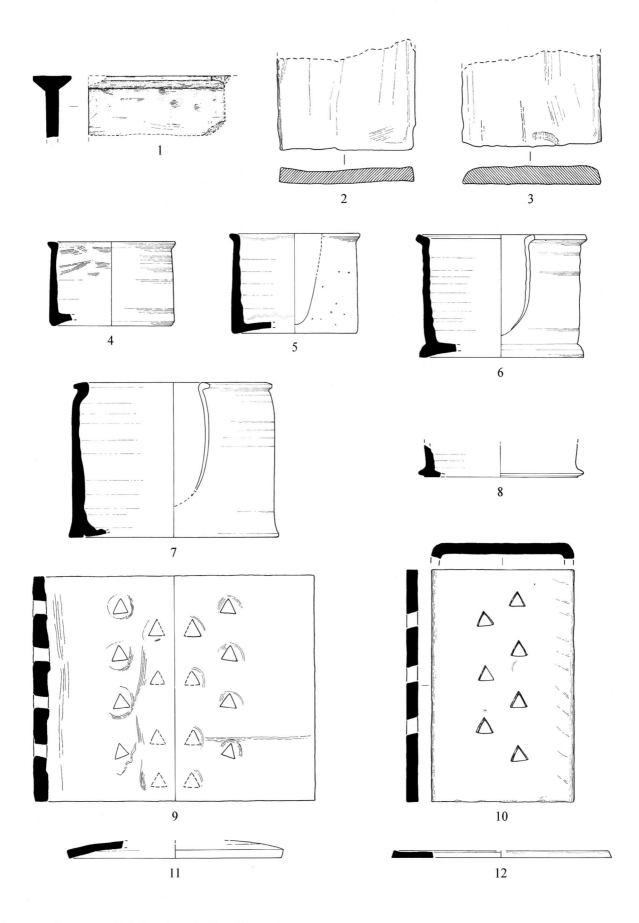

Fig. 120   Saggars and kiln furniture (scale 1:4)

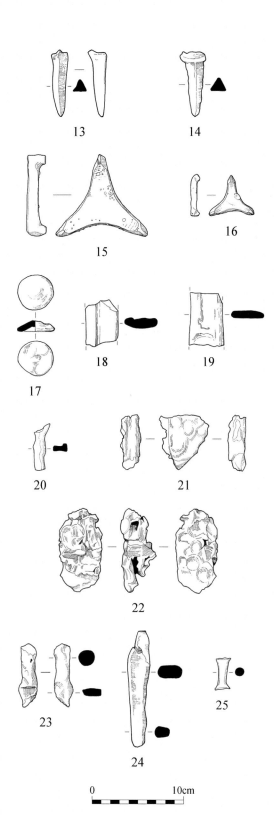

13   14

15   16

17   18   19

20   21

22

23   24   25

0   10cm

with wavy lines and rarely with scrolls (Fig. 119.6 – Fig. 119.8). This style of decorated ointment pots occurs more towards the mid 18th century. Horizontal bands are found in groups of either two or four on the shoulders of storage/dispensing jars (Fig. 119.9–Fig. 119.11) here dated *c.* 1755, but generally dated from *c.* 1690/1700 onwards.

Other geometrical designs include swags, a diamond trellis border as on a vase (Fig. 119.12), a herringbone central border (Fig. 119.13) and a spiral (Fig. 119.14) on a plate base. Most of the borders would date to the second quarter of the 18th century. The spiral, although found on mid and late 17th-century chargers, is more common on plates as part of a floral motif attributed to Lambeth in the third quarter of the 18th century (Archer 1997, A 46, A49, 97–8, B36–38, 134–5). There is also an example of a border on a plate (Fig. 119.15) dating to *c.* 1715–25 (Archer 1997, B197, 206) and a pendulous flower motif (Fig. 119.16). Many of these borders occur with Chinoiserie floral (Fig. 119.17) and landscape designs, mostly dating to the 1730s and 1740s.

Forms decorated with style H motifs are hemispherical bowls (Fig. 119.16), storage/dispensing jars (Fig. 119.9–Fig. 119.11), ointment pots (Fig. 119.6–Fig. 119.8), plates (Fig. 119.13–Fig. 119.15, Fig. 119.17, Fig. 119.18), saucers (Fig. 119.19), tea bowls (Fig. 119.20) and a vase (Fig. 119.12). The style of decoration is recognised in the waster material from 1700/30 onwards.

Kiln furniture

Kiln bars or Girders

These items were rarely encountered and appear late in the sequence (*c.* 1755). They have the appearance of girders with T-shaped ends (Fig. 120.1). Interestingly, the girders at the Norfolk House pot house were also a later development, being present only in Groups X–XII, dated *c.* 1725 –1737+ and layer 12 in Kiln B to after 1737 (Bloice 1971, 143, 147).

Shelves

Supported by the kiln bars, shelves were used within the kiln to stack the saggars on. Shelves were numerous in the deposits studied but all were fragmentary and none could be reconstructed to give their complete dimensions. As at Norfolk House, Lambeth, they were divided into two types, first as those with straight edges (Fig. 120.2) and secondly those with rounded edges (Fig. 120.3). These rectangular-shaped items have widths ranging between 152–162mm and lengths in excess of 172mm. They were made in the same way as ceramic roofing tiles, as clay forced into moulds lined with a layer of moulding sand and the top struck off. The type 1 shelves are dated from *c.* 1660 until the closure of the pot house in *c.* 1755 while the type 2 examples only occur from *c.* 1730.

Saggars

These forms were used as protective containers for vessels during firing, helping to prevent smoke and thermal damage. They are divided into two basic categories:

Type 1 saggars are generally defined as cylindrical shape vessels with bases and U-shaped cut-outs, removing part of the rim and extending to above or on the basal angle (Fig. 120.4–Fig. 120.8). On mostly larger vessels there is a central hole in the base, possibly made with a tool rather than a finger tip. These vessels are crudely made and show a wide range of sizes and shapes. Where complete profiles of saggars could be reconstructed they ranged in height between 22–182mm, while rim and base diameters both ranged between 90–300mm. The rims were variable and include slightly thickened, bevelled, collared, clubbed, hammerhead, hooked, squared, triangular and lid seated profiles, while bases were flat or concave, often with wire marks showing their removal from the wheel. Some saggar bases have a splayed embellishment (Fig. 120.6–120.8) and these may occasionally be lathed to give more angular profiles.

A few changes over time can be seen in the saggars. First, marbled fabrics occur from c. 1660 until c. 1730, indicating a cursory mixing of the clays was deemed adequate for these forms. The fabrics of these vessels from c. 1730 are uniform in appearance and all saggars are in a white coloured fabric. Turning to vessel shapes, conical and albarello (waisted at the top and bottom of the wall) profiled examples occur from c. 1700 and a shouldered jar-shaped type (Fig. 120.7) is present c. 1755. Of note were the use of clay pads, one placed on the base of a vessel and used to level it while stacking the kiln, and the other pad on a rim probably used to keep the saggars temporarily together.

Type 2 saggars (Fig. 120.9) were used in the firing of flat wares and are defined as open-ended with triangular piercings to take pegs (see below). All, except for one example of this vessel class, are cylindrical (type 2a) and these were made by rolling out a rectangle of clay, more often on a bed of moulding sand, with the ends frequently tapering. The clay rectangle was formed into a cylinder and the tapered ends allowed for an even wall thickness on the seam join. Staggered pairs of triangular piercings were then made in four discrete columns evenly spaced around the cylinder. A saggar such as that shown in Fig. 120.9 would have accommodated eight glazed plates to be fired. All the saggars were fragmentary and no complete examples could be reconstructed. Only two incidences could be found to demonstrate that four columns of piercings were used. This is in contrast to saggars from other kiln sites, such as Norfolk House where three pairs of columns were adequate to support a vessel rim contained within the saggar (Bloice 1971, 142). However, due to the fragmentary recovery of the form it is possible that this type of saggar is present at Montague Close. Surface treatment showed frequent scars from knife paring and internally the disruption of the vessel wall made by the triangular piercings was always trimmed to a flat surface. These vessels ranged in height between 402–510mm and have a diameter range of 180–380mm,

so reflecting the size of plates and dishes to be fired. The c. 1755-dated type 2 saggars have piercings made with a handled tool as the circular impression of the end of the handle is frequently found surrounding the triangle (Fig. 120.9). In the kiln these vessels were stacked on top of each other and occasionally pads of clay were found on the rim to keep them in place. The vessels are also frequently covered internally with blue and white glaze, either as splashes, runs or with extensive surface coverage.

There was a single instance of a square or rectangular saggar with triangular piercings (type b) which survives as a single wall with rounded corners, 250mm tall by 162mm wide (Fig. Fig. 120.10). It was formed by rolling out a slab of clay and the moulding sand survives on the exterior. The triangular piercings (trimmed on the inside) survive as a single column of staggered pairs. This form was present in the 1969–73 Montague Close assemblage and a fragmentary example is known from Norfolk House (Bloice 1971, 143). What it was used to protect during firing is uncertain. Square or rectangular shaped flat wares are not found amongst the wasters. However, at the Mortlake pot house, in operation between 1745–1823, a box-like vessel is reported with pairs of closely spaced rectangular holes for same shaped pegs. There is uncertainty over the use of the saggar, the pegs being unsuitable to fire glazed plates, and some doubt about its applicability in firing tiles, if it was used like an upright toast rack (Stephenson 2003, 78–79).

Saggar Lids

These are flat or slightly convex shaped circular discs of clay, some with bevelled edges (Fig. 120.11, Fig. 120.12). Although fragmentary, they range in diameter between 150–380mm. Their purpose would have been to seal off the top of the column of stacked saggars and give additional protection from the smoke in the kiln. They were recorded from between c. 1700–55 and are illustrated by Diderot (1725–65, plate VIII) in conjunction with type 2 saggars.

Pegs

There were two types of pegs recovered, the first and earliest (Fig. 120.13) has a tapering, triangular cross-section and range in length between 43mm and 62mm and occurs only in the material pertaining to c. 1700–30. These are superseded by the second type with a head (nail-shaped in plan, Fig. 120.14) and occur in two sizes, the small examples ranging between 40–54mm and the less common larger type ranging between 66–68mm. The second type of pegs (both large and small) are present only in the latest, c. 1755 dated, material.

Trivets

These three-pronged items with pinched ends were used to keep glazed vessels, such as chargers, separate during firing; the points placed on the internal glazed basal surface and the base or footring of another charger placed on the flat surface of the trivet. Glazed chargers often show the three internal scars left behind by the scars from the trivet points. Only one complete trivet was recovered from the kiln dumps (Fig. 120.15). It measured 94mm long by 86mm wide, but unlike all the other trivet fragments it did not have moulding sand on its flat surface. An unstratified smaller example is also illustrated (Fig. 120.16). Trivets were made by rolling out an area of clay, mostly onto a layer of moulding sand, then the trivet was cut to shape and the ends pinched upwards. The sandy surface not only prevented the clay sticking to the working surface during rolling, but would have helped to prevent vessels fusing together from glaze runs during firing.

Trivets were present throughout the use of Kiln 1, but only in the first phase of Kiln 2 and therefore coincide with the production of chargers, which went out of fashion by *c.* 1740. As flat wares became more common, pegs superseded trivets.

Setters

Pads and setters were used to keep vessels separated during firing or used to level stacked saggars. Most of these setters or pads were made by the kiln stacker as he required them for the purpose of loading the kiln and perhaps only the final setter described here was purpose-made for this job. The earliest setter recorded here is from a *c.* 1660–80 layer and comprises a concave (or bossed) disc (Fig. 120.17). Several examples of flat strips, rounded and cylindrical-shaped lumps of white fired clay were recovered from all phases of the kiln and its abandonment (Fig. 120.18–Fig. 120.24). They often have finger impressions, as well as the imprint of vessels. For example (Fig. 120.22) may have been partly moulded around a trivet. The sausage of clay was slightly twisted during forming and the strips of clay have a layer of moulding sand. A single item of kiln furniture has been described as a setter and has concave sides and the general shape of a 'finger bone' (Fig. 120.25). It can be paralleled amongst the Norfolk House kiln waste (Bloice, 1971, fig. 19A, 119–120).

Fig. 121   Examples of kiln furniture recovered from the excavations

DELFTWARE KILN DISCUSSION

Previous archaeological work on the site suggests that there were two kilns operating during the late 17th and early 18th centuries (Dawson 1976). With the exception of the very fragmentary remains to the west of the eastern wall of the chapter house, the kilns reinvestigated during the Millennium excavations were, according to documentary sources, located in the 'new pot house' first mentioned in a lease of 1681 (Edwards 1974, 71–72). Plans of the pottery, based on Dollman (1881) show this building immediately to the east of the 'Kiln House', a property that appears to have been remodelled from the Priory's chapter house some time between 1624 and 1634 (Dawson 1976, 57). Excavation has shown that both buildings incorporated the northern wall of the chapel of St John and the east wall of the chapter house.

The earliest meaningful kiln remains in the Kiln House had two rectangular barrel-vaulted firing chambers each with its own flue and stoke hole (Dawson 1976, 55). This kiln was later replaced by another with a single chamber, possibly around 1700 (Dawson 1976, 53,57). Although documentary evidence would suggest that the new pot house kiln existed by 1681, there was little archaeological dating evidence for the construction date of Kiln 1. The alterations to the kiln during Phase 2, however, produced pottery suggesting a 1700–1730 date range for this event. Kiln 1 was replaced by Kiln 2 in about 1730 and this remained in use, with many modifications, until *c.* 1755 when documentary records suggest the pottery closed.

The Dollman plan of the pottery implies that the 'new pot house' measured about 11m east–west by over 23m north–south indicating its eastern wall lay beyond the limit of excavation. However, a brick wall, about 1.5m short of the predicted location may well be the eastern wall of the pot house, at basement level. Other walls found nearer to the kiln are presumably internal features, built as partition walls within the pot house, or perhaps to support the other floors of the building, which is reported to have had three stories (Britton 1987, 42). Early 19th-century engravings (eg Fig. 108) show a two-storied building, but levels on the floors of the kilns suggest that, as might be anticipated, it sat within a basement. The apparent retention of an earlier flint wall foundation may indicate that the recorded dimensions of the new pot house relate to a later phase which may have evolved and expanded from the building mentioned in the 1681 lease.

In the 17th and 18th centuries the main local suppliers of pottery to the London market tended to specialise in certain vessel forms. The local redware industry made mostly kitchen, serving, storage, horticultural and industrial wares. The Surrey-Hampshire red and white Border ware industry also produced kitchen and serving wares, and in addition drinking vessels and tablewares, usually finer and smaller than the coarse redware repertoire. The stoneware industry largely restricted itself to drinking (serving and consumption) and storage forms. The delftware industry provided decorative wares: for the table, and for the drinking of tea and similar beverages, in addition to pharmaceutical and display items. Tin-glazed earthenware has a major disadvantage, for it is not a hardwearing product, so few items are associated with the kitchen and if so they are only those suitable for light duties, such as strainers, which could also be part of the table or tea wares. Although many of the same forms were manufactured by different local pottery industries (eg chamber pots, drinking wares), and some forms by all of them, despite some changes over time, such as the end of the white Border ware industry in *c.* 1700, all the different local wares complimented each other and aimed for certain niches in the market.

The larger groups of wasters from the site show that certain types of wares were more commonly made at different times than others; however, the wasters reflect what the pot house failed to make rather than what it successfully produced and marketed. Table 1 (see appendix) lists the larger waster deposits (layer [3364], Kiln 1, Phase 2, and Kiln 2, Phase 5) and the function and use groups of delftware wasters. The number of pottery categories does slowly increase over time from seven recorded in layer [3364] to eleven in the final kiln group. Ignoring the prominence of the kiln furniture in each of the groups, there are four main functional categories, namely drinking, hygiene, multi-functional and tableware vessels. The prominence of each of these groups does differ in each of the waster deposits. In the 1660–80 dated layer [3364] tablewares, such as the chargers and porringers account for 48.5% and drinking wares, including the posset pots and their lids (the covers category) account for 16.2% and 7.2% respectively. Interestingly the only occurrence of heating or lighting wares (candlesticks) is also found in this layer. Kiln 1, Phase 2, dated *c.* 1700–30 was largely dominated by hygiene wares, but exclusively as pharmaceutical forms, 70.4% by EVE's, with only drinking wares a notable component as 13.4%. There is a much more even distribution of functions associated with the final use of the kiln and end of the pot house. Tablewares (33.3%) are the main functional group and may be linked to the demands and development of the formal 18th-century dining and eating habits. However, nearly as important are the hygiene wares (36.9%), mainly as pharmaceutical forms, but also the sanitary chamber pots, which are more common in this group than ever before.

The glazed wares are fairly rare in the waster deposits studied, accounting for 1.7% EVE's in layer [3364] and in the larger pottery groups from the kiln as 1.4% in Kiln 1, Phase 2, 5.8% in Kiln 2, Phase 5 as 9.1%, and for all the deposits 8.3%. A low ratio of glazed wares was also recognised at the Norfolk House excavation and an explanation was for a greater discard rate at the biscuit firing stage, while greater care was taken in the second (glazed) and final firing of the delftware product (Bloice 1971, 141). The tin-glazed wasters from the previous excavation were commented on as having few 18th-century polychrome wares, which are almost absent from this phase of analysis. The predominance of plain blue wares would indicate that the Montague Close delftware kiln was aiming at the lower end of the market, an observation made also by Graham Dawson (*pers comm*). Otherwise, the output of forms from this pot house does appear to be similar to other pot houses and further indicates a fairly uniform London industry. There are very few indications of specialist items, such as flower bricks, pill tiles, figurines, etc, and no evidence for the decorative salts found at Hibernia Wharf and attributed to the Montague Close pot house. Work in progress on the 1750s dated wasters recovered from the 1969–73 excavation shows that urns and other forms, besides the kiln furniture reported here are diagnostic to this period, but a commonly occurring mug type with a distinctive base and colander bowls could not be easily distinguished in the contemporary 1999 excavation wasters (Dawson 2006, 5–6).

It is not clear why the Montague Close kiln closed, as tin-glazed ware was still very much in demand at this time. Even during the last five years of production, there were two major changes to Kiln 2 (Phase 3 and 4) possibly reflecting attempts to keep up with competition, although these indicated contraction of the kiln's firing chamber. Elsewhere in London, manufacturers of tin-glazed ware were diversifying into stoneware. Excavations at Fulham have revealed rectangular stoneware kilns, not dissimilar to those at Montague Close being used during the 17th and 18th century before the circular bottle kilns which dominated 19th-century production were introduced from the late 18th century onwards (Crossley 1990, 274).

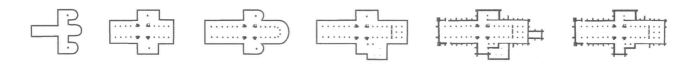

Chapter 6   Conclusions

Victoria Ridgeway

EARLY ACTIVITY

Features of prehistoric date have been found in the vicinity of Southwark Cathedral, such as the ring-ditch at Fenning's Wharf, approximately 100m to the northeast of the site, indicative of significant prehistoric activity along the edge of the river (Watson *et al* 2001, 8–10). However, no unequivocally contemporary features were identified during the Millennium excavations. The earliest deposits recorded at the site consisted of sandy layers similar to those recorded at many other sites across the north Southwark islands but not surprisingly, given the extent of later activity, these appeared to have been disturbed. Nevertheless, 32 pieces of struck flint and prehistoric pottery were recovered; the struck flint included a Mesolithic type pyramidal core and the pottery most likely dated to the Bronze Age (Bishop 2001). These demonstrate that, as across the north Southwark islands, human groups were at least visiting the site from the earliest formation of the islands onwards and reflects the potential of the area for future research.

THE ROMAN PERIOD

Road 2

The earliest evidence for intensive activities at the site comes from the Roman period. The Millennium excavations have added to the emerging picture of Roman settlement in north Southwark and more specifically the construction and subsequent maintenance of Road 2, its adjacent land use and roadside buildings. The earliest evidence for road construction identified in plan was dated *c.* AD 55–60, though an earlier and narrower manifestation was identified to the northwest at the Bonded Warehouse. Whilst details of the road's construction, its date, associated quarrying, maintenance and resurfacing were all forthcoming, there was no evidence for any associated roadside settlement until the 2nd century, perhaps reflecting a general expansion of Southwark at that time. Unfortunately, very little of the roadside buildings survived, due to truncation by the basements of warehouses built in the 19th century; those elements that did were preserved fortuitously by slumping into earlier deeply cut features, rendering ground plans incomplete and patchy.

It has been established that Road 1 was constructed in about AD 50, the bridge linking Southwark with London shortly afterwards and Road 2 by *c.* AD 60. The construction of the road was clearly a major undertaking and it was initially well-maintained, particularly through the first few decades of its use, but the motivation behind its construction remains a matter for debate, as does its course and final destination to the southwest of the site. It has been suggested that major construction projects such as this would generally be undertaken by the military and that this is the case in Southwark (e.g. Sheldon 1978, 28; Merrifield 1965, 35). The involvement of the military has been much-debated elsewhere (eg Cowan 2003; Yule 2005) and it is not the author's intention to replicate those arguments here; as Cowan (2003, 81) concludes the evidence is ambiguous and the Millennium excavations have not produced any evidence to further support or refute a military origin and presence.

As discussed in detail above (see Chapter 2, Period 1 Discussion) if, as Sheldon (1978) suggests, the road continued to a crossing point of the Thames between Lambeth and Westminster, provision would have to be made for it to cross two channels, presumably carried on a timber raft, as was Road 1 at 106–114 Borough High Street (Schwab 1978). Various scenarios have been proposed: wooden piles and puddled clay found at 51 Southwark Street in 1866 (Bird and Graham 1978, 525, site 85) on the projected line of Road 2 were interpreted as possible supports to carry the road over marshy ground. However, recent excavation has disproved this interpretation (Killock 2005); the road may have turned south, crossing the channel further east (Dillon *et al* 1991, 258), or it may not have extended beyond the island, primarily being built to service the local area (eg Heard *et al* 1990, 611). What is clear is that no conclusive evidence for the road has been found to the southwest of Southwark Cathedral. Had the road continued on the same alignment it would have passed within metres of the excavations at the Courage Brewery site, but none of the buildings found on that site were aligned with the projected route of Road 2 (Cowan 2003, 78–79). However, the road need not necessarily have extended in a straight line as the layout of settlement and associated roads on the north island may have largely been influenced by topographic factors. In summary, therefore, there is no irrefutable evidence for Road 2 extending beyond the Cathedral and, whilst not proven, the possibility must at least be considered that it extended no further than this general area. This is clearly a matter that can only be resolved by further excavation.

However, assuming the road did not extend far beyond the modern-day Cathedral, what was its purpose and where did it go? Yule (2005, 75) suggests that the 2nd- to 4th-century building complex at Winchester Palace, to the northwest of Southwark Cathedral, was linked to Road 2 to the south. Earlier developments at Winchester Palace, including clay and timber buildings dated *c*. AD 60 – AD 80 and later AD 80 –120 masonry buildings may also have been accessed via Road 2, as well as from the river. The earliest possible road identified at Winchester Palace (Road 3), founded before AD 60, was aligned parallel to Road 1 (Yule 2005, 46).

No buildings contemporary with the construction of the road were identified during the Millennium excavations. However, evidence for a 1st-century structure was uncovered during excavations in the Cathedral crypt (Hammerson 1978, 207), and the recovery of an assemblage of potentially late 1st- to mid 3rd-century statues with fragments of a votive altar and tombstone, interpreted by the excavator as possibly deriving from a mausoleum, may be significant. To this evidence may be added an assemblage of mid 2nd-century pottery recovered from a ditch to the northwest of the Cathedral, containing unusually high quantities of tazzae which may derive from a nearby shrine (see Chapter 2, Period 3 pottery). These suggest that a religious building, possibly a mausoleum or temple, may have been located in the vicinity of the Cathedral. Henig (2001) has suggested that the remains found beneath the Cathedral '...are suggestive of the presence of a temple to Attis on the approach to London bridge, at the only point of entry to the capital from the south', comparing this to the triangular temple at Verulamium, also at a boundary location (the crossing point of the Thames, in the case of Southwark Cathedral) and possibly dedicated to Attis.

For how long the road and its adjacent area remained in use remains a matter for debate; the latest building identified, Building 4, appears to have been occupied into the late 3rd century, there was a dearth of 4th-century pottery recovered, though this may be a factor of truncation.

Roadside Settlement

The site is low-lying and drainage measures appeared to be critical throughout the Roman period; the maintenance of a roadside ditch in early phases and the insertion of a box-drain (Drain 1) crossing the road and emptying into the roadside ditch reflect this concern. However, the construction of Drain 2, crossing the road from southwest to northeast, appears to have been a major undertaking. The drain ran parallel to Road 1, as did most of the buildings post-dating the construction of the drain around AD 120. It was substantial at approximately 0.9m wide and at least 1m deep and its excavation would have been demanding, the compacted surfaces of the road being difficult to dig through. Although there are no structural reasons to suggest that road surfaces did not continue above the drain, no evidence for any road resurfacing which could be confidently dated to after the drain's construction were identified. The area adjacent to the road to the southeast remained peripheral into the early 2nd century. Pits and dumps

indicate marginal activities, although this area was perhaps within the backyards of properties fronting onto Road 1. To the northwest of the roadside ditch no deep cut features were identified. Although truncation by warehousing had removed 1st- and early 2nd-century ground levels and some buildings may have been present, the threat of frequent inundation from the Thames suggests this unlikely and the area perhaps remained peripheral to the main focus of settlement. The need for drainage is certainly evidenced by ditch maintenance and drain construction, whilst the road remained important as evidenced by episodes of resurfacing.

Building adjacent to the road commenced in the second quarter of the 2nd century, although this appears to have been an intense but short-lived episode. The clay and timber buildings, which only survived patchily, appeared initially to respect the alignment of Road 2, but these were superseded by buildings in similar locations aligned to Road 1. It may be that Road 2 had been abandoned or was becoming less significant as the 2nd century drew to a close. This suggestion may be supported by the construction of Drain 2 cutting the road on a roughly north–south alignment, again parallel to Road 1, and possibly indicating Road 2's demise.

Evidence for 3rd-century occupation is less extensive. A hearth in Building 4 and an associated well were used into the late 3rd century. A well in the Cathedral crypt was constructed by or not long after AD 270 and a 4th-century well was excavated at Montague Close (Graham 1978). Although the relative lack of other features of this date may partly be a result of later truncation, elsewhere at the site, in Trenches 1, 3, 4 and 5, the earlier Roman occupation deposits were overlain by dark, predominantly sandy silt deposits. Equivalent deposits in Trench 2 had been largely truncated by the Victorian warehouse basements. These deposits resembled the 'dark earth' such as is frequently found sealing Roman occupation sites. However, excavation in Trench 1 revealed an intense sequence of intercutting pits, which had removed virtually all traces of the 'dark earth' layers suggesting that, although actual settlement of the area may have contracted, use of the land continued, albeit in a different form. Here the late 2nd-century decline in occupation appears to reflect that observed at many sites in Southwark (eg Sheldon 1978, 36–39) though this appears in contrast to sites investigated further west in northwest Roman Southwark (Yule 2005, 85).

In conclusion, the road is of substantial and early construction but questions remain as to why it was constructed and where it goes. The evidence remains inconclusive and only further excavation will elucidate the direction and final destination of the road. Well-maintained throughout the 1st century, there is little evidence of adjacent contemporaneous occupation from the Millennium excavations. Although roadside ditches and surfaces were maintained, environmental evidence and the lack of building evidence combine to indicate an area peripheral to the main focus of settlement, which was alongside Road 1 and the approach to the bridgehead. This situation changed in the early 2nd century, buildings lined the road and further drainage measures were put in place and by the middle of the century a substantial drain was constructed crossing the road aligned to Road 1.

The association of early Christian churches with Roman remains is a topic well-discussed elsewhere (eg Morris and Roxan 1980, Bell 1998) and given the density of Roman occupation within an urban context such as Southwark, the association of the Cathedral with Roman building remains *per se* might be seen as no more than coincidence. However, the religious items found by Hammerson and the tazzae found during the Millennium excavations appear to point to a religious focus, a mausoleum or perhaps temple. The siting of churches on the sites of former mausolea is not without precedent, such as at Lullingstone and Stone-by-Faversham in Kent (Taylor and Taylor 1965, Fletcher and Meates 1969), and here may be more than mere coincidence.

Although it remains very conjectural, the suggestion of a mausoleum or other possible religious focus, combined with a lack of evidence to date for the road continuing beyond the Cathedral, may indicate that the road was constructed primarily to serve such a building or complex. In his discussion of the sculptures found in the well beneath the Cathedral, Hammerson (1978, 211–212) concludes: 'It may not, of course, be entirely coincidental that a Christian Church was later founded on the same spot, and that the figures came from a building with some religious significance for which a religious tradition persisted…' That coincidence could be extended to the existence of a substantial, well-maintained road extending from the river crossing to the site of the Cathedral, with no evidence for it beyond this point. However, as Hammerson continues: '…there is as yet no archaeological evidence to bridge a very wide time-gap, the first Christian foundation on the site appearing to date from the mid-9th century.'

SAXON AND MEDIEVAL ACTIVITY

As established above, in spite of suggestions of a possible nunnery on the site as early as the 7th century (Stow 1994, 52), there is still no conclusive archaeological evidence for the construction of a church on the site before the 12th century.

Large pits excavated by Dawson (1976, 45) were interpreted by him as possible elements of a large wooden church, the *monasterium* alluded to in Domesday book. However, although numerous, morphologically similar, pits were investigated during the Millennium excavations these appeared to have been used for the disposal of domestic waste. Structural evidence for the *monasterium* is disappointingly inconclusive and, although a short length of foundation trench was revealed, it makes an unsatisfactory building element. The pits, which were predominantly dated to the latter half of the 11th century, have demonstrated relatively intense activity. It is possible that they do relate to an earlier church building, the structural elements of which were not archaeologically recognisable; the pits demonstrate domestic waste disposal in the Saxo-Norman period, their layout is well-ordered and their alignment reflects that of the Cathedral. Perhaps of interest in this regard is Hammerson's

discovery, in the Cathedral crypt, of the foundations of two walls of unknown date, but which truncated Roman building and pitting activity, one of which had been extensively robbed in or after the 16th century (Hammerson 1978, 212).

Evidence for the post-Conquest priory church and its subsequent history was more persuasive. The Millennium excavations provided only tantalising glimpses of the medieval priory, due to the 'keyhole' nature of the investigations. Nevertheless, examination of this data in conjunction with the known history of the priory and the results of the building recording have helped to illuminate the constructional history of the priory buildings.

The Millennium Project at Southwark Cathedral has enabled the collaboration of numerous disciplines and demonstrated the value of considering the upstanding masonry remains (the 'built' as opposed to the 'buried' heritage resource) in conjunction with the evidence provided by archaeological investigation, documentary references and antiquarian records. Combining these various strands of evidence has enabled the early construction history and the story of the Cathedral and its environs throughout the medieval and later periods to be fully illuminated. The detailed nature of the hand-drawn records, together with the production of a written and photographic archive also highlights the value of training in building recording techniques.

The early history of the Cathedral building was eventful and appears to have been a more-or-less continuous process of improvement and modification, with periods of more intense activity prompted by catastrophic events, such as fire and flood. The building recording works and excavation have enabled the form of the Augustinian priory church as founded in 1106 to be suggested. This model proposes a cruciform building with a central tower, a relatively short apse at the east end and apsidal chapels to the north and south. An intermediate phase of building between this and the documented 13th-century rebuilding is proposed. Two possible forms for the remodelled church are suggested. The first (as propounded by Roffey, 1998) suggests a remodelling *c.* 1120–1130 resulting in a cruciform church with a squared east end and square-ended chapels to north and south. However, a second, preferred, scenario is presented, which sees the chapels to north and south retaining their apsidal form and the choir extended to the east with a larger, apsidal ambulatory at the east end. Both building survey and archaeological excavations at the northwest of the Cathedral indicate that towards the end of the 12th century the nave was extended to the west and the cloisters rebuilt.

The fact that two such different scenarios can be presented demonstrates that there is still much to be discovered and indicates the value of continued recording work around the church.

Extensive rebuilding during the 13th and into the 14th centuries was initially prompted by the destruction of much of the Cathedral by fire in the early 13th century and subsequently hampered, throughout the century, by episodes of flooding and fire. This resulted in the more familiar ground plan for the Cathedral: a cruciform building, albeit asymmetrical with the Chapel of St Mary Magdalene built against the south transept chapel.

In addition to excavation and recording of the fabric of the church itself various other strands of evidence have been used to build the picture of the medieval priory church, including a survey of reused moulded stone within the church and study of the intricate timber vaulted ceiling, constructed in response to fire damage in 1469 but subsequently dismantled in 1831. Some 50 roof bosses survive along with 19th-century illustrations, which have enabled details of the roof construction to be determined.

Very little of the claustral buildings to the north of the church were revealed during the excavation although elements of cloister and chapter house immediately north of the church were seen. Further information on the layout and appearance of the priory buildings can be gleaned from Dollman's survey and various early 19th-century images, which show elements of claustral buildings surviving within buildings only destroyed from the 1830s onwards when the area began to be extensively redeveloped. This redevelopment resulted in the removal of much archaeology when the basements of warehouses were built. What still remains undetermined is the relationship of the priory to the Thames; the proximity of the river and inlet to the west were almost certainly critical to the situation of the priory at its foundation.

POST-MEDIEVAL ACTIVITY

The Dissolution

It is concluded above that the priory had declined in importance by the early 16th century and that buildings may already have been falling into disrepair. Nevertheless the church survived the Dissolution relatively well and did not suffer deliberate demolition; buildings to the north passed into the hands of Sir Anthony Browne and the church became the Parish Church of St Saviour. However the fabric of the building continued to deteriorate until the early 17th century when the parishioners purchased the church from the crown and began a series of repairs. Again evidence from archaeological excavation and building recording, increasingly enhanced by historical information and contemporary images, has helped to build a picture of the building's structural history. A study of post-medieval funerary monuments within the Cathedral showed that whilst the wall monuments and chest tombs survive well the ledger slabs are deteriorating rapidly and becoming cracked and worn. It is concluded that measures to protect these primary historical documents should be taken urgently, whether by preservation *in situ* or by record.

Burial evidence

The investigations also provided a glimpse of the actual people who inhabited the priory and the parishioners of the later church. The re-examination of skeletal remains of priors recovered during Dawson's excavations from the chapter house and cloister has revealed indicators of a wealthy lifestyle, including alcohol consumption and a rich diet. Indications of possible 'zoning' of burials within the churchyards were revealed through examination of skeletal remains coupled with a study of the coffin grips recovered during excavation, although only a very small percentage of the total buried population was exposed, a policy of leaving the remains as undisturbed as possible being adopted. Remains of individuals buried in a confined area of three shaft graves to the north of the church, reflect the increasing pressure on space in north Southwark by the 19th century.

The process of urbanisation had already begun; by the 17th century a terrace of houses, the Chain Gate buildings, had been constructed adjacent to the southeast corner of the church, cesspits in the back of No 6 Chain Gate were constructed against the southern wall of the Lady Chapel and further, intensive pitting was found adjacent to the chapel's northern wall. The excavation of elements of these buildings provided an opportunity to test the accuracy of Dollman's plans, a valuable source for the layout and form of the priory at the beginning of the 19th century, and to demonstrate the accuracy of this source material.

The delftware pot house

The delftware pot house, with its kilns initially constructed within the former chapter house and subsequently slightly further east, using a corner formed by the north transept wall and the eastern wall of the chapter house, are a poignant reminder of the secularisation of land around the Parish Church. From the excavated evidence it has been possible to examine the form of two phases of kiln building and modifications to these as well as to define the products of the kilns and determine how these changed over time in response to changing demands and fashions. Chemical analysis of fabrics from other London delftware pot houses has shown that subtle differences in the composition of the 'fat' clays used can be detected and potential sources of localised clay can be determined (Hughes 2008,131). Future chemical analysis of the Montague Close pot house fabrics may help determine the source of clay, which, given the built-up nature of north Southwark in this period, may not have been as local as that determined at contemporary pot houses in more rural settings.

It is not, of course, possible to follow every potential line of research when dealing with the publication of developer-led and funded excavation, but it is hoped that this synthesis of evidence, helped by the provision by CoLAT of additional resources to enable the integration of building work undertaken by SCARP, provides a welcome interpretation of the changing fortunes of Southwark Cathedral and its environs throughout the last two millennia, and to point the way for future research, should the opportunity arise.

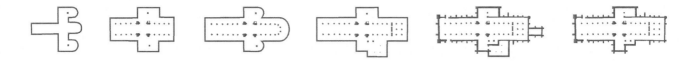

Chapter 7   Southwark Cathedral and the New Millennium: An Architectural Design Statement

Richard Griffiths Architects

The Millennium Project at Southwark Cathedral was inspired by the Dean's conviction that the much-loved Cathedral buildings needed to develop and expand in order to accommodate the ever-increasing pressure of activities that were taking place there for the Parish and for the Diocese, and to react to the challenge posed by the rapidly increasing number of people who were visiting the Cathedral by virtue of the new attractions of the Bankside area. The new Tate Gallery was planned, and the new Globe Theatre was under construction. More projects would follow, with new transport links such as the Jubilee Line extension and Thameslink 2000 planned or in the pipeline. Meanwhile, the Cathedral buildings and churchyard were difficult to find and difficult of access for people with disabilities, they were dirty and ill-lit, and their visibility and their accessibility needed to be dramatically improved. Space was needed for a new theological teaching library and for the formation of a new Girls' Choir. There was also

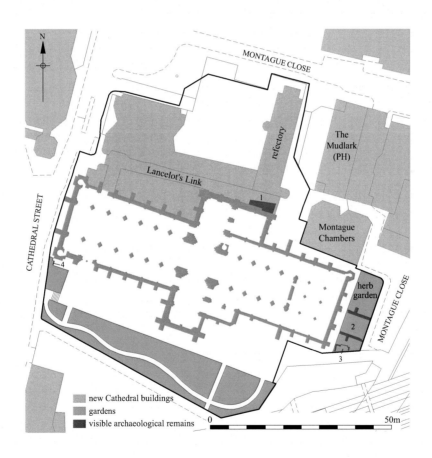

Fig. 122   The Cathedral in the New Millennium; new buildings and visible architectural remains (scale 1:1000)

1.   Remains of Roman road, Norman transept chapel, medieval Chapter House and Delftware kiln.
2.   Bishop's chapel incorporated into the herb garden
3.   Remains of no 6 Chain Gate buildings
4.   Remains of the hovel

Fig. 123   The new building from the north
© Dennis Gilbert/VIEW

advice from the Tourist Board that a ten-fold increase in the number of visitors to the Cathedral could be anticipated within a few years' time. The Dean and Chapter recognised that Southwark's moment had come, and submitted a successful first stage application to the Millennium Commission for a major grant towards their proposed Millennium Project.

The key to this bid was the purchase of Montague Chambers, a 19th-century office building just north of the Cathedral retro-choir. With its associated lands and rights of way they provided Southwark Cathedral with a tremendous opportunity. The three disjointed spaces around the Cathedral to the south, north and east could now, for the first time, be reunited into a single Cathedral precinct, to provide a worthy setting for the South Bank's most ancient and venerable building. At the same time, the accommodation offered by Montague Chambers would re-house its administrative functions, and allow the remaining Cathedral accommodation to be converted and extended to provide new and urgently required public facilities.

The Cathedral's Brief was to make the Cathedral and its precinct as welcoming, visible and accessible as possible to visitors. In detail, the aims were:

- To embrace and create a major new entrance for visitors approaching from the riverside walk to the north of the Cathedral.

- To make an exhibition, which tells the story of the Cathedral and of the surrounding area.
- To provide enlarged premises for the Cathedral shop.
- To rehouse the Cathedral refectory.
- To provide premises for a new theological teaching library.
- To provide improved accommodation for meetings and functions.
- To provide a new chair store to replace the existing store in the crypt.
- To concentrate all the Cathedral offices in Montague Chambers, and to integrate Montague Chambers into the Cathedral precinct.
- To improve landscaping and accessibility of the south churchyard.
- To integrate the inaccessible east churchyard into the precinct and to create a new formal garden.
- To allow full access the Cathedral and its buildings for those with disabilities.
- To clean the Cathedral of layers of damaging sulphurous grime to reveal the contrasting colours and textures of the flint walls with stone dressings.
- To floodlight all elevations of the Cathedral to identify it as the spiritual focus of the South Bank, by night as well as by day, and to announce its presence to visitors and passers-by alike.

Fig. 124   Construction of the new buildings, by Ptolemy Dean

Fig. 125   The permanent display within the covered street – kiln remains visible in the foreground, looking west

Fig. 126   Foundations of the Lady Chapel preserved in the herb garden to the east of the Cathedral

Richard Griffiths was appointed Cathedral Architect in 1997, shortly before the announcement that the Cathedral's project had been long-listed in the final round of the Millennium Lottery. Richard Griffiths Architects, with Ptolemy Dean as project architect, were appointed to take the project forward. A close examination of the historic layout of the area suggested the final solution. A new library and refectory wing partly encloses a court, which echoes the monastic cloister court that survived to the north of the Cathedral into the early years of the 19th century. A memory of the later 19th-century replacement of this, a densely packed cityscape of warehouses served by narrow alleyways, is recaptured with the recreation of the route of Montague Close, a glazed-over 'street' linking the Cathedral with its 1905 vestries to the 1980s chapter house, the proposed new additions and Montague Chambers. In essence a future is discovered through an understanding of the past. Following extensive consultation with the Cathedral's Fabric Commission for England, the Local Authority, national amenity societies and the public, the project received Planning and CFCE consents, and was awarded a major grant by the Millennium Lottery Fund.

Work on the archaeological excavation begun in 1998, revealing fragments of a Roman road, a Norman transept chapel, the medieval chapter house, and a remarkable 17th-century delftware kiln. These are now displayed permanently in the internal street. (Fig. 125). At the same time, substantial 19th-century brick retaining walls were uncovered from the former warehouses, which separated the Cathedral from the River Thames until the 1970s. These now line the basement link passageway between the new building and Montague Chambers. The foundations of the former Bishop's (or Lady) Chapel have also been uncovered as a part of the east churchyard works. This part of the Cathedral was demolished before the rebuilding of London Bridge in the 1830s. The foundations have now been capped and displayed permanently as a border to a new herb garden (Fig. 126).

A new two storey wing has been constructed to the north of the Cathedral, containing a refectory on the ground floor and a Cathedral library and function room on the first floor, lit by oak framed oriel windows overlooking the river. The new wing follows the form and function of the equivalent refectory range of the former Priory of St Mary Overie of which the undercroft survived into the 1830s. A further new range, containing a shop and further meeting rooms, links the new wing to the 1980s chapter house. The new building is constructed of stone walls with flint panels, with oak roofs covered in slate and copper, as exists elsewhere in the Cathedral precinct. Internally, however, the construction and detailing is clearly contemporary, with an exposed pre-cast concrete structure of ribs and vaults, and steel and glass balustrades.

The chapter house has been converted to house an exhibition about the history of the Cathedral and of the surrounding area, together with an enlarged Cathedral shop. The internal street between the Cathedral and the new buildings has been glazed over to provide a major circulation route evoking the memory of Montague Close, one of the characteristic Victorian alleyways, which used to follow this line. To the west the route is used by visitors as they leave the exhibition and enter the Cathedral. To the east the route leads to the Cathedral offices in Montague

Chambers, past the excavated remains of the 17th-century kiln for the manufacture of English delftware. School children visiting the education department in the basement of Montague Chambers will pass the archaeological remains of the kiln, exposed fragments of the Norman transepts, and the retaining walls of the former Victorian warehouses in the underground basement link.

The three disjointed spaces around the Cathedral to the south, north and east have, for the first time, been reunited into a single Cathedral precinct. The steps leading into the south churchyard from the southwest gateway have been moved to align with the main pathway through the churchyard, thereby allowing more space for the cramped roots of the magnificent plane tree. A wide bed of shrubbery has been planted against the south railings, next to a meandering path lined with a generous provision of benches. Ramps have been provided at both ends of the main path to allow unimpeded access to wheelchair users. The east churchyard, which is currently inaccessible, has been redesigned and opened to the public as a herb garden, referring to the origins of St Thomas' Hospital which originated in a chapel to the south of the Cathedral.

The Cathedral church began life as the Priory Church of St Mary Overie, became the Parish Church of St Saviour after the Dissolution, and only became Cathedral Church of the new Diocese of Southwark in 1905. The new buildings refer back to these monastic origins in both form and function, but also look forward to the future. They will allow the Cathedral church to fulfil its ever-growing role in serving the needs of parishioners, the local community and visitors alike.

The £10 million project was completed in 2001, and the new Millennium Buildings were opened by Dr Nelson Mandela on 28 April 2001.

APPENDIX 1: QUANTIFICATION OF DELFTWARE FORMS

The table presents quantification of delftware (Biscuit and Tin-glazed earthenware) forms by EVE's for layer [3364] and different phases of kilns. * indicates no EVE's could be calculated for the form.

Function	Shape	Layer [3364], c.1660-1680 EVE's	%	Kiln 1, Phase 1, c.1680/90-1700 EVE's	%	Kiln 1, Phase 2, c.1700-30 EVE's	%	Kiln 1, Phase 3, c.1730 EVE's	%	Kiln 2, Phase 1, c.1730-40 EVE's	%	Kiln 2, Phase 2, c.1730-50 EVE's	%	Kiln 2, Phase 3, c.1750 EVE's	%	Kiln 2, Phase 5, c.1755 EVE's	%
Ceramic building material	Wall tile									*						*	
Cover	Lid, domed							*									
	Lid, flanged	0.62	9.5													0.30	0.4
	Lid, teapot															1.80	2.4
	Sub-total	*0.62*	*9.5*					***								*2.10*	*2.8*
Display	Vase															0.10	0.1
Drinking	Cup					0.42	3.7									*	
	Cup, capuchine															0.10	0.1
	Cup, flared					0.07	0.6	0.12	6.5	0.09	17.6					0.30	0.4
	Cup, rounded					0.31	2.8			*		0.40	34.8			0.58	0.8
	Cup, straight-sided					0.55	4.9									0.43	0.6
	Jug					*										0.21	0.3
	Jug, barrel-shaped															*	
	Jug, rounded							*								*	
	Jug, small rounded	*															
	Mug															*	
	Mug, cylindrical															0.03	0.0
	Mug, rounded					0.20	1.8									0.18	0.2
	Mug, small rounded	*														0.11	0.1
	Posset					*		*									
	Posset, cylindrical	1.40	21.4			0.03	0.3										
	Saucer	0.08	1.2													0.50	0.7
	Tankard															*	
	Tea bowl					*				*						0.34	0.4
	Sub-total	*1.48*	*22.6*	***	***	*1.58*	*14.0*	*0.12*	*6.5*	*0.09*	*17.6*	*0.40*	*34.8*	***	***	*2.78*	*3.7*
Heating or lighting	Candlestick	*															
Hygiene	Albarello	*				3.25	28.9	0.10	5.4			0.24	20.9			1.33	1.8
	Barbers bowl															0.17	0.2
	Chamber pot					*		*		*		*		0.14	35.9	8.77	11.6
	Jar, spouted															0.49	0.6
	Jar, storage					0.98	8.7	*								1.98	2.6
	Ointment pot					*		0.33	17.8	0.17	33.3					4.69	6.2
	Ointment pot A					*											
	Ointment pot B					*										0.07	0.1
	Ointment pot C					4.08	36.2	0.32	17.3							2.41	3.2
	Ointment pot D							0.25	13.5							0.96	1.3
	Ointment pot E											0.30	26.1	0.25	64.1	7.94	10.5

		Layer [3364], c.1660-1680		Kiln 1, Phase 1, c. 1680/90-1700		Kiln 1, Phase 2, c. 1700-30		Kiln 1, Phase 3, c. 1730		Kiln 2, Phase 1, c. 1730-40		Kiln 2, Phase 2, c. 1730-50		Kiln 2, Phase 3, c. 1750		Kiln 2, Phase 5, c. 1755	
Function	*Shape*	*EVE's*	*%*	*EVE's*	*%*	*EVE's*	*%*	*EVE's*	*%*	*EVE's*	*%*	*EVE's*	*%*	*EVE's*	*%*	*EVE's*	*%*
	Ointment pot F															0.35	0.5
	Ointment pot G															0.92	1.2
	Sub-total	*				8.31	73.8	1.00	54.1	0.17	33.3	0.54	47.0	0.39	100	30.08	39.8
Kitchen	Strainer															*	
Kitchen/ table	Dish, pedestal					0.18	1.6									0.27	0.4
Multi-functional	Bowl	*				0.05	0.4										
	Bowl or dish	0.05	0.8					0.20	10.8							0.05	0.1
	Bowl, flared															0.13	0.2
	Bowl, hemispherical															4.51	6.0
	Bowl, hemispherical 1					0.05	0.4	0.26	14.1	0.04	7.8					4.29	5.7
	Bowl, hemispherical 2															0.06	0.1
	Bowl, rounded			0.10	58.8	*										*	
	Bowl, straight-sided					0.07	0.6										
	Unknown					0.06	0.5										
	Urn															0.09	0.1
	Sub-total	0.05	0.8	0.10	58.8	0.23	2.0	0.46	24.9	0.04	7.8					9.13	12.1
Storage	Patty pan					0.40	3.6									0.35	0.5
	Jar	0.08	1.2														
	Jar rounded											0.07	6.1			0.83	1.1
	Sub-total	0.08	1.2	*		0.40	3.6	*		*		0.07	6.09	*		1.18	1.56
Table ware	Dish	0.25	3.8													*	
	Charger	*		0.07	41.2	0.16	1.4			0.07	13.7					*	
	Charger C	2.95	45.1														
	Charger E							0.17	9.2							0.27	0.4
	Charger K															0.16	0.2
	Dish, flared															*	
	Dish, flared 1															0.32	0.4
	Dish, flared 2															0.28	0.4
	Dish, small, flared									0.06	11.8					0.27	0.4
	Dish, fluted					*				*							
	Dish, oval															*	
	Dish, pedestal					0.28	2.5										
	Dish, rounded	*														0.86	1.1
	Dish or charger															0.26	0.3
	Plate					*		*		0.08	15.7	0.07	6.1			1.57	2.1
	Plate H					*										0.17	0.2
	Plate I															20.57	27.2
	Plate J															0.10	0.1
	Plate K															2.99	4.0
	Porringer											0.07	6.1			0.33	0.4
	Porringer A	0.88	13.5			0.12	1.1										
	Porringer B	0.10	1.5														
	Porringer C							0.10	5.4							1.93	2.6
	Sub-total	4.18	63.9	0.07	41.2	0.56	5.0	0.27	14.6	0.21	41.2	0.14	12.2	*		1.18	39.4

Function	Shape	Layer [3364], c.1660-1680		Kiln 1, Phase 1, c. 1680/90-1700		Kiln 1, Phase 2, c. 1700-30		Kiln 1, Phase 3, c. 1730		Kiln 2, Phase 1, c. 1730-40		Kiln 2, Phase 2, c. 1730-50		Kiln 2, Phase 3, c. 1750		Kiln 2, Phase 5, c. 1755	
		EVE's	%	EVE's	%	EVE's	%	EVE's	%	EVE's	%	EVE's	%	EVE's	%	EVE's	%
Indeter-minate	Salt/wet drug jar					*										0.22	0.3
	Unknown	0.13	2.0			*		*		*		*		*			
	Sub-total	0.13	2.0	*		*		*		*		*		*		0.22	0.3
	Total	6.54	100	0.17	100	11.26	100	1.85	100	0.51	100	1.15	100	0.39	100	75.67	100
Kiln furniture	Kiln bar															*	
	Lid, sagger					0.12	21.8			0.18	69.2	0.07	100	*		0.17	36.7
	Peg 1					*											
	Peg 2															*	
	Sagger	*														*	
	Sagger 1	1.92	81.0	*		0.43	78.2	*		*						8.89	62.1
	Sagger 2A	0.45	19.0							0.08	30.8	*		*		5.25	36.7
	Sagger 2B															*	
	Setter			*		*										*	
	Shelf, 1	*				*		*		*		*		*		*	
	Shelf, 2									*		*				*	
	Trivet			*		*				*							
	Total	2.37	100	*		0.55	100	*	*	0.26	100	0.07	100	*	100	14.31	100
Kiln products		6.54	73.4	0.17	100	11.26	95.3	1.85	100	0.51	66.2	1.15	94.3	0.39	100	75.67	84.1
Kiln furniture		2.37	26.6	*		0.55	4.7	*		0.26	33.8	0.07	5.7	*		14.31	15.9
	Total	8.91	100	0.17	100	11.81	100	1.85	100	0.77	100	1.22	100	0.39	100	89.98	100

APPENDIX 2: GLOSSARY OF ARCHITECTURAL TERMS USED

Abacus	Flat slab forming the top of a capital.
Ambulatory	A covered passage around a cloister; sometimes (as here) applied to the procession way around the east end of a cathedral or large church and behind the high altar, continuing the line of the aisles lining the nave in a half circle running behind the apse.
Apse	Semicircular or polygonal end of an apartment, especially of a chancel or chapel.
Arcade	Series of arches supported by piers or columns.
Ashlar	Masonry of large blocks wrought to even faces and square edges.
Aumbry	A cupboard or recess in which sacred vessels can be stored.
Blind arcading	Series of arches applied to the wall surface.
Boss	Ornamental projection covering intersection of ribs or vaults in a ceiling
Bressumer	A horizontal timber which carries a wall above.
Caen stone	Oolitic limestone generally imported from Normandy. It saw its main period of use in the late 11th and 12th century.
Capital	Head or crowning feature of a column or pilaster.
Chancel	Part of the east end of a church set apart for the use of the officiating clergy.
Chapter house	Place of assembly for abbot or prior and members of a monastery.
Choir	The area of a church where divine service is sung. The choir is usually situated in the chancel usually in the western part, to the east of the nave.
Clerestory	The upper stage of the main walls of a church above the aisle roofs, pierced by windows.
Cloister	Enclosed space within a monastery, in the form of an open court or garden (the garth) surrounded by roofed or vaulted passages with open arcades or colonnades on the inner sides and plain walls on the outer.
Column	An upright structural member of round section with shaft, a capital, and usually a base.
Compound pier	Grouped shafts, or a solid core surrounded by shafts.
Corbel	Projecting block, usually of stone, which may support a beam or similar
Decorated	The decorated style of English architecture was in use in the late 13th to mid 14th centuries. It was characterised by the use of ogee (double or 'S') curves, particularly in arches and window tracery
Early English	The Early English period (1180-1275) period, simple, almost austere, Early English emphasizes height. The most obvious difference between this and the preceding Romanesque, or Norman style of architecture is the use of the pointed arch.
Feretory	A shrine for relics designed to be carried in processions, kept behind the high altar.
Gothic	Relating to the style of architecture that was used in Western Europe from the 12th to the 16th centuries, characterised by the lancet arch, the ribbed vault and the flying buttress.
Lady Chapel	Chapel dedicated to the Virgin Mary, usually built at the east end of the chancel and projecting from the main building.
Lancet	Slender, single-light pointed-arched window. The arch has two centres.
Ledger Slab	A stone slab set flush in the floor of a church.
Moulding	Shaped ornamental strip of continuous section.
Nave	The body of a church west of the crossing or chancel often flanked by aisles.
Nook-shaft	A shaft set in the angle of a pier, a respond a wall or the jamb of a window or doorway.
Pier	Large freestanding masonry or brick support, often for an arch.
Plinth	Projecting courses at the foot of a wall or column, generally chamfered or moulded at the top.
Purbeck marble	An Upper Jurassic shelly limestone from the Upper Purbeck beds quarried on the Isle of Purbeck, Dorset.
Reigate stone	A limey sandstone of the Upper Greensand.
Reredos	Painted and/or sculptured screen behind and above an altar.
Retro-choir	The space behind the high altar.
Roll moulding	Medieval moulding of part-circular section.
Romanesque	Otherwise known as Norman, architecture, dated to the years 1066-1180

Shaft — Vertical member of round or polygonal section.

String course — Horizontal course or moulding projecting from the surface of a wall.

Tracery — Openwork pattern of masonry or timber in the upper part of an opening.

Transept — The transverse arms of a cross-shaped church usually between nave and chancel.

Transitional style — Generally used for the phase between the Romanesque and Early English (*c.*1175–*c.*1200).

Trefoil — Three lobes formed by the *cusping* (q.v.) of a circular or other shaped in tracery.

Triforium — Middle storey of a church treated as an arcaded wall passage or blind arcade, its height corresponding to that of the aisle roof.

Vault — Arched stone roof.

Vaulting rib/ arch — Masonry framework of intersecting arches (ribs) supporting vault cells, used in Gothic architecture.

RÉSUMÉ

Agnès Shepherd

Le projet 'Millenium' de la Cathédrale de Southwark était l'un des nombreux programmes menés à travers l'Angleterre pour marquer le début du nouveau millénaire. Le nettoyage et la conservation des murs de la cathédrale, l'aménagement des jardins, la réorganisation du cimetière ainsi que la construction de nouveaux bâtiments à son côté nord ont constitué le tout des travaux menés. Ces travaux ont été l'occasion de revenir sur les lieux de fouilles conduits auparavant par Graham Dawson à la fin des années 60, début 70, et d'explorer des éléments de structure de la cathédrale grâce à des fouilles et des enregistrements du bâtiment en lui-même.

L'historique archéologique de la Cathédrale de Southwark commence dès les premières années de l'occupation romaine, avec la construction d'une route se dirigeant vers le sud-ouest, démarrant à l'endroit où un passage traversait la Tamise, fournissant ainsi un accès à la ville de Londinium, près du pont actuel appelé aujourd'hui 'London Bridge'.

La destination finale de cette route vers le sud-ouest reste toutefois inconnue, quoique les fouilles aient fourni l'opportunité d'explorer plus entièrement ses origines, sa construction et les bâtiments adjacents.

Les objets et matériaux environnementaux trouvés nous ont fourni un aperçu du style de vie des habitants, comme par exemple les fragments d'amphores qui indiquent peut-être le vin bu par des ouvriers lors de la construction de la route, ou encore les fruits sauvages et les noix ayant peut-être complété un régime de viande de bœuf, mouton et porc, de légumineuses et grains d'orge.

Bien que nous imaginions l'origine de la Cathédrale comme étant Saxonne, aucune preuve certaine de ceci n'est apparue. Le creusage de fosses, aux Xème et XIème-siècles, est peut être associé à une première église, mais pourrait également refléter l'expansion graduelle de l'occupation autour du point de passage sur la Tamise, avant l'établissement du Prieuré Augustinien de St Mary en 1106. Une série de fouilles menées en petites tranchées éparpillées autour du périmètre de la cathédrale, a révélé des parties de fondations et de structures du bâtiment, fournissant ainsi un stage de formation d'étudiants créé par l'Institut d'Archéologie de Londres (Institute of Archaeology, University College London) et permettant ainsi l'enregistrement de divers éléments de la structure de la cathédrale.

Les résultats des différentes informations recueillies lors des fouilles ont été réunis pour former un récit, qui est présenté aujourd'hui sous forme 'd'un tour' de la Cathédrale. Celui-ci commence dans la nef médiévale et continue progressivement à travers le bâtiment, pour enfin arriver au cloître du prieuré, situés peu ordinairement au nord de l'église, mais qui fournissait ainsi un accès à la Tamise. Les découvertes et données historiques sont combinées dans la description de l'église et des bâtiments associés. De nouvelles recherches menées sur les ossements trouvés par Dawson dans la salle capitulaire ont fourni un aperçu du style de vie opulent et du régime alimentaire riche des prieurs. L'église du prieuré a réchappé à la dissolution remarquablement bien. Bien que l'église n'ait été démolie, elle a cependant souffert d'une période de négligence. Les cloîtres et autres bâtiments auxiliaires au nord de l'église sont devenus des propriétés privées et ont été convertis en bâtiments d'utilisation domestique et industrielle, ensuite de nouvelles constructions ont été faites dans l'ancienne enceinte puis contre la structure même de l'église. L'église, reconsacrée au St. Sauveur (St Saviour), s'est détériorée jusqu'au début du XVIIème siècle, l'époque où les paroissiens ont acquis l'église et ont entrepris toute une série de réparations. Une analyse de la structure de l'église post-médiévale montre une structure semblable à celle du prieuré.

Les enquêtes archéologiques ont fourni l'occasion d'examiner certaines des constructions non religieuses qui entouraient l'église après la Réforme et elles ont aussi révélé des parties du cimetière. L'interprétation des vestiges visibles et ensevelis qui ont été enregistrés a été élargie par une richesse de sources historiques incluant de nombreux plans et illustrations du secteur. Beaucoup ont été reproduit ici, révélant ainsi l'état changeant de la Cathédrale de Southwark au cours du temps.

Un événement évocateur du changement d'utilisation des anciens bâtiments du prieuré, est la conversion de l'ancienne salle capitulaire en un atelier de potier pour la fabrication de Delft. Le tout premier four a été par la suite prolongé à l'est, utilisant le mur de transept nord dans sa construction. La publication comprend un rapport détaillé de la forme des fours, des vases produits dans cet atelier et des méthodes de fabrication.

Ayant examiné les résultats du travail sur le terrain, l'ouvrage se termine par une idée de l'avenir de la Cathédrale, produite par Richard Griffiths et par une illustration de la construction des nouveaux bâtiments créés par Ptolemy Dean, les deux architectes rattachés au projet. L'ouvrage fournit aussi un guide des vestiges archéologiques préservés pendant les travaux de construction, qui sont encore visibles dans les alentours de la Cathédrale.

Aucune publication seule ne pourrait englober chaque aspect des 2000 ans de l'histoire fascinante de la Cathédrale de Southwark et cet ouvrage ne couvre qu'une petite partie de cette histoire. Cependant, nous espérons qu'autant les étudiants en architecture d'église, que les archéologues et les visiteurs de la Cathédrale de Southwark trouveront dans cette publication une grande source d'intérêt.

ZUSAMMENFASSUNG

Sylvia Butler

Das Millennium Projekt an der Southwark Kathedrale war eines von vielen Programmen, die innerhalb des Landes durchgeführt wurden, um den Beginn des neuen Millenniums zu markieren. Die Arbeiten umfassten die Reinigung und Konservierung des Mauerwerkes der Kathedrale, die landschaftliche Gestaltung und Reorganisation des Kirchhofes und die Konstruktion neuer Gebäude an ihrer nördlichen Seite. Dies ergab die Gelegenheit die Stätte einer früheren Ausgrabung, durchgeführt bei Graham Dawson in den späten sechziger und frühen siebziger Jahren, nochmals zu besuchen und die Elemente des Mauerwerkes der Kathedrale mittels Ausgrabungen und Erfassung der noch stehenden Gebäude zu untersuchen.

Die archäologische Geschichte der Southwark Kathedrale beginnt in den ersten Jahren der römischen Besetzung mit der Konstruktion einer Strasse, die von einem Knotenpunkt der Themse südwestlich zeigend Zugang zu der Stadt "Londinium" herstelle, nahe der heutigen London Bridge. Der letztendliche Zielort dieser Strasse zum Südwesten hin bleibt unbekannt, jedoch lieferte die Ausgrabung die Möglichkeit die Herkunft, Konstruktion und die anliegenden Gebäude vollständiger zu untersuchen. Artefakts und Ecofakts lieferten einen Einblick in den Lebensstil der Anwohner und Amphora Fragmente zeigen vielleicht an, welcher Wein von den Straßenbauern getrunken wurde, während Wildfrüchte und Nüsse vielleicht eine Ernährungsweise, die auf Rind, Schaaf und Schwein sowie Hülsenfrüchte und Körner wie Gerste basierte, ergänzt haben.

Obwohl angenommen wird, dass die Kathedrale einen sächsischen Ursprung hat, gab es keine definitiven Beweise hierfür. Grubenbildung aus dem 10. und 11. Jahrhundert steht vielleicht mit einer frühen Kirche in Verbindung, könnte aber ebenso eine schrittweise Erweiterung der Besiedlung, die vor der Etablierung des augustinischen Priorates von St Mary in 1106 nahe des Knotenpunktes der Themse stattfand, darstellen. Stückweise Ausgrabungen in kleinen Schnitten um das Gebiet der Kathedrale herum entblößten Bestandteile der Fundamente und des Mauerwerkes des Gebäudes, während ein Studenten Trainings Programm, welches vom Institute of Archaeology, University College London organisiert wurde, das Aufzeichnen von verschiedenen Bestandteilen des Kathedralen Mauerwerkes ermöglichte.

Die Ergebnisse der verschiedenen Fasern des Beweismaterials wurden hier in einer Beschreibung zusammengeführt, die die Form einer Tour um die Kathedrale herum annimmt. Diese Tour beginnt im mittelalterlichen Kirchenschiff, führt weiter durch das Gebäude hindurch und schließlich nach draußen in den Kreuzgang des Priorates, welcher sich ungewöhnlicherweise im Norden der Kirche befindet, hier aber durch seine Lage den Zugang zur Themse ermöglicht. Funde und historische Daten sind in die Beschreibung der Kirche und ihrer angegliederten Gebäude eingewoben. Die erneute Untersuchung von Skelettüberresten, die von Dawson im Kapitelsaal freigelegt wurden, gibt einen Einblick in den Wohlstand und die üppige Ernährungsweise der Priors.

Die Prioratskirche überlebte die Auflösung der katholischen Klöster durch Heinrich VIII erstaunlich gut. Obwohl die Kirche dem Abriss entkommen war, war sie jedoch einer Periode der Vernachlässigung ausgesetzt. Das Kloster und die Nebengebäude nördlich der Kirche fielen in Privatbesitz und wurden für den häuslichen und industriellen Gebrauch umgebaut, neue Gebäude wurden innerhalb des ehemaligen Bezirkes errichtet und letztendlich sogar gegen das Kirchenmauerwerk selbst. Die Kirche, nun dem Heiligen St Saviour gewidmet, war bis zum frühen 17. Jahrhundert dem Verfall ausgesetzt, zu welcher Zeit Gemeindemitglieder die Kirche erworben und eine Reihe von Reparaturen begannen. Eine Untersuchung des nachmittelalterlichen Kirchemauerwerkes folgt einer ähnlichen Struktur wie die der Prioratskirche.

Die archäologische Untersuchung lieferte die Gelegenheit einige der säkularen Gebäude um die Nach-Reformationskirche herum zu untersuchen und deckte ebenfalls Elemente des Friedhofes auf. Die Interpretation der aufgezeichneten, stehenden und begrabenen Überreste konnte erweitert werden durch eine Fülle von historischen Quellen, einschließlich zahlreicher Pläne und reichhaltiger Illustrationen des Gebietes, viele welcher hier reproduziert worden sind und somit anzeigen, welchen wechselnden Schicksalen die Southwalk Kathedrale über die Zeit ausgesetzt war.

Vorausgehend dem Wechsel der Nutzung der ehemaligen Prioratsgebäude ist die Konvertierung des ehemaligen Kapitelsaales in ein Töpferhaus für die Herstellung von Delftware; der früheste Brennofen wurde folglich zum Osten hin erweitert unter Verwendung der nördlichen Transeptmauer in seiner Konstruktion. Diese Publikation beinhaltet einen detaillierten Bericht über die Form der Brennöfen, die Produkte des Töpferhauses und die Methoden der Verarbeitung.

Einer Auswertung der Ergebnisse der Feldarbeiten folgend, schließt diese Ausgabe mit einer Vision für die Zukunft der Kathedrale ab. Diese wurde erstellt von Richard Griffiths und enthält eine Illustration der Konstruktion des neuen Gebäudes von Ptolemy Dean, beide Architekten für dieses Projekt. Sie liefert ebenso eine Richtlinie für verbleibende, archäologische Überreste, welche während der Konstruktionsarbeiten erhalten wurden und um die Kathedrale herum sichtbar sind.

Keine einzelne Publikation könnte alle Aspekte von 2000 Jahren der faszinierenden Geschichte der Southwalk Kathedrale umfassen, und diese Ausgabe behandelt nur einen kleinen Teil dieser Geschichte. Es wird jedoch gehofft, dass diese Publikation gleichermaßen für Studenten der Kirchenarchitektur, Archäologen und den Besucher der Southwalk Kathedrale etwas von Interesse bereitet.

BIBLIOGRAPHY

Ainsley, C. 2002. The Animal Bones. In: J. Drummond-Murray, and P. Thompson, with C. Cowan *Settlement in Roman Southwark: archaeological excavations (1991–8) for the London Underground Limited Jubilee Line Extension Project*. Museum of London Archaeology Service Monograph 12, 259–274.

Ajmar, M. and Sheffield, C. 1994. The Miraculous Medal. An immaculate conception or not. *The Medal* 24, 37–51.

Anderson, S. 1998. *A human skeleton from Marmont Priory, Upwell, Norfolk*. Available from: http://www.spoilheap.co.uk/giblet [Accessed 18 November 2004].

Anderson, S. 2000. *Guisborough Priory*. Available from: http://www.spoilheap.co.uk/ahyp.htm. [Accessed 18 November 2004].

Archer, M. 1997. *Delftware: The Tin-glazed earthenware of the British Isles, a catalogue of the collection in the Victoria and Albert Museum*. London: HMSO.

Armitage, P. L. 1994. Unwelcome Companions: ancient rats reviewed. *Antiquity* 68, 231–240.

Armitage, P. L. West, B. and Steedman, K. 1984. New evidence of black rat in Roman London. *The London Archaeologist* 4, 375–383.

Askew, P. 1998. Early Medieval Purbeck Marble Grave Slabs from Southwark. *Journal of the Church Monuments Society* 8, 15–16.

Audoin-Rouzeau, F. 1994. *La Taille du Cheval en Europe de L'Antiquité aux Temps Modernes*. Fiches d'Ostéologie Animale pour L'Archéologie Serie B: Mammiferes No. 5, Centre de Recherches Archeologiques du CNRS.

Bass, W.M. 1992. *Human Osteology: A laboratory and field manual*. Columbia, Missouri Archaeological Society, Inc.

Bateman, N. Cowan, C. and Wroe-Brown, R. 2008. *London's Roman Amphitheatre: excavations at the Guildhall, City of London*. Museum of London Archaeology Service Monograph 35.

van Bath, B. H. S. 1966. *The Agrarian History of Western Europe A.D. 500–1850*. Londo.

Beagrie, N. 1989. The Romano-British Pewter Industry. *Britannia* 20, 169–91.

Bell, T. 1998. Churches on Roman Buildings: Christian associations and Roman masonry in Anglo-Saxon England. *Medieval Archaeology* 42, 1–18.

Benson S. 1885. *A Guide to St. Saviour's Church, Southwark*. London: William Drewett.

Binns, A. 1989. *Dedications of Monastic Houses in England and Wales*. Woodbridge: Boydell Press.

Bird, J. and Graham, A. H. 1978. Gazetteer of Roman Sites in Southwark. In: J. Bird, A. H. Graham, H. Sheldon, and P. Townend (eds), *Southwark Excavations 1972–74*. London and Middlesex Archaeological Society and Surrey Archaeological Society Joint Publication 1, 517–526.

Bird, J. Graham, A. H. Sheldon, H. and Townend, P. (eds), 1978. *Southwark Excavations 1972–74*. London and Middlesex Archaeological Society and Surrey Archaeological Society Joint Publication 1. London.

Bishop B. 2001. The Lithics. In: D. Divers, *Assessment of an Archaeological Excavation at Southwark Cathedral, London Borough of Southwark SE1: Phases 1 and 2*. Pre-Construct Archaeology Ltd Unpublished Report.

Black, J. 2001. *British Tin-glazed Earthenware*. Shire album 390. Princes Risborough, Buckinghamshire: Shire Publications Ltd.

Blackmore, L. 1999. Aspects of Trade and Exchange Evidenced by Recent Work on Saxon and Medieval Pottery from London. *The Transactions of the London and Middlesex Archaeological Society* 50, 38–54.

Blackmore, L. 2005. The Pottery. In: J. Schofield and R. Lea, *Holy Trinity Priory, Aldgate, City of London: an archaeological reconstruction and history*. Museum of London Archaeology Service Monograph 24.

Blagg, T. F. C. 1980. Roman Pewter-Moulds. In: C. Heighway and P. Garrod, Excavations at Nos. 1 and 30 Westgate Street, Gloucester: The Roman Levels 1. *Britannia* 11, 73–114.

Blair, J. 1990. St.Frideswide's Monastery: problems and possibilities. In J. Blair (ed) *St. Frideswide's Monastery, Oxford*. Alan Sutton Publishing, 221–259.

Blair, J. 1991. *Early Medieval Surrey: landholding, church and settlement*. Stroud: Sutton Publishing Ltd.

Bloice, B. J. 1971. Norfolk House, Lambeth: excavations at a Delftware kiln site, 1968. *Post-Medieval Archaeology* 5, 99–149.

Brickley, M. Miles, A. and Stainer, H. 1999. *The Cross Bones Burial Ground, Redcross Way, Southwark, London: archaeological excavations (1991–1998) for the London Underground Limited Jubilee Line Extension Project*. Museum of London Archaeology Service Monograph 3.

Britton, F. 1987. *London Delftware*. London: Jonathan Horne.

Brooks, S. T. and Suchey, J. M. 1990. Skeletal Age Determination Based on the Os Pubis: a comparison of the Acsádi-Nemeskéri and Suchey-Brooks methods. *Human Evolution* 5, 227–238.

Brothwell, D. 1981. *Digging Up Bones*. London: British Museum (Natural History).

Brigham, T. 1998. The Port of Roman London. In B. Watson (ed), *Roman London: recent archaeological work*. Journal of Roman Archaeology Supplementary Series 24. Portsmouth, Rhode Island: Journal of Roman Archaeology.

Buikstra, J. E. and Ubelaker, D. H. (eds), 1994. *Standards for Data Collection from Human Skeletal Remains*. Arkansas Archaeological Survey Research Series 44. Fayetteville: Arkansas Archaeological Survey.

Carlin, M. 1996. *Medieval Southwark*. London: The Hambledon Press.

Carruthers, W. J. 1999. The plant remains. In: A. Douglas, *Assessment of an Archaeological Excavation at Long Lane, Southwark SE1*. Pre-Construct Archaeology Ltd Unpublished Report.

Carruthers, W. J. 2002. Roman plant remains. In: R. Taylor-Wilson, *Excavations at Hunt's House, Guy's Hospital, London Borough of Southwark*. Pre-Construct Archaeology Monograph 1.

Carter, S. and Shepherd, J. 2004. *Southwark Cathedral, Montague Close, The Glass*. Pre-Construct Archaeology Ltd Unpublished Report.

Cave, C. J. P. 1948. *Roof Bosses in Medieval Churches: an aspect of Gothic sculpture*. Cambridge: Cambridge University Press.

Chadwick, E. 1843. *A Supplementary Report on the Results of a Special Inquiry into the Practice of Interment in Towns*. London: House of Lords.

Chamberlain, A. 1999. Teaching Surgery and Breaking the Law. *British Archaeology* 48, 6–7. Cherry, B. 1990. Some New Types of Late Medieval Tombs in the London Area. In L. Grant (ed), Medieval Art, Architecture and Archaeology in London. *The British Archaeological Association Conference Transactions for the year 1984*, 140–154.

Cherry, B. and Pevsner, N. 1983. *The Buildings of England, London 2: South*. Harmondsworth: Penguin Books Ltd.

Clanchy, M. T. 1989. *England and its Rulers (1066-1272)*. London: Fontana Press.

Clapham, A. W. 1934. *English Romanesque Architecture After the Conquest*. Oxford: Clarendon Press.

Clifton-Taylor, A. 1972. *The Pattern of English Building*. London: Faber and Faber Ltd.

Cohen, N. 1994. *Church Investigation in the City of London 1878-1968*. Unpublished BA dissertation, University of London.

Coldstream, N. 1994. *The Decorated Style, Architecture and Ornament 1240-1360*. Toronto: University of Toronto Press.

Concanen, M. and Morgan, A. 1795. *The History and Antiquities of the Parish of St Saviour's, Southwark*. London: J. Delahoy.

Concetta di Natale, M. and Abbale, V. 1995. *Il Tesoro nascosto, gioie e argenti per la Madonna di Trapani*, Museo Regionale Pepoli Trapani, 109–119.

Coppack, G. 1990. *Abbeys and Priories*. Stroud: Tempus.

Cowan, C. 1992. *A possible mansio in Roman Southwark: excavations at 15-23 Southwark Street, 1980-86*. Transactions of the London and Middlesex Archaeological Society 43, 3–191.

Cowan, C. 2003. *Urban development in North-West Roman Southwark: excavations 1974-90*. Museum of London Archaeology Service Monograph 16.

Cross, F. L. and Livingstone, E. A. (eds), 1977. *The Oxford Dictionary of the Christian Church*. Oxford: Oxford University Press.

Crossley, F. H. 1943. *The English Abbey, Its Life and Work in the Middle Ages*. London: Batsford.

Crossley, D. 1990. *Post-Medieval Archaeology in Britain*. London, Leicester and New York: Leicester University Press.

Crouch, K. R. and Shanks, S.A. 1984. *Excavations in Staines 1975-76. The Friends' Burial Ground Site*. London and Middlesex Archaeological Society and Surrey Archaeological Society Joint Publication No. 2.

Cunningham, C. M and Drury, P. J. 1985. *Post-Medieval Sites and their Pottery: Moulsham Street, Chelmsford*. Council for British Archaeology Research Report 54.

Daniell, A. E. 1897. *London Riverside Parish Churches*. London: Archibald Constable and Co.

Davies, B. Richardson, B. and Tomber, R. 1994. *The Archaeology of Roman London Volume 5. A Dated Corpus of Early Roman Pottery from the City of London*. Council for British Archaeology Research Report 98.

Dawson, G. 1971a. Two Delftware Kilns at Montague Close Southwark, Part 1. *London Archaeologist* 1 (10), 228–231.

Dawson, G. 1971b. Montague Close, Part 2. *London Archaeologist* 1 (11), 250–251.

Dawson, G. J. 1976. Montague Close Excavations 1969–73. *Research Volume of the Surrey Archaeological Society* 3, 37–58.

Dawson, G. J. 1999. Southwark in Domesday Book. *Southwark and Lambeth Archaeological Society Newsletter* 79, 4–5.

Dawson, G. J. 2000. The Saxon Minster at Southwark – Some Late Evidence. Southwark and Lambeth Archaeological Society Newsletter 84, 4–6.

Dawson, G. 2006. Processing at Montague Close. *Southwark and Lambeth Archaeological Society Newsletter* 106, 5–6.

Dawson, G. J. and Edwards, R. 1974. The Montague Close Delftware factory prior to 1969. *Research Volume of the Surrey Archaeological Society* 1, 47–64.

Dean, M. 1980. Excavations at Arcadia Buildings, Southwark. *London Archaeologist* 3 (14), 367–373.

Dickinson, J. C. 1950. *Origins of Austin Canons*. London: S.P.C.K.

Diderot, D. 1756. *Encyclopedié, ou Dictionnaire Raisonne des Sciences, des Arts et des Métiers*. Paris.

Dillon, J. Jones, H. and Jackson, S. 1991.Excavations at the Courage Brewery and Park Street 1984–1990. *London Archaeologist* 6, 255–262.

Divers, D. 2001. *Assessment of an Archaeological Excavation at Southwark Cathedral, London Borough of Southwark SE1: Phases 1 and 2*. Pre-Construct Archaeology Ltd Unpublished Report.

Divers, D. 2002. The Post-Medieval Waterfront Development at Adlards Wharf, Bermondsey, London. *Post-Medieval Archaeology* 36, 39–117.

Dodwell, N. 2001. The Human Remains. In: D. Divers, *Assessment of an Archaeological Excavation at Southwark Cathedral, London Borough of Southwark SE1: Phases 1 and 2*. Pre-Construct Archaeology Ltd Unpublished Report.

Dollman, F. T. 1881. *The Priory of St Mary Overie, Southwark*. London: W. Drewett.

Drummond-Murray, J. and Thompson, P. with Cowan, C. 2002. *Settlement in Roman Southwark: archaeological excavations (1991-8) for the London Underground Limited Jubilee Line Extension Project*. Museum of London Archaeology Service Monograph 12.

Dubois, S. Mille, B. with Binet, E. 1994. La Céramique à Pâte Blanche à quartz: contribution à l'élaboration d'un faciès regional. In: M. Tuffreau-Libre and A. Jacques, (eds) *La Céramique du Haut-Empire en Gaule Belgique et dans les Régions Voisines: facies regionaux et courants commerciaux*. Nord-Ouest Archéologie 6, 103–130.

Edwards, J. 1999. A Group of Biscuit and Glazed Wares from Holy Trinity Priory, London. In: D. Gaimster (ed), *Maiolica in the North: the archaeology of tin-glazed earthenware in North-West Europe c.1500-1600*. London: British Museum.

Edwards, J. (in prep). *Post-Medieval Pottery in London, 1500-1700, Vol 2: tin-glazed wares*.

Edwards, J. and Stephenson, R. 2002. Production and Use of Tin-Glazed Wares in Late 16th and Early 17th Century London. In: J. Veekman, C. Dumortier, D. Whitehouse, and F. Verhaeghe (eds), *Majolica and Glass from Italy to Antwerp and Beyond: The transfer of technology in the 16th–early 17th century*. Antwerp.

Edwards, Rhoda, 1974. London Potters circa 1570–1710. *Journal of Ceramic History* 6.

Edwards, Roy, 1981. The Vauxhall Pottery, Part 1. *London Archaeologist* 4 (5), 130–136.

Edwards, Roy, 1982. The Vauxhall Pottery, Part 2. *London Archaeologist* 4 (6), 148–154.

Edwards, Roy, 1984. An Early 18th-century Waste Deposit from the Vauxhall Pottery. *English Ceramic Circle* 12 (1), 45–56.

Egan, G. 1978. Kiln Material from the Thames Foreshore in the City. *Transactions of the London and Middlesex Archaeology Society* 29, 156–159.

Egan, G. 1998. *The Medieval Household c.1150 – c.1450*. Medieval Finds from Excavations in London 6. London: HMSO.

Farid, S. 2000. An Excavation at 6–16 Old Church Street, Royal Borough of Kensington and Chelsea. *Transactions of the London and Middlesex Archaeology Society* 51, 126–135.

Fletcher, B. 1987. *A History of Architecture*, 19th edition, John Musgrove (ed). London: Butterworth.

Fletcher, E. and Meates, G.W. 1969. The Ruined Church of Stone-by-Faversham. *Antiquaries Journal* 49, 273–294.

Foster, R. 2000. *The roof bosses at Southwark Cathedral: a case study of late 15th-century carpentry, vaulting design and symbolism*. Unpublished BA dissertation, University of London.

Frere, S. 1972. *Verulamium Excavations Vol.1.* Report of the Research Committee of the Society of Antiquaries London 28. Oxford.

Frere, S. 1984. *Verulamium Excavations Vol. 3.* Oxford University Committee for Archaeology Monograph 1.

Funari, P.P.A. 1996. *Dressel 20 Inscriptions from Britain and the Consumption of Spanish Olive Oil; with a Catalogue of Stamps.* British Archaeological Reports (British Series) 250.

Garner, F. H. 1946. London Pottery Sites. *English Ceramic Circle Transactions* 2 (9), 179–187.

Garner, H. and Archer, M. 1972. *English Delftware.* London: Faber.

Gem, R. 1990 The Romanesque Architecture of Old St Paul's Cathedral and its late Eleventh Century Context. In: L. Grant (ed), Medieval Art, Architecture and Archaeology in London. *The British Archaeological Association Conference Transactions for the year 1984.* 47–63.

Gibbard P. L. 1994. *The Pleistocene History of the Lower Thames Valley.* Cambridge: Cambridge University Press

Gilchrist, R. and Sloane, B. 2005. *Requiem: the medieval monastic cemetery in Britain.* Museum of London Archaeology Service Surveys and Handbooks Series. London.

Goffin, R. 1995. The Pottery. In: P. Mills, Excavations at the Dorter Undercroft, Westminster Abbey. *Transactions of the London and Middlesex Archaeological Society* 46, 79–87.

Gose, E. 1976. *Gefasstypen der Romischen Keramik im Rheinland. Beihefte der. Bonner Jahrbucher.* Band 1.

Graham, A. 1978. The Bonded Warehouse, Montague Close. In: J. Bird, A. H. Graham, H. Sheldon and P. Townsend (eds), *Southwark and Lambeth Archaeological Excavation Committee Southwark Excavations 1972–1974.* London and Middlesex Archaeological Society and Surrey Archaeological Society Joint Publication 1, 237–290.

Graham, A. 1988. District Heating Scheme. In: P. Hinton (ed*), Excavations in Southwark, 1973–76, Lambeth 1973–79.* London and Middlesex Archaeology Society and Surrey Archaeology Society Joint Publication 3, 26–54.

Gray, L. 2002. The Botanical Remains. In J. Drummond-Murray and P. Thompson, with C. Cowan, *Settlement in Roman Southwark: archaeological excavations (1991–8) for the London Underground Limited Jubilee Line Extension Project.* Museum of London Archaeology Service Monograph 12, 242–274.

Green, C. 1999. *John Dwight's Fulham Pottery: excavations 1971–79.* London: English Heritage.

Greene, J. P. 1992. *Medieval Monasteries.* Leicester: Leicester University Press.

Greene, K. 1978. Mould-Decorated Central Gaulish Glazed Ware in Britain. In: P. Arthur and G. Marsh (eds), *Early Fine Wares in Roman Britain.* British Archaeological Reports (British Series) 57.

Greig, J. 1981. The Investigation of a Medieval Barrel-Latrine from Worcester. *Journal of Archaeological Science* 8, 265–282

Greig, J. 1984. The Palaeoecology of some British Hay Meadow Types. In: W. van Zeist and W. A. Casparie (eds), *Plants and Ancient Man*, 6th IWGP, 213-66. Rotterdam: A. A. Balkema.

Grieve, M. 1995. *A Modern Herbal.* Available from http://www.botanical.com/botanical/mgmh/comindx.html_

Grimes, W. F. 1968. *The Excavation of Roman and Medieval London.* London: Routledge & Kegan Paul.

Hadley, D. M. 2001. *Death in Medieval England: an archaeology.* Stroud: Tempus.

Hall, A. 2000. *A Study of the Evidence for a Change in Construction of the East End of St Mary Overie's Priory, Southwark, from the 12th to the 13th Centuries.* Unpublished BA dissertation, University of London.

Hall, A. R. Jones, A. K. G. and Kenward, H. K. 1983. Cereal Bran and Human Faecal Remains from Archaeological Deposits – some Preliminary Observations. In: B. Proudfoot (ed), *Site, Environment and Economy.* British Archaeological Reports (International Series) 173, 85–104.

Hammer, F. 2003. *Industry in North-West Roman Southwark: excavations 1984–8.* Museum of London Archaeology Service Monograph 17.

Hammerson, M. 1978. Excavations Beneath the Choir of Southwark Cathedral 1977. *London Archaeologist* 3 (8), 206–212.

Heard, K. 1997. *Bermondsey Square, London SE1, London Borough of Southwark: an archaeological desktop assessment.* Museum of London Archaeology Service Unpublished Report.

Heard, K. Sheldon, H. and Thompson, P. 1990. Mapping Roman Southwark. *Antiquity* 64 (233), 608–619.

Henig, M. 2001. Religion and Art in St Alban's City. In: M. Henig and P. Lindley (eds.) *Alban and St Albans: Roman and Medieval architecture, art and archaeology.* London: The British Archaeological Association Conference Transactions 24, 13-29.

Henig, M. 2006. Two-Part Mould. In: E. Hartley, J. Hawkes, M. Henig, and F. Mee (ed) *Constantine the Great. York's Roman Emperor.* York Museums Trust, 158.

Higham, F. 1955. *Southwark Story.* London: Hodder and Stoughton.

Hill, J. and Rowsome, P. (forthcoming). *Roman London and the Walbrook Stream Crossing: excavations at 1 Poultry and vicinity, City of London.* Museum of London Archaeology Service Monograph 37.

Hines, J. Cohen, N. and Roffey, S. 2004. Iohannes Gower, Armiger, Poeta: records and memorials of his life and death. In S. Echard (ed), *A Companion to Gower. Cambridge: D. S. Brewer.*

Hinton, P. 1988. *Excavations in Southwark, 1973-76, Lambeth 1973-79.* London and Middlesex Archaeology Society and Surrey Archaeology Society Joint Publication 3.

Hinton, P. Orton, C. and Yule, B. 1988. Mark Brown's Wharf. In: P. Hinton (ed), *Excavations in Southwark, 1973-76, Lambeth 1973-79. London and Middlesex Archaeology Society and Surrey Archaeology Society Joint Publication* 3, 133–156

Hull, M. R. 1963. *The Roman Potters' Kilns of Colchester.* Report of the Research Committee of the Society of Antiquaries London, 21. Oxford

Hughes, M. J. 2008. Inductively Coupled Plasma Analysis of Tin-Glazed Tiles and Vessels Produced at Several Centres in London. In: K. Tyler, I. Betts and R. Stephenson, *London's Delftware industry: the tin-glazed pottery industries of Southwark and Lambeth.* Museum of London Archaeology Service Monograph 40.

Isings, C. 1957. *Roman Glass from Dated Finds.* Groningen: Djakarta.

Jalland, P. 1996. *Death in the Victorian Family.* Oxford: Oxford University Press.

Jarrett, C. 2002. The Pottery. In: D. Divers, The Post-Medieval Waterfront Development at Adlards Wharf, Bermondsey, London. *Post-Medieval Archaeology* 36, 102–108.

Jarrett, C. 2003. Pottery Production in the 17th and 18th centuries. In: D. Killock, J. Brown and C. Jarrett, The Industrialisation of an Ecclesiastical Hamlet: stoneware production in Lambeth and the sanitary revolution. *Post-Medieval Archaeology* 37 (1), 34–42.

Jarrett, C. 2000. The Post-Medieval Pit Group [97]. In: S. Farid, An Excavation at 6–16 Old Church Street, Royal Borough of Kensington and Chelsea. *Transactions of the London and Middlesex Archaeology Society* 51, 126–135.

Jones, D. M. 1980. *Excavations at Billingsgate Buildings "Triangle", Lower Thames Street, 1974.* London and Middlesex Archaeological Society Special Paper 4.

Killock D. 2005. Roman River Bank Use and Changing Water Levels at 51–53 Southwark Street, Southwark, London. *Transactions of the London and Middlesex Archaeological Society* 56, 27–44.

Killock, D. (forthcoming). *Assessment of an archaeological excavation at Tabard Square, London Borough of Southwark*, Pre-Construct Archaeology Ltd Unpublished Report.

Killock, D. Brown, J. and Jarrett, C. 2003. The Industrialisation of an Ecclesiastical Hamlet: stoneware production in Lambeth and the sanitary revolution. *Post-Medieval Archaeology* 37 (1), 29–78.

Kjølbye-Biddle, B. 1992. Dispersal or Concentration: the disposal of the Winchester dead over 2000 years. In: S. Bassett (ed), *Death in Towns: urban responses to the dying and the dead, 100-1600.* London: Leicester University Press.

Kruger, A. 1992. *The Pocket Guide to Herbs.* London: Parkgate Books.

Langley, B. 1748. *The London Prices of Bricklayers Materials and Works.* London: Archimedes Langley.

Lethaby, W. R. 1914. The Cloister of Southwark Priory and Other Early Cloisters. *Archaeological Journal* 71, 155–160.

Lever, J. and Harris, J. 1993. *Illustrated Dictionary of Architecture 800–1914.* London: Faber and Faber Ltd.

Litten, J. 1991. *The English Way of Death: the common funeral since 1450.* London: Robert Hale.

Llewellyn, N. 1991. *The Art of Death: visual culture in the English death ritual c 1500–c 1800.* London: Reaktion Books.

Luard, H. R. (ed.) 1866. *Annales Monastici, Vol. III.* London: Longman, Green and Dyer.

Luff, R. M. 1982. *A Zooarchaeological Study of the Roman North-western Provinces.* British Archaeological Reports (International Series) 137.

Lyne, M. A. B. 2003. *The Pottery from the Southwark Cathedral Site.* Pre-Construct Archaeology Unpublished Report.

Lyne, M. A. B. and Jefferies, R. S. ,1979. *The Alice Holt/Farnham Roman Pottery Industry.* Council for British Archaeology Research Report 30.

Malden, H. (ed), 1914. *The Victoria History of the Counties of England: Surrey. Vols I–IV, 1902-14.* London: Archibald Constable and Co Ltd.

Malden, H. (ed), 1967. *The Victoria History of the Counties of England: Surrey, Vol IV,* London.

Marsh, G. 1978. Early Second Century Fine Wares in the London area. In: P. Arthur and G. Marsh (eds), *Early Fine Wares in Roman Britain.* British Archaeological Reports (British Series) 57.

Martin-Kilcher, S. 1983. Les Amphores Romaines a Huile de Betique (Dressel 20 et 23) d'Augst (Colonia Augusta Rauricorum) et Kaiseraugst (Castrum Rauracense), Un rapport Preliminaire. In: J. M. Blasquez-Martinez and J. Remesal Rodriguez (eds), *Produccion y Comercio del Aceite en la Antigüedad.* II Congresso, Madrid, 337–47.

Mellor, M. 1994. A Synthesis of Middle and Late Saxon, Medieval and Early Post-Medieval Pottery in the Oxford Region. *Oxoniensa* 59, 17–217.

Merrifield, R. 1965. *The Roman City of London.* London: Earnest Benn Ltd.

Mills, S. 2004. *All Hallows, Goodmanham: myth and reality in the pre-Conquest past.* MA dissertation in the Archaeology of Buildings, Department of Archaeology, University of York.

Milne, G. 1995. *Roman London. Urban Archaeology in the Nation's Capital.* London: Batsford/English Heritage.

Milne, G. 1997. *St Bride's Church London: archaeological research 1952-60 and 1992-5.* English Heritage Archaeological Report 11.

Monaghan, J. 1987. *Upchurch and Thameside Roman Pottery: a ceramic typology for northern Kent, first to third centuries A.D.* British Archaeological Reports (British Series) 173.

Moore, G. 1967. *An Introduction to English Canon Law.* Oxford: Clarendon Press.

Morley, J. 1971. *Death, Heaven and the Victorians.* London: Studio Vista.

Morris, J. (ed and trans.), 1975. *Domesday Book. 3: Surrey.* Chichester.

Morris, R. and Roxan, J. 1980. Churches on Roman Buildings. In: W. Rodwell (ed.), *Temples, Churches and Religion: recent research in Roman Britain*, Oxford, British Archaeological Report (British Series) 77 (i).

Moss, W. G. and Nightingale, Rev. J. 1818. *The History and Antiquities of the Parochial Church of St. Saviours Southwark.* London: W. G. Moss.

MPRG, 1998. *A Guide to the Classification of Medieval Ceramic Forms.* Medieval Pottery Research Group Occasional Paper 1.

Newman, C. 1988. *The Anglo-Norman Nobility in the Reign of Henry I.* Philadelphia: University of Pennsylvania Press.

Noël Hume, I. 1977. *Early English Delftware from London and Virginia.* Williamsburg.

Oliver, A. 1984. *Early Roman Facetted Glass.* Journal of Glass Studies 26, 35–58.

Orton, C. 1975. Quantitative Pottery Studies: some progress, problems and prospects. *Science and Archaeology* 16, 30–35.

Orton, C. 1988. Post-Roman Pottery from Mark Browns Wharf. In: P. Hinton (ed*), Excavations in Southwark, 1973-76, Lambeth 1973-79.* London and Middlesex Archaeology Society and Surrey Archaeology Society Joint Publication 3, 307–348.

Orton, C. R. and Pearce J. E. 1984. The pottery. In: A. Thompson, F. Grew and J. Schofield, Excavations in Aldgate, 1974. *Post-Medieval Archaeology* 18, 34–68

Pace, G. G. 1971. *Southwark Cathedral: historical and archaeological notes.* Friends of Southwark Cathedral.

Page, W. (ed), 1974. *The Victoria History of the Counties of England: London. Vol. I.* London.

Payne, S. 1973. Kill-off patterns in sheep and goats: the mandibles from Asvan Kale. *Anatolian Studies* 23, 281-303.

Peacock, D. P. S. and Williams, D.F. 1991. Amphorae and the Roman Economy. An Introductory Guide. London/New York: Longman.

Pérez-Sala Rodés, M. and Shepherd, J. 2008. The Cullet Dump and Evidence of Glass-Working at Guildhall Yard, London. In: N. Bateman, C. Cowan, and R. Wroe-Brown, *London's Roman Amphitheatre: excavations at the Guildhall, City of London.* Museum of London Archaeology Service Monograph 35,

Perring, D. with Brigham, T, 2000. Londinium and its Hinterland, the Roman period. In: Museum of London 2000, *The Archaeology of Greater London, An assessment of archaeological evidence of human presence in the area now covered by Greater London.* 119–170. London: Museum of London Archaeology Service,

Price, E. 2000. *A Romano-British Settlement, its Antecedents and Successors*, Vol. 2. Gloucester and District Archaeological Research Group.

Price, J. and Cottam, S. 1998. *Romano-British Glass Vessels: a handbook.* Council for British Archaeology Practical handbook in Archaeology 14.

Proctor, J. and Bishop, B. 2002. Prehistoric and Environmental Development on Horsleydown: excavations at 1-2 Three Oak Lane. *Surrey Archaeological Collections*, 89, 1–26.

Quevillon, D. 1999. *A Catalogue of Worked Stone from St Mary Overy Priory, Southwark.* Unpublished University of London Dissertation

Ragnar Hagland, J. and Watson, B. 2005. Fact or Folklore: the Viking attack on London Bridge. *London Archaeologist* 10 (12), 328–332.

Ray, A. 1968. *English Delftware Pottery in the Robert Hall Warren Collection*. Oxford: Ashmolean Museum.

Raymond, F. 1999. *An Archaeological Impact Assessment of Southwark Cathedral Steps, London SE1*. AOC Archaeology Unpublished Report.

Reeve, J. 1998. A View from the Metropolis: post-medieval burials in London. In: M. Cox (ed), *Grave Concerns: death and burial in England 1700 to 1850*. Council for British Archaeology Research Report 113, 213-237.

Reeve, J. and Adams, M. 1993. *The Spitalfields Project: Volume 1, the archaeology. Across the Styx*. Council for British Archaeology Research Report 85.

Richardson, B. 1981. Excavation Round-up 1980. *London Archaeologist*, 4 (2), 44–51.

Roberts, H. and Godfrey, W. 1950. *Survey of London, Vol. XXII, Bankside (Parishes of St. Saviour and Christchurch, Southwark)*. London.

Rodwell, W. 1993. The Development of the Choir of Lichfield Cathedral: Romanesque and Early English. In: J. Maddison (ed), Medieval Archaeology and Architecture at Lichfield. *The British Archaeological Association Conference Transactions for the year 1987*.

Rodwell, W. and Bentley, J. 1984 .*Our Christian Heritage*. London: George Philip.

Roffey, S. 1998a. *The Early History and Development of St Marie Overie Priory, Southwark: the 12th century Chapel of St. John and associated cloistral buildings*. Unpublished University of London Dissertation.

Roffey, S. 1998b. The Early History and Development of St Marie Overie Priory, Southwark: the 12th century Chapel of St John. *London Archaeologist* 8 (10), 255–262.

Roffey, S. 1999. The Southwark Cathedral Archaeological Recording Project. *Church Archaeology* 3, 45–47.

Rogers, J. and Waldron, T. 1995. *A Field Guide to Joint Disease in Archaeology*. Chichester: John Wiley & Sons Ltd.

Royal Commission on Historical Monuments (England), 1930. *London East: Volume 5*. London: HMSO.

Southwark Archaeological Excavation Committee, 1973. Excavations at New Hibernia Wharf. *London Archaeologist* 2 (5), 99–103.

Sayer, D. 2001. *Carver Street Methodist Chapel, Sheffield*. ARCUS Unpublished Report.

Schofield, J. and Lea, R. 2005. *Excavations at Holy Trinity Priory, Aldgate, London*. Museum of London Archaeology Service Monograph 24.

Sheldon, H. 1978. The 1972-4 excavations: their contribution to Southwark's history. In: J. Bird, A. H. Graham, H. Sheldon and P. Townend (eds), *Southwark Excavations 1972-74, 11–49*. London and Middlesex Archaeological Society and Surrey Archaeological Society Joint Publication 1. London.

Sidell, J. Wilkinson, K. Scaife, R. and Cameron, N. 2000. *The Holocene Evolution of the London Thames*. archaeological excavations (1991–1998) for the London Underground Limited Jubilee Line Extension Project. Museum of London Archaeology Service Monograph 5.

Sidell, J. Cotton. J. Rayner, L and Wheeler, L. 2002. *The Prehistory and Topography of Southwark and Lambeth*. Museum of London Archaeology Service Monograph 14,

Smith, J. T. 1958. The Pre-Conquest Minster at Southwark. *Transactions of the London and Middlesex Archaeological Society* 19 (3), 174–179.

Stace, C. 1997. *New Flora of the British Isles*. Cambridge: Cambridge University Press.

Steele, D. G. and Bramblett, C. A. 1988. *The Anatomy and Biology of the Human Skeleton*. Texas: A & M University Press.

Stephenson, R. 1999. Tin Glazed ware in London: A review. In G. Egan, and R. L. Michael (eds), *Old and New Worlds*. Oxbow Books, 264–268.

Stephenson, R. 2003. Pottery. In: B. Sloane and S. Hoad, with J. Cloake, J. Pearce, and R. Stephenson, *Early Modern Industry and Settlement: excavations at George Street, Richmond, and High Street, Mortlake in the London Borough of Richmond upon Thames*. Museum of London Archaeology Service, Archaeology Studies Series 9, London, 69–79.

Stevens, T. P. 1954. *Southwark Cathedral 606-1931*. London: Sampson Low, Marston & Co Ltd.

Stow, J. 1931 edition. *A Survey of London*.

Stow, J. 1994 edition. *A Survey of London*. Dover: Alan Sutton Publishing Ltd.

Symonds, R. P. and Tomber, R. S. 1994. Late Roman London: an assessment of the ceramic evidence from the City of London. *Transactions of the London and Middlesex Archaeological Society* 42, 59–100.

Tatton-Brown, T. 1989. *Great Cathedrals of Britain*. London: BBC Books.

Tatton-Brown, T. 1990. *Building Stone in Canterbury. In D. Parsons (ed), Stone: quarrying and building in England AD43–1525*. Phillimore, in association with the Royal Archaeological Institute.

Taylor, H. M. and Taylor, J. 1965. *Anglo-Saxon Architecture Volumes 1 and 2*. Cambridge: Cambridge University Press.

Taylor, W. 1833. *The Annals of St. Mary Overy: an historical and descriptive account of St. Saviour's Church and Parish*. London: Nichols and Son.

The Mirror of Literature, Amusement and Instruction, 1832. http://www.fullbooks.com/The-Mirror-of-Literature-Amusement-andx1268.html (accessed 13th June 2005).

Thomas, C., Sloane, B. and Phillpotts, C. 1997. *Excavations at the Priory and Hospital of St Mary Spital, London*. Museum of London Archaeology Service Monograph 1.

Thompson, A., Grew F. and Schofield. J. 1984. Excavations in Aldgate, 1974. *Post-Medieval Archaeology* 18, 1–148.

Thompson, A., Westman, A. ,and Dyson, T. (eds), 1998. *Archaeology in Greater London 1965-90: a guide to records of excavation by the Museum of London*. The Archaeological Gazetteer Series Volume 2, Museum of London.

Thompson, Rev. W. 1894. *The History and Antiquities of the Collegiate Church of St. Saviour*. London.

Thompson, W. 1904. *The History and Antiquities of the Collegiate Church of St Saviour (St Marie Overie) Southwark (2nd ed)*. London: Elliot Stock.

Trotter, M. and Gleser, G. C. 1958. A Re-evaluation of Estimation Based on Measurements of Stature Taken During Life and of Long Bones After Death. *American Journal of Physical Anthropology* 16, 79–123.

Tyers, I. 1988. Environmental Evidence from Southwark and Lambeth. In: P. Hinton (ed), *Southwark 1973-76 Lambeth 1973-79*. Museum of London Department of Greater London Archaeology Joint Publication 3, 443–477.

Tyler, K. 1999. The Production of Tin-Glazed Ware on the North Bank of the Thames: excavations at the site of the Hermitage pothouse, Wapping. *Post-Medieval Archaeology* 33, 127–163.

Tyler, K. Betts, I. and Stephenson R. 2008. *London's Delftware Industry: the tin-glazed pottery industries of Southwark and Lambeth*. Museum of London Archaeology Service Monograph 40.

Tyson, M. 1925. The Annals of Southwark and Merton. Surrey Archaeological Collections 36, 24–58.

Vince, A. and Jenner, A. 1991. The Saxon and Early Medieval Pottery of London. In A. Vince (ed), *Aspects of Saxo-Norman London: finds and environmental work*. London and Middlesex Archaeological Society Special Paper 12, 19–119.

Waldron, T. 1985. DISH at Merton Priory: evidence for a 'new' occupational disease? *British Medical Journal* 291, 1762–1763.

Walford E. 1878. Southwark: St Saviour's Church. In: E. Walford, *Old and New London* 6, 16–29.

Watson, B. Brigham, T. and Dyson, T. 2001. *London bridge: 2000 years of a river crossing*. Museum of London Archaeology Service Monograph Series 8.

Watson, B. 1999. Medieval London Bridge and its Role in the Defence of the Realm. *Transactions of the London and Middlesex Archaeological Society* 50, 17–22.

Weatherill, L. M. and Edwards, R. 1971. Pottery Manufacture in London and Whitehaven in the Late 17th Century. *Post-Medieval Archaeology* 5, 160–181.

Weinreb, B. and Hibbert, C. (eds.), 1995. *The London Encyclopaedia*. London, Macmillan.

Welsby, P. A. 1958. *Lancelot Andrewes 1555 – 1626*. London: SPCK.

West, J. J. 1980. Haughmond Abbey, Salop. *Medieval Archaeology* 24, 240.

Whitehead, R. 2003. *Buckles 1250-1800*. Essex.

Willcox, G. H. 1977. Exotic Plants from Roman Waterlogged Sites in London. *Journal of Archaeological Science* 4, 269-282.

Wilson, D. G. 1975. Plant Foods and Poisons from Mediaeval Chester, Goldsmith House Site, Goss Street, Chester, 1972. *Journal of the Chester Archaeological Society* 58, 55–67.

Yule, B. 2005. *A Prestigious Roman BuildinCcomplex on the Southwark Waterfront: excavations at Winchester Palace, London, 1983–90*. Museum of London Archaeology Service Monograph Series 23.

Anonymous Periodicals

The Builder, 8 March 1912, 265-6

The Building News, 11 July 1879, 51-2

The Daily Graphic, 4 February 1910, 4

The Gentleman's Magazine, February 1832, 101

The Mirror of Literature, Amusement, and Instruction,

Vol. XVI, No. 456, 1830

Vol. XIX, No. 534, 1832

Reference Sources

C.L.R.O. ref. P.D.151.3, 1823 An Act for the Rebuilding of London Bridge and for Improving and Making Suitable Approaches Hereto; 4 Deo. IV, cap. 50; Schedule of Property to be Acquired [Royal Assent 4 July 1823]

C.L.R.O. ref. P.D.151.3, 1829 Minutes of Evidence Taken Before the Lords Committees on the Bill Entitled 'An Act for Improving the Approaches to London Bridge'

C.L.R.O. ref. P.D.29.8, 1829 Act for Improving the Approaches to London Bridge; 10 Deo. IV, c. 136; Schedule of Property to be Acquired (extract) [Royal Assent 24 June 1829]

INDEX

by Trevor Ashwin